Collins
POCKET GUIDE

Alan Mitchell
John Wilkinson

tr

of Britain and
Northern Europe

HarperCollins*Publishers*

HarperCollins*Publishers*
77–85 Fulham Palace Road
London
W6 8JB

The HarperCollins website address is:
www.**fire**and**water**.com

Collins is a registered trademark of HarperCollins*Publishers* Ltd.

First published 1982

Second edition 1988

Reprinted 1989

Reprinted 1991

Reprinted 1995

Reprinted 1997

Reprinted 2001

A **Domino Books** production

Design consultant Hermann Heinzel

ISBN 0 00 219857 6

Printed in Hong Kong

Contents

CONTENTS

Walnut Family

Birch Family

Hornbeam Family

Hazel Family

Beech and **Elm** Families

Mulberry Family

Magnolia Family

Spur-leaf Family   **Katsura** Family

Protea Family   **Laurel** Family

Winter's Bark Family

Witch Hazel Family

Rose Family

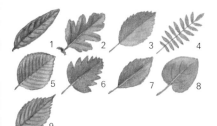

Pea Family

Maple Family

CONTENTS

Introduction

This book covers the trees to be seen in the woods, forests, hedges, parks, gardens and town streets of the British Isles and Northern Europe – over 600 species and varieties. However, it omits the numerous extreme rarities which can be found in certain botanic gardens and specialist collections and nowhere else. Their inclusion would have hopelessly swamped the book and left it much harder to use.

Some very rare species have been deliberately included – either where a fine specimen is prominent in a major garden, such as the Chestnut-leafed Oak at Kew; or for their particular botanical and general interest, e.g. Tetracentron, Lacebark Pine, Osage Orange; or for striking features, such as Sassafras; or as first-class trees which should be better known and more widely planted, such as Amur and Mongolian Limes and the Chinese Cork Oak.

Shrubs have also been generally excluded, though we have allowed one or two, like the Common Hazel, which do not usually meet the criterion of a tree – the ability to grow over 6m tall on a single stem. Nor have we attempted to cover varieties of orchard fruiting trees.

Practically every tree, common or rare, able to grow in northern Europe is to be found in Britain. Thus a guide which covers all but the very rarest trees in this country will be found to 'work' throughout northern Europe.

The text

English names. Some trees have more than one in common use. We have given priority to those which seem less misleading (Rowan), or more accurate (Ashleaf Maple), or less parochial (Giant Sequoia), or aesthetically more pleasing (Dove Tree). Where a tree has no English name in general use, we have either derived them from botanical names (Hupeh Crab, Sargent Rowan) or sometimes invented them (Pillar Apple, Railway Poplar).

Botanical names used are those accepted by the most recent authorities: *Trees and Shrubs Hardy in the British Isles* by W. J. Bean, 8th Ed., 1970–80; Hillier's *Manual of Trees and Shrubs*; *A Handbook of Coniferae and Ginkgoaceae* by Dallimore and Jackson, revised by G. Harrison, 1966. The *meaning* of Latin names has been added for each species, except where obvious.

Descriptions. A blue spot indicates the start of a new Family.

The descriptions are meant to complement the illustrations: they do not mention features clearly shown in the paintings unless there are variations to point out or where, as in some barks, further details can be helpful.

The natural ranges of exotic trees are not mentioned if they are obvious from the English name. The distribution in Britain is generally indicated. For exotic species this varies considerably. Some, like the Sycamore and Horse Chestnut, completely hardy and grown here for 400 years, are common everywhere that trees have been planted: others will only grow well in the climate of certain regions. Many rather tender evergreen species thrive only in western coastal areas with little frost and high humidity – though there are locally sheltered, damp areas in Sussex, Kent, Suffolk and as far north as

Northumberland which support species normally only seen in the far west. Other trees, notably from the eastern USA and northern China, are restricted to S and E England by their need for hot summers, though small, perhaps non-flowering and struggling specimens of them may be found elsewhere.

Dates of introduction, together with the location and measurements of notable specimens in the British Isles, will be found on pp. 264–81.

Height is indicated at the end of each descriptive text, as three figures. These are the height in metres to be expected after 10 and 20 years' growth in reasonably good conditions, and the ultimate height attained in better areas by the tallest trees.

There is no figure for **spread** of branches, because this depends too much on surroundings and individual variation to be of any real use.

Gardenworthiness is rated after the figures for height, as I, II, III, or X. We have assessed the trees for their general worth in parks and gardens in regions where they grow well, taking account of health, vigour, crown shape, foliage, bark, autumn colour, flowers and general interest.

I A first-class tree, with excellent shape, health and foliage, often with good flowers in profusion or fine autumn colour, and no notable faults. These are trees of great character, for choosing for prominent positions or where only one or a few can be planted.

II Either a good tree but lacking special personality or obvious class; or one which might be in category I but for a defect like unreliable health or a gaunt winter aspect. Thus good for general planting but not in a focal point.

III An ordinary, mediocre tree, rather dull and lacking any striking feature, though without serious fault.

Or a tree with good points but also marked faults.

Or a poor thing in this country, but perhaps of great interest botanically or with a brief period of glory, like Adam's Laburnum, and therefore worth having.

X A tree with little or nothing to recommend it. There are many better ones for every site, and all too many of it already planted. Its faults are seen all year round, like a badly shaped crown, or throughout a season, like dreary foliage.

Note. Japanese Cherries on pp. 192–3 are rated for their flowers only. Otherwise they would nearly all be X.

An element of subjectivity may be discerned in these ratings. But the author considers he knows a good tree when he sees one, and by any standards of aesthetics the Hungarian Oak has class and Pissard's Plum has none. Not all, however, are so clear-cut, and with some it is arguable whether II or III is the fairer rating.

Propagation. Where a whole Family or genus is raised in the same way, it is mentioned in the introduction to that group, and not repeated at species level unless there is some difficulty or special method for a particular tree. For different methods of propagation, see page 12.

Illustrations

The characters of each tree chosen for illustration – crown, bark, shoot, leaf, flower or fruit – are those important for identification. The leaf is always illustrated. Where a bark, fruit or flower is neither illustrated nor described, it is generally too similar to those of closely related species illustrated to be of special use.

With minor exceptions the illustrations are all from living trees and fresh specimens of shoots, flowers and fruits. All are of *typical* examples. It should be borne in mind that the leaves as well as the fruits of most trees change considerably in colour through their season; and that variations of leaf-shape frequently occur, either together or on different trees of the same species; and that the shape of crowns can vary with age, surroundings, degree of exposure to wind and cold, and treatment by man and animals, especially in their youth.

The **height** of the specimen illustrated is given beside each tree picture, as is the **diameter** of the bole at the point where the bark is illustrated. How to estimate the age of a tree from the bole's circumference ($\pi \times$ the diameter) is explained on page 17.

Flowering times. The months during which the majority of flowers or fruits appear are given beside the pictures in *italic* figures. Thus '♂ *4–5*' indicates male flowers appearing in April–May.

Winter. How to identify deciduous trees in winter, when their crowns and shoots are bare of leaves, is dealt with immediately after the book's main section, on pages 256–63, where both the winter key and silhouette captions have page references back to the tree's main treatment.

Trees

A tree is a mode of growth, not a botanical class of plants. Trees occur sporadically throughout the two Classes of flowering plants – Gymnosperms and Angiosperms. Gymnosperms (meaning 'naked seed' because the ovule is borne naked on a bract) include Ginkgo and the conifers. They are nearly all trees. Angiosperms (meaning 'hidden seed' because it is concealed in an ovary) include all our familiar garden plants and wild flowers, bulbs, palms, and grasses. Some of the Angiosperm families like Beech, Elm and Lime are nearly all trees; in others like Pea and Rose, trees are in a minority; the Figwort/Foxglove Family has only one genus of tree, Paulownia; the Primrose Family has none.

Where a tree (or shrub) differs from other forms of growth is in making **wood**. A bud growing on any plant leaves behind a shoot of pith-cells which conduct sap. In non-woody plants, that is all, and the shoot dies back at the end of the season. But in woody plants the shoots, stem and roots are all enclosed by a single layer of cells called cambium, which spend the growing season actively dividing and making new cells, both inside and out. This thickens and hardens the stem, which can then survive the winter and continue its growth the next season.

The cambial growth on the outside lays down cells, called the *bast*, for conducting *down* to the roots foods manufactured in the leaves by photosynthesis. If this thin layer, just beneath the tree's bark, is cut right round the trunk, the tree is 'ring-barked' and will die.

The cambial growth on the inside – which pushes the cambium further out each year – conducts sap *up* from the roots; the water and liquid nutrients extracted from the soil. This inner growth also has to support the tree. Broadleafed trees have evolved specialised cells: *vessels* for carrying sap with 'sieve-plates' at the top of each for the sap to pass through, and *fibres* for strength. Conifers, relatively primitive trees, use the same cells, called *tracheids*, for both purposes. They have to be thick walled and have long overlaps for the sap to pass from one to the next through little holes. These differences give broadleafed and conifer wood their different characteristics, but the term 'hardwoods' and 'softwoods' for them can be quite misleading. The softest woods known, such as Balsa, are all broadleafed, and some conifers like Yew are extremely hard.

Three broadleafed trees are so primitive that they have tracheids like a conifer. Two are in this book – Katsura and Tetracentron. The third is a rather bushy, very rare Japanese evergreen, Trochodendron.

As sap-carriers, both conifer and broadleafed inner cells have a limited life of some 15–20 years. After this they are taken out of service, a ring each year, and filled by a substance called lignin to become part of the darker-coloured *heartwood* – inactive, but essential to the tree for resisting the stresses of wind and bearing the weight of branches.

The **annual rings** visible in wood are formed because growth is quickest in the spring, when cells are large to allow sap to flow freely. Later in the season growth slows, cells can be smaller and have thicker walls for strength. So the smallest cells of all are those laid down just before the winter rest – next to the following spring's very open cells.

Bark is laid down by a small cambium layer of its own, and protects the bast and main cambium from damage and from scorching by the sun or extreme cold. The form of bark matches the species' environment. The beech, growing in shady woods, has a smooth thin bark. Oaks, growing in more open, broken woods, have a thick rough bark able to stand heat.

Leaves. A big oak has some quarter-million leaves manufacturing food from carbon dioxide in the air and water and nutrients from the roots. A large spruce has about three million, each remaining at work on the tree for four or five years. Those of conifers and other evergreens which have to withstand freeze-drying tend to have a reduced area and to be covered in polished wax or dense hairs. Leaves may emerge red, brown or yellow, but soon turn green from the pigment chlorophyll except in the unfortunate forms where this is masked by brownish purple.

The **roots** have both to find, extract and transport nutrients and to give stability. To some extent the two functions are separated into feeding roots and 'sinkers'. Feeding roots extend well beyond the spread of the crown. They are shallow, most only a few centimetres from the surface, all within 15–20cm. In open soils they tend to be deeper than in clays, and to extend further. The absorption of water and nutrients is at the root-hairs – fine white structures which live for only some three weeks: growth depends on constant extension of new roots. The energy needed for the initial burst of root-growth each spring – before the first leaves unfold – is stored over-winter by the tree in the wood.

The 'root-plate' helps to stabilise the tree, but most rely on sinkers. These grow vertically downwards from the main roots, here and there. In open soils where the water-table is far below sinkers will penetrate perhaps 10m. When it is in reach they go down to it and fan out above it, which also gives a source of water in times of drought. Beech roots will not enter very wet soils, and when beeches grow on shallow sand over clay they have huge root-plates but no real sinkers.

Flowers. All trees have flowers but only those which need to attract insects for pollination have showy flowers with petals. Forest trees do not rely on insects but on wind. They need to bear masses of pollen, and to do so before the leaves divert and slow down the wind. Hence the male, pollen-bearing catkins of beech, oak, hornbeam, hazel, with the female seed-bearing flowers separate.

Bisexual flowers, combining both male and female organs, are called *perfect*; it is a comparatively recent arrangement. Where the flowers are separate, of different sexes, the males and females may either occur on different trees (called *dioecious*, 'two households', the most primitive arrangement though some advanced trees like Holly and willows have reverted to it), or on the same tree (*monoecious*, 'one household').

Monoecious trees can have their flowers variously arranged. In pines the females are near the shoot tip and the males around the base; in oaks the females are strung along the new shoot and male catkins are at the tip of the old shoot; in larch, beech and plane they are fairly random. Sometimes male and female flowers are separate but on the same structure, which is then called *androgynous*. A few trees have whole branches either male or female. With some the situation is quite chaotic: the Common Ash may have a female or perfect branch on an otherwise male tree, and some maples exhibit every possible variation.

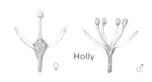

Holly ♀ Holly ♂   ♂ ♀ Sorbus

perfect

Flower types

Monoecious trees
male and female flowers
on same tree

Holly ♀ ♂

Dioecious tree
male and female
flowers on separate trees

London Plane,
similar structures,
spread at random

Hazel, male
and female
dissimilar

Chinese Necklace
Poplar, androgynous –
a single flowerhead
with male and
female flowers

Tree cultivation

Growing from **seed** is the best and easiest method of raising most tree species, but cannot be used to reproduce cultivars. In general it is always unwise to use seed collected from an isolated tree, or one surrounded by trees of other species, because nearly all trees are out-breeding – they do best when pollinated by another tree of their kind: 'selfed' seedlings are often weakly and of poor shape, or they may yield hybrids, crossing with related close neighbours.

. The ability to grow from **cuttings** varies greatly. Oaks, hollies and maples seldom or never make 'root-initials' – buds from which roots may grow. Beeches and horse-chestnuts will sometimes be found to have layered themselves, but neither is a good rooter. Willows and poplars, however, will make root-initials almost anywhere: even when sawn up and used for fence-posts they will sprout. Mulberries were traditionally propagated by 'truncheons' – 4–6' long sections of stout branches inserted in the ground to about half their length.

Most trees are in between such extremes; they will root from cuttings but need to be treated sympathetically to do so. Take the cutting either in winter, when the need for roots is almost nil and when deciduous plants have no leaves to feed, so that roots will grow as soon as the soil warms up and before new leaves emerge, or in June–July when growth is past its spring surge but when root-growth is still strong. With either method, it is crucial that most of the cutting should be buried, with plenty of buds below ground to make roots, and only one or two above to sprout. Poplars and willows will grow 2–3m in the year in which a stout shoot is nine-tenths inserted, but left to themselves will make poor, often bowed, slow trees: they should be cut to the base before growth next spring, and this time the shoot will be stout and strong.

Grafting. Cultivars – being chance forms selected from seedlings – cannot themselves be reproduced by seed, and if they are of a tree which will not strike from cuttings, they must be grafted. Grafting is also used where a species is rather tender and may survive better with the roots of a hardier relative; and extensively in fruit-trees to produce earlier fruiting or to influence – sometimes drastically – the vigour of the top growth.

The techniques of grafting are various and elaborate. For all there are two golden rules. First, the root-stock must be further into growth than the scion. The scion is taken when the plant is dormant and kept in the soil under a north wall or in cold store while the rootstock is grown in a warm position until its leaf-buds are bursting. The second rule is to 'match up the cambia'. The greater the length of cambia placed exactly together the more rapid and certain the union.

Forestry. Growing trees commercially is very different from growing them singly or as specimen groups. The outlay on buying, draining and preparing the land is such that unless there are some returns in the early stages, the final crop can never make enough money to be profitable. This is achieved by periodic thinnings. Where some 2500 trees are planted to the hectare – spaced in rows 2m each way, usually 30cm high and 2–3 years old – only about 250 remain as the final crop, the others being taken out at about the 15th year and every 3–5 years thereafter. There are a dozen different systems: forestry is very largely the art of thinning.

The market is 90% for softwoods, and the land available almost entirely that which is too poor for agriculture: high quality hardwoods will not grow well on it but many conifers will make splendid crops. Sitka Spruce out-grows and outyields any other over huge areas with high rainfall, but according to height and soil conditions other species may do better: Douglas Fir, Grand Fir, Japanese Larch, Shore Pine; or where spring frosts or low rainfall rule out Sitka Spruce, Norway Spruce; and on southern sandy heaths Corsican Pine and now also Monterey and Bishop Pines. On south-ern high open chalkland the forest will eventually be Beech but Beech will not grow there unaided at first, and will yield no early return at all. So they are planted with a mixture of Western Hemlock, European Larch, Western Red Cedar or Lawson Cypress to shelter the Beeches and to be removed periodically, making the early years profitable.

In a few areas where planting can be done on rich southern lowland soils, old oakwoods were until recently replaced by fast-growing Douglas and Grand Fir or European Larch. But now there is a policy to conserve these fine oakwoods and Common and Sessile Oaks are planted, although they can never be financially profitable.

There is almost no forestry now for specialised timbers. The *Bat Willow* is grown for cricket bats, in small groups and along ditches and rivers in the south-east. *Hybrid Black Poplars* are used for making match-boxes, pallets and fruit-trays. *Common Ash* is the best wood for high-quality sports goods, if grown fast and regularly. For this it needs deep, damp, base-rich soils. *Sycamore* is best for kitchenware, having a hard, smooth, white surface that takes no stain from food nor gives it any taint. *Horse Chestnut* is used for toys and artificial limbs since it does not splinter when broken. *Lime* is similar and carves well. *Yew* is very strong and hard; it is used in some furniture, often for the arms of chairs. *Elm* has a good figure and is hardwearing, so is used for seats, benches and staircase treads. It also withstands frequent drying and wetting, so like *Alder* (which is even better, but not found in big sizes) it is used in canal and dock constructions.

Native and introduced trees

The primeval richness in species of temperate forests is no longer found in N Europe, but only in China, Japan, and North America, where the moun-tain ranges run north–south and provided areas of southerly refuge during Ice Ages. As the ice came south, the plants could retreat before it at their preferred altitude, and then return. Thus in the Allegheny Mountains of the eastern USA today, an American beech is not, as it would be in Europe, surrounded by other beeches, in a beechwood. It is among a profusion of other trees. The next beech may be 40 species away.

But in Europe the mountains formed a nearly complete barrier from Spain to Poland, and immediately south of them, sealing the gaps, lay the Medi-terranean Sea. Also, the old flora had already been gradually thinned for millions of years by the northward movement of the land-mass, so that much of Europe now has the same latitude as from Hudson Bay to the Great Lakes, with a similar paucity of species.

For the British Isles it was worse still. At the height of the ice, there were no trees at all left in what is now Britain, and the only species that could return were those near the land-connection and a few in SW Ireland (and a south-western land refuge, now gone). Then melting ice raised sea-levels, Britain was an island, and no more trees could come.

Our only **native** conifers are thus Scots Pine, Common Juniper, and Yew. Of broadleafed trees, Silver and Downy Birches, Bay Willow, Aspen, Wych Elm, Sallow, Alder and Bird Cherry were early invaders, then Rowan, Hazel, Holly, Ash, Sessile Oak and Small-leafed Lime. This last was to become the dominant woodland tree in England until man over-utilised it and favoured the oaks. Common Oak, Crack and probably White Willow were followed by Wild Cherry, Black Poplar, Whitebeam, Hawthorn and Midland Thorn. Latecomers were Wild Service Tree, Crab Apple, Beech, Field Maple, Hornbeam, Broad-leafed Lime and Box. That adds up to our 33 native species. A complex series of Whitebeam hybrids with tiny populations in places like the Avon Gorge, Bristol, could add a dozen more, but they are not full species. All other trees, in this country and this book, have been introduced by man.

Introductions. Moving in after the Ice, early man will probably have brought some trees to give quick shelter: White and Grey Poplars, and before the Iron Age, English and Smooth-leafed Elms. He will also have brought some fruit trees: Pear, Medlar, possibly the Myrobalan Plum. The Romans may have brought Walnut, Fig and Sweet Chestnut. The Almond came early too.

But until 1548 there were no records of what trees were being grown and by that time several S European species were being planted – Stone and Maritime Pines, Norway Spruce, Italian Cypress, Holm Oak, Mulberry. Some Chinese trees, such as the Peach, had long been brought over the old trade routes to the Middle East and thence into Europe and Britain. Others like White Mulberry and Date-plum came during the 16th century. With them came species native to the Middle East, and by 1600 we had Oriental Plane, Common and Scotch Laburnums, Phillyrea, Bay and Judas Tree.

The first trees from **eastern North America**, White Cedar and Balsam Poplar, had arrived before 1600 and over the next 200 years introductions from that vastly species-rich area were almost continuous, with three periods of maximum activity: 1660–1700, 1732–60 and 1785–96.

The finest tree specimens in the world mostly grow near the **Pacific coast** of North America. Many were discovered by Archibald Menzies, a scientist with a naval squadron which sailed round Cape Horn and up to Alaska in 1792–4. He sent foliage specimens to Kew but could not introduce the plants. That was begun by David Douglas, who between 1826 and 1833 sent Grand, Noble and Douglas Firs, Sitka Spruce, Sugar, Ponderosa and Monterey Pines. Douglas was tough, and after those years often alone, covering 4000 miles in unmapped forest in one year alone, he proposed to walk home to Perth across Siberia and Europe. He stopped off to climb the highest peaks in Hawaii and was killed when he fell into a pit-trap for buffaloes with one already in it, in 1834. Douglas's trees were very popular with landowners around his native Perth, where they grow as well as anywhere else on earth. A demand for more soon arose and by 1849 Scottish gardeners had formed an association to send out John Jeffrey, while Veitch's Nurseries in Exeter sent William Lobb: by 1854 they had between them sent back nearly all the West Coast trees, including more Giant Sequoia and Coast Redwood, which were both sent slightly earlier.

The first tree from **South America** was the Monkey-puzzle, brought home by Archibald Menzies in 1797. Many fine trees were sent by Lobb from Chile in 1844, but the three most important Southern Beeches – Rauli, Roble and Dombey's – only came in the first 23 years of this century.

The **Himalayan** trees came singly after the first Morinda Spruce arrived in 1818: Himalayan Fir in 1822, Bhutan Pine in 1823, Deodar in 1831, Pindrow Fir in 1837, Himalayan Hemlock in 1838, Indian Horse Chestnut in 1851.

Collecting the vast wealth of trees in **China** was a slow and fitful process until the flood of species after 1900 from Wilson, Forrest, Purdom and Rock, and after a gap since 1935 it resumed in 1980. The first trees were brought out by Pierre d'Incarville; by 1760 Ginkgo, Tree of Heaven, Pagoda Tree and Chinese Thuya were in Britain. Then there was a period when access was limited to the Treaty Ports, and only a few south coastal species could be brought: Robert Fortune made four journeys in 1842–58, bringing the Chusan Palm, Lacebark Pine and Golden Larch. In the interior only some French Jesuit priests could travel until around 1880 an Irish doctor, Augustine Henry, attached to customs was sent to Yunnan. He heard from the Jesuits, Armand David, Paul Farges and Jean-Marie Delavay, something of the wealth of plants of which they were sending herbarium specimens to France, and became himself a great collector, sending over 5000 specimens to Kew and introducing a few, now very scarce, trees. Ernest Wilson's first call in China was on Henry in 1899, to be given the location of the Dove Tree in Szechuan. In six journeys, the last in Korea, Japan and Taiwan, Wilson sent many hundreds of plant species now frequent in gardens.

Japan was a closed country until 1854. The few Japanese plants grown in Europe before then came either from some growing in a Javanese botanic garden or were brought out by travellers privileged to enter. The most famous of these was a German eye-surgeon, Philip von Siebold, whose services were so valued that despite transgressions he was allowed back. He brought out the Smooth Japanese Maple in 1820.

Japanese gardeners had for centuries been selecting and breeding bizarre varieties. A flood of these reached Europe in 1861, collected by Fortune and James Veitch. Their movements were largely restricted to around Tokyo and Yokohama where there were many nurseries, so it was the remarkable cultivars that they often collected. Travel restrictions were eased after 1870 and the great number of new species from the interior were collected between 1872 and 1890, trees like Nikko and Hornbeam Maples and Japanese Horse Chestnut. Most of the flowering cherries arrived after 1900.

The arrival of trees from **Australasia** is poorly documented, but several were here before 1850, including Mimosa (1820), Blue Gum (1829) and Cider Gum (1846) from Tasmania and Cabbage Tree from New Zealand in 1823.

The first tree from the **Caucasus** Mountains was Zelkova (1760), then Caucasian Wingnut (1782). But apart from a minor wave when Cappadocian Wingnut, Persian Ironwood and Oriental Spruce all came between 1838 and 1841, the trees came at long and irregular intervals.

The age of trees

The maximum possible **lifespan** of a given species cannot be given very precisely since trees dying at an advanced age have very rarely been of known date of planting, and they are usually hollow, so that their age cannot be found by counting rings. Old age in itself is not the immediate cause of death, in trees or humans; it merely allows damage or disease to take a fatal course.

Many of our introduced trees have not been growing in Britain long enough to reach senility – unlike the Sycamore, Sweet Chestnut and others with a long history here. It is not at all safe to assume these newcomers will attain with us the ages they can in their own sites. The conditions of soil and climate where the Bristlecone Pine grows to be 5,000 years old, for example, are nowhere remotely matched in Britain.

The table below gives the maximum known, estimated, or simply likely ages achieved by some trees in Britain where sufficient data are available to make them not too vague. Where the oldest known specimen is still in good order, its age is rounded up and given a '+' sign.

1500++	Yew	200	Walnut
500+	Common Oak		Common Alder
			Red Oak
450+	Sweet Chestnut		Tree of Heaven
400+	London Plane	180	Maritime Pine
	Sycamore	150+	Grecian Fir
	Common Lime		Chusan Palm
			Norway Maple
350+	Cedar of Lebanon		
	European Larch	150	Monkey Puzzle
350	Horse Chestnut		Bhutan Pine
			Lombardy Poplar
300	Scots Pine		Scarlet Oak
	Hornbeam		Mulberry
	English Elm		Wild Cherry
	Tulip-tree		Silver Maple
			Catalpa
250+	Ginkgo		
	Locust Tree	120	Black Italian Poplar
	Pagoda Tree		Rowan
250	Common Silver Fir		Cider-gum
	Wych Elm		Hiba
230	Common Beech	100	Aspen
	Common Ash		Crack Willow
220+	Zelkova	80	Veitch's Silver Fir
	Lucombe Oak		Silver Birch (in South)
	Silver Birch (in far North)		Paulownia
	Tupelo	50	Pacific Dogwood
200+	Norway Spruce		
	Field Maple		

The Yew owes its position as clear leader in the table opposite not only to its ability to sprout again after clipping, lopping, breakage and general damage, but also to the enormous strength of its wood. Old trees can be very hollow, yet they hold together and support long branches in a way that no other tree can.

Estimating the age. With age the height and spread of a tree reach a maximum and then decline. They cannot be used to estimate age in a tree which has passed its prime. Every year that it is alive, however, a tree must add a ring of wood to its bole (and its branches), so the circumference of the bole is a measure of age. It so happens that a *fully-crowned* specimen of nearly any species able to make a big tree, on any site or soil, reaches a point in middle age or after when its circumference is one inch (2.5cm) for each year of growth. Few trees 15 feet round the bole at 5 feet (1.5m) up are much more or less than 180 years old. They grow in early life at nearer an inch and a half, but from an age of 80–100 years they slow down to less than an inch. So they must cross the line where the mean growth is an inch a year, and they cross it so slowly that this is about true for a long time.

Note that this is the rate for *fully-crowned* trees, not those with their growth restricted by other trees. Since it is leaves that in the end make the wood, a tree growing with others in normal woodland will grow at only about half the rate of one with a full crown growing in the open.

There are many trees which grow much *faster* than this 'normal' rate. Nearly all Giant Sequoias have grown 2–3 inches a year in circumference, and some 4–5 inches, in their first 50 years. One of these 20 feet round (194cm diameter) is seldom more than 100 years old. Similar growth is shown by Grand Fir, Low's White Fir, Hybrid Wingnut, Bat Willow, some hybrid Poplars and most Eucalypts. Some Red Oaks, Silver Limes, Larches and Paulownia add 2 inches in a year.

There are fewer trees which grow much *slower* than the normal rate (apart from trees growing in a wood – see above). The Yew is the obvious example: although a few have been known to attain the one inch a year for 100 years, many grow less than half as fast, and for big Yews an addition of an inch in 6 years is reasonable – making the estimation of their age a hazardous affair involving graphs.

Scots Pine, Horse Chestnut and Common Lime grow at the normal speed for perhaps 100 years and then slow down very markedly, while the Spanish Fir seems almost to stop: one tree has added only 6 inches in the last 70 years.

A foot of circumference means just under 10cm of diameter. Each 10cm of diameter measured at 1.5m up the bole indicates roughly 12 years of growth. Some 75–100cm of diameter is achieved by most trees in 100 years, 145–190cm in 200 years. (The diameters given for the boles illustrated in this book, however, are simply to indicate the thickness of the bole or branches at the point where the bark is painted. For it is sometimes the case that the bark on the older, thicker, lower parts of the bole differs markedly from the younger bark higher up.)

Key to Conifers

Leaves in whorls of 10 or more
  whorls directly on shoot — Japanese Umbrella Pine, 54
  whorls on short spurs
    leaves spined, hard, evergreen — Cedars, 68
    leaves soft, pale, deciduous — Larches, 70–3

Leaves in bundles of 2, 3, or 5, needle-like — Pines, 88–107

Leaves in whorls of 3
  spined; outer face not striped — Junipers, 42–5
  blunt, short, striped white — Patagonian Cypress, 40

Leaves single
  deciduous, pale fresh green, soft, on slender
    deciduous shoot
      in opposite pairs — Dawn Redwood, 53
      alternate, spiral, or all round shoot — Swamp Cypress, 52
  evergreen, usually dark green, firm
    scale-like
      closely pressed, flat
        striped white above — Chilean Incense Cedar, 31
        pairs, parallel-sided at long drawn-up base — Incense Cedar, 31
        mixed in spreading spiny scales — Junipers, 42–5
        in flattened systems
          cone pea-like, woody — 'False Cypresses', 32–6
          cone pear-shaped, leathery — Thujas, 46
          cone knobbly-globular; scales broad — Hiba, 49
        in angular, feather-like systems — True Cypresses, 49
      tips spreading, incurved
        tips short — Summit Cedar, 54
        tips long
          dark green or blue-green — Giant Sequoia, 50
          bright green or yellow-green — Japanese Red Cedar, 50
          white-banded inside — King William Pine, 54
    free-standing, awl-shaped
      yellowish; dark red in winter — Japanese Red Cedar, 50
      blue-green, soft, fluffy — Sawara Cypress, 35
      spined, hard, incurved — Tasmanian Cedars, 54
    leaves 7–12cm long, leathery, linear — Willow Podocarp, 28
    leaves 4–7cm long, spined tip
      broad, triangular, rigid — Monkey-puzzle, 30
      slender, linear, flexible — Chinese Fir, 55
      shoot green second year, ribbed — Nutmeg Trees, 26
      shoot red-brown, bud brown, pointed — Santa Lucia Fir, 67
    shoot green for 2–3 years
      scale-leaves on shoot — Coast Redwood, 50
      shoot striped white — Saxegothaea, 29
      leaves broad, leathery, pale — Cowtail Pines, 37
      leaves hard, spined, all round shoot
        yellowish beneath — Totara, 28
        silver-banded beneath — Chilean Totara, 28
      leaves linear
        yellowish bands beneath — Yews, 24
        blue-white bands beneath, soft — Plum-fruited Yew, 28
    second year shoot not green
      leaves with pale margin, hard — California Nutmeg, 26
      leaves with peg-like base left on shoot — Spruces, 74–81
      leaves with sucker-like base, leaving shoot
        smooth — Silver Firs, 56–67
      leaves slender, terminal bud pointed — Douglas Firs, 86
      leaves flattened, buds rounded — Hemlocks, 82–5

Key to Broadleafed Trees in Summer

For broadleaves in winter (without foliage), see p. 256.

This key uses primarily the leaf itself. It avoids reliance on flower or fruit as these are not there for inspection during much of the year.

COMPOUND LEAF

Doubly compound (bi-pinnate)
    leaflet untoothed
        silver-blue-green; divisions very fine   **Mimosa**, 197
        bright green; compound leaflets at base only   **Honey Locust**, 199
        pale green, whitish beneath; leaf to 1m long   **Kentucky Coffee Tree**, 201
    leaflet toothed, deeply at base; broad   **Pride of India**, 236

Palmate-leaflets radiating like fingers of a hand   **Horse Chestnuts**, 226

Singly compound (pinnate) with 5 or more leaflets
    1 or 2 broad teeth at one side of leaflet base with a
raised lump on each   **Tree of Heaven**, 204
    leaflets few; big, broad, set alternately   **Yellowwood**, 196
    leaflet base untoothed; outer $\frac{2}{3}$ sharply toothed   **Rowan**, 177
    leaflet untoothed to near tip, where a few teeth   **Manna Ash**, 247
    leaflet fully untoothed
        notched at tip; 2 thorns at base of leaf   **Robinia**, 198
        5–7 leaflets, biggest towards tip of leaf   **Common Walnut**, 118
        7–20 leaflets, smallest towards tip
            3–5cm long   **Pagoda Tree**, 199
            15–20cm long   **Varnish Tree**, 206
    leaflet wavy-edged, obscurely toothed; leaves
      opposite   **Cork Trees**, 202
    leaflet minutely toothed; leaves opposite   **Euodia**, 203
    basal leaflets with lobules and a few small teeth   **Ashleaf Maple**, 225
    leaflets saw-toothed
        15–25 leaflets
            leaf-stem densely hairy; bud pink   **Butternut**, 118
            leaf-stem finely downy; bud grey to pale brown   **Black Walnut**, 118
            leaf-stem smooth; bud 2 leaves, dark brown   **Wingnuts**, 116
        5–13 leaflets
            leaflet slender, up to 12cm long; leaves opposite   **Ashes**, 246
            leaflets near tip biggest, 15–35cm long,
                10–20cm broad, leaves alternate   **Hickories**, 120

Trifoliate – 3 leaflets
    leaflet untoothed; stalk green, smooth   **Laburnum**, 200
    stalk red, hairy   **Maples**, 210–25
    leaflet with a few big teeth or many or many irregular
      ones   **Maples**, 210–25
    leaflet regularly sharp-toothed; leaf dark, evergreen;
      very short stalk   **Eucryphias**, 234

SEMI-COMPOUND LEAF

Free leaflets at base of lobed leaf   **Bastard Service Tree**, 181

SIMPLE LEAF

see next page

SIMPLE LEAF – some special cases

Knob-like 'glands' on stalk
  knob reddish, sometimes green or yellow; leaf oblong — **Cherries, Plums etc,** 189–95

  knob green; leaf round with slender tip — **Poplars**, 108–11
Leaf twisted on twisting shoot — **Corkscrew Willow**, 115
Leaf torn across shows strings of hardening sap
  leaf toothed, dark glossy green — **Gutta-percha Tree**, 171
  leaf wavy, untoothed, pale or bright green — **Dogwoods**, 241
Leaf with a single spine at base — **Osage Orange**, 160

SIMPLE LEAF – EVERGREEN – hard; dark green or blue-grey

Margin spined
  leaf flat; underside densely hairy, white — **Holm Oak**, 150
    underside tufted in vein-angles — **California Live Oak**, 150
    underside smooth green — **Highclere Hollies**, 209
  leaf buckled; spines alternately up and down — **Holly**, 208
Margin toothed
  leaf 1–5cm long
    underside shows midrib only – no veins — **Southern Beeches**, 133–5
    underside prominently veined; leaves opposite — **Phillyrea**, 280
    leaf papery, thin; 10–12 large teeth — **Red Beech**, 134
  leaf 6–10cm long
    margin finely crinkled; aromatic — **Bay**, 168
    margin flat; not aromatic — **Strawberry Trees**, 242
    margin flat; teeth near tip only — **Bamboo-leaf Oak**, 152

Margin wavy-entire
  leaf 10–14cm long; dark green — **Japanese Evergreen Oak**, 152
  leaf 3–5cm long, very buckled; pale green — **Pittosporum**, 237

Margin entire
  leaf 1cm long; alternate; dull, dark green — **Southern Beeches**, 133
  leaf 2–3cm long; opposite; glossy — **Box**, 207
  leaf 5–10cm long
    blue-grey; aromatic — **Gum Trees**, 238
    dark green
      glossy; stalk green; opposite — **Chinese Privet**, 250
      glossy; underside golden; alternate — **Chinkapins**, 139
      matt green
        aromatic; stalk green — **California Laurel**, 169
        not aromatic; stalk red and broad — **Strawberry Trees**, 242
  leaf 15–25cm long
    blue-grey, slender, aromatic — **Gum Trees**, 238
    broad
      hairy beneath — **Magnolias**, 162–5
      smooth and pale or silver-blue beneath — **Winter's Bark**, 168

SIMPLE LEAVES – DECIDUOUS – Rarely hard or dark

Lobed deeply – half way to midrib or more

many lobes each side down the stem	Oaks, 140–53
5–7 lobes radiating, nearly equal	
teeth fine, hard	Prickly Castor-oil Tree, 235
teeth big, occasional	Oriental Plane, 175
big lobe each side and many smaller	
teeth few, irregular, big	
leaf 10cm; alternate	Wild Service Tree, 180
leaf 5–7cm; shoot thorny	Thorns, 174
leaf 5–7cm; shoot not thorny	Mongolian Lime, 233
untoothed; leaf 25–35cm	Fig, 160

Lobed to less than half way to midrib

lobes prominent – more than just big teeth	
entire	
5–7 lobes; leaves broad, opposite	Cappadocian Maple, 211
4 lobes – no central lobe	Tulip Trees, 166
3 lobes	
widely spread, soon dark green	Montpelier Maple, 223
forward-pointing, near tip	Trident Maple, 222
2–3 lobes, asymmetric, aromatic	Sassafras, 169
toothed	
7–11 lobes, finely and sharply toothed	Downy Japanese Maple, 216
5–7 lobes, fairly equal	
leaf 7–9cm long	Smooth Japanese Maple, 216
leaf 13–15cm long; lobes shallow	Prickly Castor-oil Tree, 235
lobes unequal – 3 big, 2 small	
teeth numerous, fine; leaf alternate	Sweetgum, 170
teeth numerous, irregular; leaf opposite	Maples, 210–35
teeth few, big, irregular	Planes, 172–3
3 lobes	
large; teeth jagged and hard	Chinese Sweetgum, 170
small; leaves opposite	Snakebark Maples, 218–16
2–3 lobes on a few leaves; asymmetric	Mulberries, 160
lobes like big entire teeth, on a big leaf	
leaf 40–50cm; lobes near base	Paulownia, 253
leaf 25–35cm; lobes on outer half	Hybrid Catalpa, 252
leaf 15cm, nearly round	Bigleaf Storax, 245
lobules – small toothed lobes like big teeth	
around tip of leaf	
stalk very short; leaf up to 18cm long	Wych Elm, 154
stalk 2cm long; leaf 15–18cm, round in shape	Bigleaf Storax, 245
along each side of leaf	
densely hairy beneath	Swedish Whitebeam, 181
leaf slender, oblong, tapered	Oaks, 140–53
leaf broadly oval, dark, 10–12cm long	Alders, 128
leaf; narrowly oval, 5–8cm long	Roble, 133
lobed and unlobed leaves mixed on shoot	
entire, aromatic	Sassafras, 169
toothed	
hairy on shoot and leaf, or only on veins	Mulberries, 160
smooth all over; leaves opposite	Hers's Maple, 218
	or Trident Maple, 222

Leaves unlobed
  MARGINS UNTOOTHED
    leaves elliptic   **Magnolias**, 162–5
      12–50cm, smooth
        narrowed to base, aromatic, pale beneath; stalk
          dark red;
      leaf slender, 10–12cm long
        scent of aniseed, heliotrope   **Willow-leafed Magnolia**, 165
        scent of vanilla, orange   **Sassafras**, 169
      margin crinkled; leaf 13–18cm long   **Shingle Oak**, 152
      leaf-stalk 1–2cm long
        stalk dark red; leaf oval   **Tupelo**, 240
        stalk yellow-green; leaf slender   **Willow Oak**, 152
        stalk densely hairy
          leaf broad   **Goat Willow**, 112
          leaf slender   **Himalayan Tree-cotoneaster**, 176
    leaves round, fan-veined   **Judas Tree**, 196

  MARGINS WAVY; teeth obscure
    leaf 15–18cm long
      with pointed tip, dark glossy green   **Persimmon**, 251
      rounded, pale matt green   **Bigleaf Storax**, 245
    leaf up to 10cm long
      obtuse – broad tip
        thick leaf on 0.5cm stalk   **Persian Ironwood**, 171
        Thin leaf on 1–1½cm stalk   **Beeches**, 136–7
      pointed tip
        stalk 5cm; leaf broad; a spine at base   **Osage Orange**, 160
        stalk 0.5cm; leaf not broad   **Snowbell Tree**, 245

  TOOTHED MARGINS
    teeth confined to one side or tip of leaf   **Nettle Trees**, 159
    leaf toothed except for long, entire tip; leaf-base unequal   **Limes**, 230–3
    teeth well separated
      teeth like minute blunt pegs; leaf 5cm   **Manchurian Cherry**, 194
      teeth with whiskers; leaf 20cm long
        leaf green beneath, tip long pointed   **Sweet Chestnut**, 138
        leaf silvered beneath, tip nearly obtuse   **Chinese Cork Oak**, 151
      stalk with glands   **Japanese Cherries**, 192
    teeth close together
      teeth hooked
        stalk 12–30cm, scarlet   **Idesia**, 237
        stalk 3–6cm, flattened   **Poplars**, 108–11
        stalk 1–2cm; leaf with 13–18 pairs of parallel veins   **Armenian Oak**, 151
      teeth very small and very close
        teeth rounded; leaf rounded; opposite   **Katsura Tree**, 167
        teeth sharp
          leaf underside glossier than upper   **Deciduous Camellia**, 235
          leaf underside with white midrib only   **Sorrel Tree**, 244
          leaf underside with hairy veins   **Snowdrop Tree**, 244
          leaf underside smooth, green or grey   **Willows**, 112–15
          teeth hard, thickened; leaf on spur   **Spur-leaf**, 166
    leaf unequal at base
      stalk 1–2cm   **Elms**, 154–7
      stalk 5–8cm; leaf with fine untoothed tip   **Limes**, 230–3
    teeth with broad round bases
      stalk 1.5cm; leaf-base equal   **Caucasian Elm**, 158
      stalk 5–8cm; leaf-base unequal   **Limes**, 230–3

teeth triangular
  stalk 15cm, pink; teeth coarse **Dove Tree**, 240
  stalk 6−8cm, red
    leaf broad, opposite **Père David's Maple**, 218
    leaf slender, alternate **Hupeh Crab**, 186
  stalk less than 6cm *see below*

[Leaves unlobed, margins toothed, teeth close together and triangular, stalk less than 6cm]

Leaf with 10−20 pairs of prominent, parallel veins
  leaf oblong, much longer than broad
    blunt-tipped, shallowly toothed **Rauli**, 133
    pointed, sharply toothed **Hornbeam**, 130
    finely pointed, 15−17cm long **Hornbeam**, 130
    veins beneath silky and tufted **Chinese Red-barked Birch**, 124
    smooth beneath; leaves opposite **Hornbeam Maple**, 223
  leaf nearly as broad as long
    stalk 0.5cm, softly hairy, vein-end teeth projecting **Hop-Hornbeam**, 131
    leaf-margin finely but sharply bent under **Red Alder**, 128
    teeth at vein-ends projecting
      leaf shiny **Monarch Birch**, 126
      leaf matt; skinned shoot scent oil of wintergreen **Yellow and**
Cherry Birches, 126

Leaf with only 4 pairs of veins **Antarctic Beech**, 134

Leaf broadly blunt-ended **Common Alder**, 128

Leaf 10−12cm long × 6−10cm broad
  underside densely downy **Pillar Apple**, 187
  underside with hairy veins
    strongly toothed **Mulberries**, 160
    with irregular small teeth **Hazels**, 132

Leaf 3−8cm long
  very sharply toothed; gland on stalk **Plums, cherries etc**, 189−95
  finely toothed; heart or strap-shaped leaf **Pears**, 188
  lightly toothed **Birches**, 122−6

● **GINKGO FAMILY** Ginkgoaceae (from a Japanese name for the tree meaning 'silver plum', referring to the fruit). Ginkgos were the dominant form of tree some 200 million years ago, before the conifers and broadleaved trees we know today had evolved. Many species of them are known from fossils. Only one has survived into historic times. Propagation by seed, always imported.

MAIDENHAIR TREE Ginkgo biloba (two-lobed; leaf) was found by Europeans in Japan, but is native only to China. The first Ginkgo in Britain was the old tree at Kew, planted in 1761 and still in good health today. It likes hot summers so thrives best in southern cities like London and Bath, and is little planted in Scotland or Ireland. It is incredibly tough, almost the only tree able to grow well in the canyons between American skyscrapers. Only a few old trees flower at all regularly, and most of these are males. The females in Britain are tall and narrow, but in America they may sprawl widely. The fruit on female trees rots with an evil smell. 5–9–28m. l.

fruit, 9

● **YEWS** Taxus (Family Taxaceae). Eight similar and closely related species, five of them low shrubs, are found across the northern hemisphere. They are primitive conifers with separate male and female trees, and poisonous seeds surrounded by a deep, succulent red cup called an aril. The foliage, especially when drying out, is also poisonous to most animals but apparently not to deer. Propagation by seed, cuttings and grafting.

fruit
(fleshy aril)
10

COMMON YEW Taxus baccata (bearing berries). This native tree can easily outlive any other, partly because its wood is exceedingly strong: a very hollow bole can hold together and support heavy branches. Many of the big churchyard yews must be over 1000 years old. Just why so many yews should have been planted in churchyards is unclear. The bark is purplish-brown, scaling and stripping away to show bright red-brown patches. 2–4–28m. II.

Irish Yew 'Fastigiata'. All the plants of this form derive from one survivor of two found on a hillside in Co. Fermanagh before 1780. They are tall and narrow in western areas, more squat in the east.

fruit 10

'Adpressa Variegata' is a bushy female plant with very small oval leaves broadly margined bright yellow. It is a first-class golden shrub in the winter with an orange tinge on its new growth in the spring. 2–3–4m. l.

Another striking cultivar is the **West Felton Yew**, 'Dovastoniana', with a central stem and long, level branches arching out at the ends, with curtains of foliage hanging from them. 2–5–17m. l.

JAPANESE YEW Taxus cuspidata (abruptly sharp-pointed) is the only other yew which can grow as big as the Common Yew. But it does so only in Japan: with us it remains low and bushy except in the shade. Two specimens under other trees at Bedgebury Pinetum in Kent are around 10m tall. It differs from Common Yew in its leaves standing more upright, yellow beneath, and in its larger clusters of fruit. It crossed with Common Yew in an American garden and the hybrid Taxus ×media has an erect form, 'Hicksii', sometimes seen in Britain; it is like the Irish Yew but broader and with the leaves of Japanese Yew. III.

underside

leaf spray and twig

♀

♂

Yew fl.
2–3

autumn **20m**

MAIDENHAIR TREE

young tree

'Irish Yew'

COMMON YEW 12m

'Adpressa Variegata'

25

NUTMEG TREES *Torreya* (John Torrey, American botanist). Six species in the Yew Family, found only in California, Florida, China and Japan. The fruit resemble nutmegs but have no connection with them. The foliage differs from that of Cow's-tail Pines in being hard, sharply spined, dark shining green, and more widely spaced.

fruit 10

♂ 5

◁ **CALIFORNIA NUTMEG** *Torreya californica* is much the largest and least rare species, but most of the specimens in Britain and all the biggest ones are in western and southern gardens. A few of these have stout boles 1m in diameter, and in the open they make broad trees with long, level branches, from which hang lines of slender shoots. The crushed foliage has a strong, heavy sage-like scent. The trees are mostly either male or female, but some have whole branches of the opposite sex. The timber is of high quality and durable in the open, but being scarce and taking a good polish is more used indoors: it is pale brownish-cream, faintly grained. The top of the desk at the Westonbirt Arboretum's Visitor Centre is made from a large tree which was blown down there. 3–6–20m. II.

◁ **JAPANESE NUTMEG** *Torreya nucifera* (nut-bearing) was one of the very few trees to be brought out of Japan when it was a country closed to foreigners, before 1854. It came to Britain in 1764 but has been planted very little since. It makes a slender, thinly crowned tree, often yellowish and not thriving. The foliage has the same oily-sage scent as the Californian species, but is smaller and the shoots become red-brown in two years. 2–4–12m. III.

fruit 10

● **COWTAIL PINE FAMILY** Cephalotaxaceae (with a yew-like head). Seven bushy species grow between eastern India and Korea, across China and Japan. Each plant is either male or female. They differ from Nutmeg Trees in their soft, leathery, unspined leaves; and the similar fruits are borne in bunches.

fruit, var. *drupacea* 10

♂ 5

♀ 5

var. *drupacea*

◁ **JAPANESE COWTAIL PINE** *Cephalotaxus harringtonia* was named as the main species when two Cowtail Pines were brought from Japan in 1829 but was later found to be a garden form. The other one, named var. *drupacea* (bearing drupes or plum-like fruits) was the wild species and is the broad shrub commonly seen. The first named form has leaves spreading and curving at various angles. It is very rare. 1–3–5m. III.

Var. *drupacea* holds its leaves nearly vertically, showing their silvery-green undersides, on shoots that bend elegantly downwards towards the tips. 1–3–5m. II.

'**Fastigiata**' is an erect, blackish form seen in formal gardens with leaves 7cm long, decreasing in length towards the tip of each year's growth. 2–3–6m. II.

16m
CALIFORNIAN NUTMEG

14m
JAPANESE NUTMEG

10m
CHINESE COWTAIL PINE

bark at 40cm

seed

fruit, *10*

CHINESE COWTAIL PINE *Cephalotaxus fortuni* (Robert Fortune, plant collector who took tea plants from ▷ China to India and collected many other plants during 18 years' travels). This little tree is mainly seen in older established gardens in the west and south, where some are from the original seed of 1849. In damp soils and sheltered warm sites it makes exceedingly luxuriant shoots but never becomes more than a small tree. The heavy foliage makes the branches (at first very level) droop ever lower and the whole tree may lean to the ground. There are often two or three boles, tending to splay out. The shoot remains bright green for three years. 3–5–10m. II.

bark at 20cm

27

● **YELLOW-WOOD FAMILY** Podocarpaceae (foot-fruit, from the fleshy thick stalks on the fruit of e.g. Largeleaf Podocarp). A large and diverse family mainly in the tropics and southern hemisphere but with a few species in India and Japan. Many have large, leathery leaves; some have edible fruit-stalks. Propagation by seed or late summer cuttings.

PLUM-FRUITED YEW *Podocarpus andinus* (from the Andes) is not a yew, nor is Prince Albert's Yew (below) for which this is often mistaken. This tree differs from both in its smooth dark grey bark and soft leaves. Many grow with several boles and upswept branches; those with single stems have level branches. It is very hardy and can take clipping as a hedge, but is far from common. In young trees the leaves are harder and minutely spined, and less than half as long as the adult leaf. The green fruit ripens black, bloomed. 4–7–20m. II.

TOTARA *Podocarpus totara* (the Maori name) is tender and can thrive only in Ireland and in sheltered western gardens. In the south-east it will grow, but hardly thrive, if well above frosty valley bottoms. Its leaves are hard, leathery and spined, with a yellowish-grey tinge. The bark is grey-brown and peels coarsely. It was introduced from New Zealand – where it makes a large tree – in 1847. 3–6–18m. III.

CHILEAN TOTARA *Podocarpus nubigenus* (born among the clouds; it grows in very wet, cloudy areas of southern Chile). The English name, invoking a Maori name, is not a good one. 'Cloud Podocarp' would be better, emphasising its need for moist air and plenty of rain. In Ireland and Cornwall there are a few with boles 80cm through, but except in the west it is scarce and small. It differs from the true Totara in its foliage being more dense, a bright green, and striped silver beneath. 3–5–17m. II.

WILLOW PODOCARP *Podocarpus salignus* (like a willow) seeds itself quite freely in some far western gardens. It will also grow in eastern Britain but is smaller, and more likely to have many stems, making a thin though handsomely foliaged bush. The bark is dark orange-brown and on old trees it peels away in long, rough, dark strips. The leaf can be 12cm long and is leathery but soft and flexible. The shoot stays green for two years and the bud is just a small green thickening at its tip. In its native Chile, where it grows in small scattered groups, it yields valuable timber for building. 4–8–20m. II.

LARGELEAF PODOCARP *Podocarpus macrophyllus* (large-leafed) is one of the few Podocarps native to the northern hemisphere, occurring in various forms from Burma across SE Asia to Japan. Considered to be tender, it has been planted only in the mildest parts of the south and west, but it is unaffected by the rare severe winters that kill some plants around it. Very slow-growing, it becomes a remarkably leafy and healthy upright bush, of a distinct yellow-green, and has seldom become a real tree so far in Britain. The bark is dark grey and scaly. The fruit, not seen here but common in cities of the southern USA, has a swollen, club-shaped blue-bloomed stalk. 2–3–7m. II.

♀
6

♂
6

Plum-fruited Yew

bark at 30cm

15m
PLUM-FRUITED YEW fruit
8

12m
PRINCE ALBERT'S YEW

bark at 30cm

PRINCE ALBERT'S YEW *Saxegothaea conspicua* (out-standing) comes from the southern parts of Chile and Argentina and requires a moist site with shelter from drying east winds. Given these it grows well, even in Kent and Sussex, but it is a bigger tree growing much faster in Ireland and the south-west. The curved, hard leaves emerge tinged dark purple and give a grassy scent when crushed. The finer shoots are pendulous. The little blue-grey flowers may be found at any time. The bole is ribbed and hollowed smoothly with bark like the Common Yew's but in big round flakes. 2–5–18m. I.

▽
♀ flower
6–10

underside

conelet

29

NORFOLK ISLAND PINE 15m

fruit
9

20m
MONKEY-PUZZLE

bark at 40cm

● **MONKEY-PUZZLE FAMILY** Araucariaceae (first found in the lands of the Arauca Indians in Chile). Some 30 species, only from S America and Australasia. The mode of growth makes forked stems nearly impossible. All trees either male or female. Raised from seed.

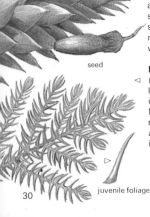

seed

MONKEY-PUZZLE or CHILE PINE *Araucaria araucana* is native to a small area in the southern Andes and was first brought to Europe (Kew) in 1795 after Archibald Menzies had pocketed some seed (nuts) from the Governor of Chile's dining-table and sowed them on board ship. It was a rarity until a big seed-lot arrived in 1844. To give fertile seed the two sexes need growing close together, but the sex cannot be told until they flower. Both can be either narrowly or extremely broadly domed. Biggest mainly in western Britain. 3–7–29m. II.

NORFOLK ISLAND PINE *Araucaria heterophylla* (variously leaved: young plants have spreading, sharp leaves but older ones have closely incurved leaves, covering the shoot). It is native only to the one island north of New Zealand, but its curiously layered crown is a feature of many warm countries now. In Britain it has been popular as a pot plant and recently inside large buildings. Out of doors it succeeds only at Tresco Abbey on the Scilly Isles. (I).

30

juvenile foliage

● **CYPRESS FAMILY** Cupressaceae (from the classical name for the Italian Cypress). A large and varied group of evergreen conifers widely spread over both hemispheres. Cypresses have very small leaves, usually scale-like; very small or no buds; and cones that are small, leathery, conic or round, woody or in Junipers fleshy. There are 18 genera, mostly growing slowly into middle-sized trees, long-lived and yielding strong, fragrant timber; this led to many being called 'cedars' by early colonists. Seedlings all have free, spreading, narrow leaves regardless of their adult foliage.

INCENSE CEDARS. Eleven species from the Pacific shores and islands, in five genera. Their nearest relatives are the Thujas with similar flask-shaped leathery cones. Only two species are hardy here. Raised from seed (or cuttings).

INCENSE CEDAR *Calocedrus decurrens* (decurrent – the leaves run down the shoots) makes impressive narrow columns in lines or groups in many gardens. They have short, very upright branches, but the wild trees in Oregon and California have sparse, level branches and broadly conic crowns. British trees increase in spread towards the west and Irish trees are quite broad. In exposed, dry areas the tops become tufted, losing greenery behind the branch-tips. Bruised foliage smells of turpentine. Cuttings strike easily but good seed can be had in most years and gives better results. 5–11–35m. I.

cone, 2cm

INCENSE CEDAR

bark at 50cm

incense Cedar   25m

cone, 1cm

CHILEAN INCENSE CEDAR

CHILEAN INCENSE CEDAR *Austrocedrus chilensis* is much less frequent, slower and smaller than the Californian tree. It is rather short-lived and a little tender, so largely grows in western and southern areas. The slender branches sweep up in a curve to make an egg-shaped crown, but the tree sometimes forks low and is less shapely. The foliage is flattened to a thin section and may lack in places the white stripes above, when it resembles that of Hinoki Cypress (p.34). The bark is very distinctive. It seldom bears flowers in this country. 3–6–15m. II.

bark at 30cm

31

LAWSON CYPRESS   'Allumii'   'Fraseri'   'Erecta'   'Wisselii'
                          'Green Spire'   'Columnaris'

'FALSE CYPRESSES' *Chamaecyparis* ('dwarf cypress', an unfortunate name for a tree growing to 60m or more). Foliage more flattened than *Cupressus* and cones smaller. Male flowers red or yellow, shedding pollen in spring; females smaller, green. Cones ripen in first or second year. Propagation by cuttings or seed. Three American species, two Japanese, one each from China and Taiwan.

under   ♂ 3   ♀ 4

flowers

6   cones 9   12

LAWSON CYPRESS *Chamaecyparis lawsoniana* (introduced by Lawson's Nurseries, Edinburgh, in 1854), one of the most abundant of all trees in gardens, both town and country, and in parks and churchyards, even without reckoning the 200 or more variant forms raised. It seeds itself freely and comes up almost any shade of green from yellowish to nearly blue, though cultivars are propagated from cuttings. Hedges of Lawson Cypress are often seen with no two trees quite the same green, being grown from seedlings collected locally. Very tough, hardy, and tolerant of any but ill-drained soils.

Invaluable for shelter, screening, and for giving winter form to a garden they also provide ideal cover for birds: town goldcrests, goldfinches and greenfinches rely on them for nesting sites, and the small finches are starting to eat the always abundant seeds.

No Lawson Cypress in Britain has yet stopped growing. Big trees are liable to be blown down and only in shelter are they now reaching 40m, but they should go on well above this. Young trees will often grow shoots of 60 or 70cm in a year – slender, and drooping in a broad curve to the tip. They clip well, if started young, to make a good hedge or topiary. The crushed foliage of every form of Lawson has a scent of parsley and resin. Some old trees hide behind a ring of branches that have rooted; if then the original bole and crown die back, the result is ugly. The species is native to Oregon and NW California, and all forms prefer a good moist soil. The bright pink male flowers adorn the ends of every shoot in spring, and shed pollen in April before falling. The powder-blue female flowers are set further back.

'Pottenii' 'Ellwoodii' 'Fletcheri' 'Lutea' 'Stewartii' 'Intertexta' 'Triumph of Boskoop'

Lawson Cypress cultivars number more than for any other tree species in cultivation: we show here some of the commonest and distinctive forms. They began to appear from the earliest seed imports raised in British and Dutch nurseries, and continue to do so. All are easily raised from cuttings. It is still too early to forecast the ultimate heights of any but the oldest cultivars: **'Erecta'** can reach 33m, **'Triumph of Boskoop'** is already 26m, and **'Stewartii'** 18m.

'Allumii'

'Lutea'

'Intertexta'

'Fletcheri'

'Pottenii'

'Ellwoodii'

bark at 50cm

'Wisselii'

'Filiformis'

33

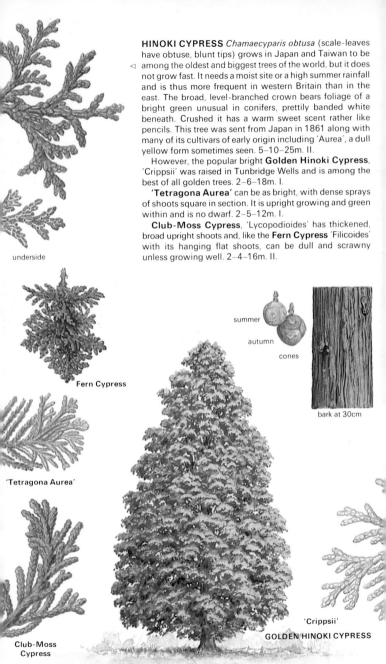

HINOKI CYPRESS *Chamaecyparis obtusa* (scale-leaves have obtuse, blunt tips) grows in Japan and Taiwan to be ◁ among the oldest and biggest trees of the world, but it does not grow fast. It needs a moist site or a high summer rainfall and is thus more frequent in western Britain than in the east. The broad, level-branched crown bears foliage of a bright green unusual in conifers, prettily banded white beneath. Crushed it has a warm sweet scent rather like pencils. This tree was sent from Japan in 1861 along with many of its cultivars of early origin including 'Aurea', a dull yellow form sometimes seen. 5–10–25m. II.

However, the popular bright **Golden Hinoki Cypress**, 'Crippsii' was raised in Tunbridge Wells and is among the best of all golden trees. 2–6–18m. I.

'Tetragona Aurea' can be as bright, with dense sprays of shoots square in section. It is upright growing and green within and is no dwarf. 2–5–12m. I.

Club-Moss Cypress, 'Lycopodioides' has thickened, broad upright shoots and, like the **Fern Cypress** 'Filicoides' with its hanging flat shoots, can be dull and scrawny unless growing well. 2–4–16m. II.

underside

Fern Cypress

'Tetragona Aurea'

Club-Moss Cypress

summer

autumn

cones

bark at 30cm

'Crippsii'
GOLDEN HINOKI CYPRESS

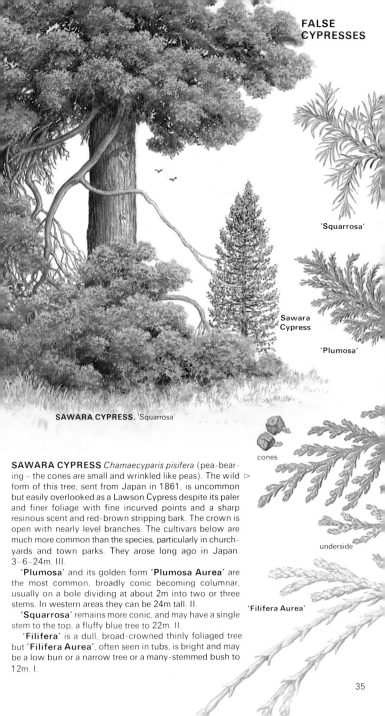

'Squarrosa'

Sawara Cypress

'Plumosa'

SAWARA CYPRESS, 'Squarrosa'

cones

underside

'Filifera Aurea'

SAWARA CYPRESS *Chamaecyparis pisifera* (pea-bearing – the cones are small and wrinkled like peas). The wild ▷ form of this tree, sent from Japan in 1861, is uncommon but easily overlooked as a Lawson Cypress despite its paler and finer foliage with fine incurved points and a sharp resinous scent and red-brown stripping bark. The crown is open with nearly level branches. The cultivars below are much more common than the species, particularly in churchyards and town parks. They arose long ago in Japan. 3–6–24m. III.

'**Plumosa**' and its golden form '**Plumosa Aurea**' are the most common, broadly conic becoming columnar, usually on a bole dividing at about 2m into two or three stems. In western areas they can be 24m tall. II.

'**Squarrosa**' remains more conic, and may have a single stem to the top, a fluffy blue tree to 22m. II.

'**Filifera**' is a dull, broad-crowned thinly foliaged tree but '**Filifera Aurea**', often seen in tubs, is bright and may be a low bun or a narrow tree or a many-stemmed bush to 12m. I.

35

FALSE CYPRESSES

WHITE CEDAR 12m

bark at 45cm

FORMOSAN 10m
CYPRESS

Nootka 'Pendula' 15m

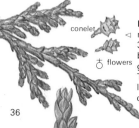

conelet, 5–8

fl., 5

♂ ♀
12
open
cone

conelet

♂ flowers

NOOTKA CYPRESS *Chamaecyparis nootkatensis* (discovered at Nootka, Vancouver I.). Growing just below the glaciers and snow from Oregon to Alaska, this will tolerate almost anything except chalky soil. It can be known from a great distance by its regularly conic crown, narrow in the east, broader in the west and very wide in Ireland where the lowest branches tend to root and send up stems. The foliage has a heavy scent of turpentine when crushed, and is harsh to the touch when rubbed the wrong way. The cones take two years to ripen and are navy blue in their first year; each scale has a beak. 7–11–30m. III.

'**Pendula**' has longer shoots hanging from upcurved branches. 7–11–25m. II.

WHITE CEDAR *Chamaecyparis thyoides* (like a Thuja) is a neat little conic tree with a round top found only in some large gardens in the south and east. It needs warm summers to enable it to grow well, since it comes from the coastal plain of the eastern USA. The foliage of each tree is either yellowish or dark blue-green and when crushed it has a warm gingery scent. The bark has spiralled grey stringy ridges. 3–9–17m. II.

FORMOSAN CYPRESS *Chamaecyparis formosensis* is now rare in its native Taiwan where a few are reputed to be 3000 years old and are immense. Since 1910 some have been planted in large gardens in the south and west and it grows a distinctive crown of widely U-shaped branching. The foliage is like Sawara Cypress but has a bronze tint, lacks the white markings beneath and has a scent when crushed of old seaweed. 4–8–16m. II.

36

'Castlewellan'

'Robinson's Gold'

cones

'Leighton Green'

NOOTKA CYPRESS
20m

LEYLAND CYPRESS
29m

25m
MONTEREY CYPRESS
(p.38)

'Haggerston Grey'

'Naylor's Blue'

HYBRID CYPRESSES ×*Cupressocyparis leylandii* (*Cupressus* + *(Chamae) cyparis*) includes all the hybrids between trees of these two groups. Only one is common at present, Leyland Cypress. All are raised from cuttings, though can be grafted on to Monterey Cypress.

LEYLAND CYPRESS ×*Cupressocyparis leylandii* (C. J. Leyland raised the first six trees) is a series of hybrids between the Nootka and Monterey cypresses. They were raised from seed from a Nootka Cypress in 1888, then two more from a Monterey Cypress in 1911. They all grow very fast in any site not too shaded or boggy and are now abundant in towns and suburbs, often clipped into a tall hedge. The commonest is **'Haggerston Grey'** with sprays at all angles, and the next most seen is **'Leighton Green'** with thicker foliage in long, flattened sprays. **'Naylor's Blue'** arose from the same seed batch and has slender dark grey-blue foliage, pale when new. **'Castlewellan'** has foliage at all angles, brightest gold at the tips and **'Robinson's Gold'** less seen at present, has flat, fernlike sprays; both arose recently in Northern Ireland. 11–19–35m. l.

TRUE CYPRESSES *Cupressus* (classical name for Italian Cypress) are distinguished from 'False Cypresses' (pp.32–6) by the foliage being in sprays of shoots arising at varying angles and by the usually bigger, more woody cones. Of the 20 species, 10 are confined to small groves in California and 5 more are in Arizona or Mexico. One grows in the Sahara Desert, with only a few surviving trees. Best raised from seed.

ITALIAN CYPRESS *Cupressus sempervirens* (evergreen). Native to S Europe north to Switzerland and east to Iran. Truly wild trees are of spreading habit, but the species was first named botanically from the narrowly conic form most usually seen, a selection of ancient origin. It is a form, however, which comes true from seed and it is common to see slender young trees growing 80cm a year from seeds brought back from a Mediterranean holiday. At that age a hard winter will often kill the top shoots but they are replaced and old trees are unharmed even in eastern Scotland. On old flowering shoots the foliage is short and thick. Unlike most other true Cypresses it has no distinctive scent when crushed. 8–12–22m. II.

cone
×½

MONTEREY CYPRESS *Cupressus macrocarpa* (large fruit or cone). There are more Monterey Cypresses in almost any Devon parish than in the entire wild populations on low cliffs at Point Lobos and Cypress Point near Monterey, California. It grows very much faster too in Britain, and when at its best, by our south coast and in Ireland, is three times as big as any wild tree. In the Midlands and east it is a narrow, erect tree but in the west it is enormously spreading. In Ireland, young trees are broader than they are tall, as in Monterey. Once widely planted for garden hedges, it has now been superseded by the Leyland, which keeps its lower foliage better. The crushed foliage has a lemony scent. 8–15–36m. III.

'**Lutea**' tends to be more branchy and is good in seawinds. It has golden foliage. 6–14–26m. II.

ripe
cone

seeds

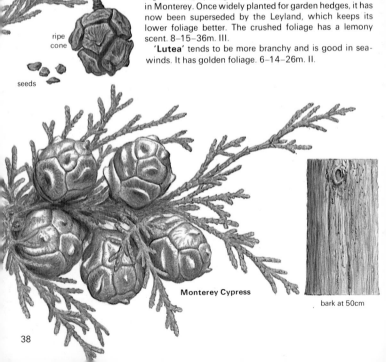

Monterey Cypress

bark at 50cm

20m

ITALIAN CYPRESS

25m

MONTEREY CYPRESS

GOWEN CYPRESS *Cupressus goveniana* (after James Gowen, Scottish horticulturist) has very few trees in the wild, in two tiny groves near Monterey, California. A fire in one in 1950 left one tree 14m tall among a mass of seedlings. It is a gaunt tree with few spreading branches, but in Britain the tree is typically a dense column, sometimes narrow. The short, noticeably right-angled shoots give a rich scent of thyme and lemon when crushed. The bunches of shiny red-brown cones on last year's shoots are typical and are borne within about 15 years from seed. 5–12–24m. II.

cone
×½

39

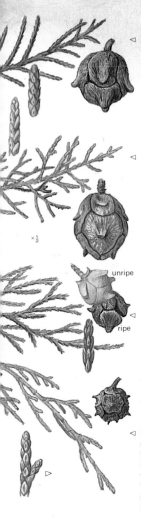

×½

unripe

ripe

cone

ARIZONA CYPRESS *Cupressus arizonica* was not distinguished from the smooth-barked form (below) until after they were both introduced but it seems to have been the one to be sent first. Most of the oldest and biggest trees have the stringy, fissured bark and green, almost unspotted foliage of this form. 5–9–23m. II – generally inferior to *C. glabra* below.

SMOOTH ARIZONA CYPRESS *Cupressus glabra* (smooth, from the bark) grows in central Arizona with long, level, closely-set branches, but in Britain it is neat and upright with an egg-shaped crown. It is a common feature of decorative planting in England but not in Scotland although it is completely hardy. It may need hot summers. It tolerates soils from chalky to peat and never suffers from drought yet grows well with high rainfall. It can be clipped and is frequently used for garden hedges. It grows at a moderate speed and remains neat. The grey-blue foliage, freely spotted white has a grapefruit scent when crushed and may be tipped with yellow male flowers through the winter. 5–11–22m. I.
    'Pyramidalis' has erect outer shoots, bluer with more spots.

MEXICAN CYPRESS *Cupressus lusitanica*. (Lusitania, the part of Portugal from which it was introduced. The tree had been brought earlier from Mexico by missionaries. They also took it to Goa, whence the alternative name 'Cedar of Goa'.) It is not fully hardy in Britain away from the south-west coasts; many inland trees died in the winter of 1962. Young trees are slender with sinuous pink stems and grey foliage, growing 1m in a year. Old trees are dark green and grow rather slowly. The crushed foliage has no distinctive scent. 9–15–25m. II.
    'Glauca' has smoother foliage in erect tufts of blue-grey. 8–12–18m. I.

BHUTAN CYPRESS *Cupressus torulosa* (tufted) is scarce but very hardy; several of the biggest are in Perthshire. The crown is egg-shaped, with raised branches from which the foliage hangs in loose, open sprays. Seedling trees are blue-grey with drooping shoots for some years but older trees have green, widely spaced, finely divided long shoots. When crushed they have an aroma like mown grass. The shallow ridges of the bark tend to be in spirals. Growth is rather slow. 3–6–27m. II.

PATAGONIAN CYPRESS *Fitzroya cupressoides* (cypress-like) is named in honour of Admiral Fitzroy who commanded *The Beagle* on which Charles Darwin sailed. It is called 'Alerce' in Chile, where it grows to a great age and size. In Britain it is slow and reaches its best size in the west from Devon to Argyll and in Ireland. Its rising branches are hung with shoots in dense masses often thickly dotted with cones. It has strong branches from low on the bole curving sharply up to be erect. The hard, blunt, outcurved scale-leaves, striped white on both sides, are distinctive. 2–4–16m. II.

TRUE CYPRESSES

15m

ARIZONA
CYPRESS

bark at 40cm

bark at 40cm

15m

12m

'Pyramidalis'

SMOOTH ARIZONA CYPRESS

2m

18m

16m

PATAGONIAN CYPRESS

MEXICAN
CYPRESS

BHUTAN
CYPRESS

41

JUNIPERS *Juniperus* (the classical name) are spread right across the northern hemisphere, north to the Arctic and south to the deserts. The cone scales turn fleshy and coalesce to resemble a berry. None makes a big tree nor grows other than slowly. Raised from seed or cuttings.

COMMON JUNIPER *Juniperus communis* has a wider range than any other tree and is the only species native to both sides of the Atlantic. It is also one of the very few to grow from coast to coast across America. High on mountains it is more like a mat than a tree and on better sites it rarely is the 6m tall required to be called a tree but is an erect bush. It is native to the chalk hills of S England, on the northern limestones and on peat in Scottish pinewoods. In gardens it is almost unknown other than as a cultivar. The prickly foliage has a scent of apples when crushed. Male and female flowers are on different plants as a rule and the fruit takes 3 years to ripen, from green to dark blue with a white bloom and finally black. Young shoots are triangular in section and bear the leaves in whorls of three. 2–3–6m. III.

Irish Juniper 'Hibernica' is much planted in small shrubberies and amongst heaths and dwarf conifers. Its slender vertical shape offsets the rounded or flat shapes of the other plants. 2–3–7m. II.

Swedish Juniper 'Pyramidalis' has long been grown as 'Suecica' and is like the Irish Juniper but looser in habit with the shoot-tips turning down and out showing silver. 1–2–5m. II.

Swedish ▽

△
Irish

TEMPLE JUNIPER *Juniperus rigida* comes from Japan, Korea and Manchuria but British stock is probably all from Japan and although hardy in the south of England is not seen in the north. There seems nothing rigid about this tree as the foliage, although finely pointed, is fairly soft and hangs on slender shoots in rather sparse curtains. It grows very slowly but usually keeps to a single straight stem and wide U-shaped branching. From a distance, the foliage appears slightly bronzed yellowish-green. Female trees bear lines of lumpy rounded fruit, bluish-green ripening dark purple-brown, closely held along the hanging shoots. The bark peels away in long grey strips leaving dull brown. 2–5–15m. II.

SYRIAN JUNIPER *Juniperus drupacea* (bearing fruit like plums) is the best Juniper for foliage, growth, shape and hardiness and grows on limestone or acid sands. It is seen only in rather few gardens. It may have an extraordinarily slender columnar crown or it may divide and be somewhat broader but is always a bright, fresh green. It has orange-brown, shredding bark and the longest leaf of any Juniper, to 2.5cm, rigid and spined with two white bands beneath. All the flowering trees so far noted here have been male, which bear numerous little egg-shaped flowers, bright green in bud. The 2cm fruit is purple-brown and woody, more like a cypress than a juniper. 3–6–18m. I.

Swedish

Irish

5m

COMMON JUNIPER

10m

TEMPLE JUNIPER

18m

SYRIAN JUNIPER

43

JUNIPERS

'Keteleerii' 10m
CHINESE JUNIPER 12m
'Aurea' 10m
PENCIL CEDAR 12m old tree 16m

♂ 4

fruit 4

fruit 6

CHINESE JUNIPER *Juniperus chinensis* is much the commonest Juniper grown in town parks and gardens and also the biggest. It is however, no great ornament, being dull, dark and ever more sparse with age. The adult shoots of scale-leaves have at their base numerous shoots of the prickly projecting juvenile leaves arranged in opposite pairs or in threes. Crushed foliage has a sour, resinous, catty scent. The bole is so deeply ribbed and hollowed that it is almost two stems. The ribs are smoothly rounded and often spiralled. The pale red-brown bark strips in long threads. Trees are usually either male or female, the males with yellow flowers through the winter shedding pollen in early spring. 5–7–20m. X – a dull plant.

    Golden Chinese Juniper 'Aurea' is a good little tree in towns, growing slowly as a neat broad column. It is male. The juvenile foliage is hard and prickly. 2–4–13m. II.

    'Keteleerii' is a rare tree but good. Its neat conic crown of adult shiny dark green foliage bears brightly blue-bloomed fruit. 4–6–10m. II.

PENCIL CEDAR *Juniperus virginiana* springs up like a weed on roadsides and in disused fields throughout much of the eastern USA, in a great variety of greens from black-ish to pale blue-grey. It has long been cultivated in Britain but is far less seen than Chinese Juniper and is often short-lived although there are a few big, battered old trees. The shoots are more slender than in the Chinese tree, the scale-leaves smaller, patterned by pale margins, and when crushed they emit a scent of paint or kitchen-soap. The fluffy looking but spined juvenile foliage is nearly all at the tips of shoots. 5–6–17m. X – poor in growth, shape and foliage.

44

MEYER'S BLUE JUNIPER *Juniperus squamata* 'Meyeri' was found by Frank Meyer in a Chinese garden and taken to New York in 1910. It is a form of the Flaky Juniper of the Himalayas and China, a very rare and uninteresting plant. Meyer's form is deservedly popular; almost metallic blue and conic when young, it tolerates any soil and hardship, and is ideal for low shrubberies bordering carparks. It may, however, grow with un-Juniper-like speed and send out long upcurved branches. It can then be moved out and a new cutting put in. The bark is in pink-brown papery scales. 2–4–11m. I.

under

DROOPING JUNIPER *Juniperus recurva* (bent down; branch-tips) grows high in the Himalayas and through Burma to China. In Britain it prefers the cool damp summers of the north and west to the warmer, drier east and the biggest trees are found from Perthshire to western Ireland. Young plants have many vertical branches from low on the bole and form a conic crown of drooping, thick foliage. Old trees may be broadly conic with a spire top, or open, wide bushes. The foliage rustles drily in the hand and smells of paint. 3–5–14m. II.

fruit
9

Cox's Juniper var. *coxii* (first sent by Euan Cox in 1920) from Burma has brighter, pale more hanging foliage and more orange, even shaggier bark. 3–6–15. I.

seed

8m

MEYER'S BLUE JUNIPER

11m

DROOPING JUNIPER

trunk

45

THUJAS *Thuja* (Greek 'thuia' a name given to an aromatic wood) are 6 species from N America and E Asia. Several are commonly called 'cedar' but they are a form of Cypress. Best raised from seed, they also grow from cuttings and the slow-growing Asiatic ones are sometimes grafted on to *T. plicata*.

'Zebrina'
22m

25m
WESTERN RED CEDAR

bark at 60cm

cone

'Zebrina'

WESTERN RED CEDAR *Thuja plicata* (plaited – from the appearance of the scale-leaves) is native from Alaska to California and inland to Montana. It can grow to 60 × 3m and withstands a good deal of shade and needs a damp climate. It is very commonly planted everywhere in Britain for shelter, specimens, hedges, and less commonly for timber. It gives a rapid yield of light, strong timber, once the favourite for ladder-poles and still for rugby-posts. In Canada it is the tree for totem-poles, as can be seen in Windsor Great Park, Berkshire. At first confused with Lawson Cypress, it differs in shiny, flat foliage easily aromatic (pineapple), stringy bark, erect leader and leathery cones. 8–15–40m. II.

'Zebrina' varies in the intensity and amount of yellow in the foliage. 6–11–26. I – one of the best golden trees, for size and shape.

18m
JAPANESE THUJA
bark at 40cm

12m
NORTHERN WHITE CEDAR

'Lutea'

'Spiralis'

cones

underside

cone

underside

NORTHERN WHITE CEDAR *Thuja occidentalis* ('west-ern'; discovered when the only other Thuja known was from China) was probably the first tree from America to be grown in Europe, perhaps by 1539, more than 300 years before Western Red Cedar was introduced. It tolerates wet soils but does not live very long or achieve much size. Old trees tend to lean over and lie down. It is sometimes grown as a hedge and less often as a specimen. 3–5–20m. III.

'**Lutea**' is more vigorous and stands up better. The new shoots stand out from the green interior crown which, like all forms of the species, bronzes in winter. 4–7–20m. I.

'**Spiralis**' has congested foliage prettily set in spirals on the shoot, erect on the short branches, and scarcely bronzes in winter. 3–6–11. I.

JAPANESE THUJA *Thuja standishii* (John Standish, Ascot nurseryman raised some of the first seeds sent from Japan) is easily identifiable at a distance by the broad U-shaped branching and the nodding shoot-tips of pale green or silvered grey-green. The foliage is hard and rounded, unlike Western Red Cedar, and when well crushed it yields a glorious scent of lemon and eucalyptus. The bark is unlike any other Thuja with its shiny patches of rich deep red and big plates lifting away. It is found in many of the major gardens in all parts, being hardy, but it grows rather slowly. 3–6–22m. I – a tree of great character.

47

'Elegantissima'

8m

12m

CHINESE THUJA

bark at 30cm

♂

cone

♀

cone

CHINESE THUJA *Thuja orientalis* came in 1752 – one of the first trees to be brought out of China. It is the only Thuja to hold its foliage in vertical flat sprays. This gives equal light to both surfaces, so both are of the same green colour – another feature not found in other Thujas. A third is the prominent hooked beaks on the cone, and a fourth is the lack of any distinct, strong scent when the foliage is crushed. This tree likes warm summers and is most often seen in the English Midlands, particularly in small, stone-walled village front gardens. 2–5–16m. III.

'**Elegantissima**' starts dwarf, pointed, narrowly upright, becoming broader. Foliage brightly tipped gold in summer, yellowish-green in winter. 1–3–7m. II.

KOREAN THUJA *Thuja koraiensis* is the only Thuja or tree with similar foliage with the underside almost entirely snow-white. The upper side of the shoot can be fresh green or, on some trees blue-green with a silver sheen when new. The foliage has the most appetisingly sweet scent of any conifer when crushed, like a rich fruit cake with plenty of almonds and a trace of lemon. The tree is uncommon and slow growing. Cuttings make good plants growing some 15cm in good years. 2–3–11m. I – for its silver foliage and delicious scent.

HIBA *Thujopsis dolabrata* (hatchet-like, from the shape of the white on the underside of each scale-leaf). This ▷ Japanese tree is frequent mainly in western and northern gardens, preferring a high rainfall or damp soil and growing much less luxuriantly in drier areas. Even in the west, many of the oldest trees are now going bare at the top and some have died. Most are many-stemmed with a central group of nearly equal size but some have a stout single bole with short, sharply upcurved branches and hanging shoots. The underside of the leaves has a well-defined pattern of thick white markings and glossy pale green margins 3–5–20m. I – for its glossy foliage of reptilian scales, almost like a green lizard.

underside

old cone

fresh cone

10m

KOREAN THUJA

15m

HIBA

bark at 30cm

Korean Thuja underside

49

●REDWOOD FAMILY

Taxodiaceae (*Taxodium*, yew-like, from the leaves of Coast Redwood, the first species described). A very ancient family, once included and diverse. Today, the ten genera total only 15 species. One genus, *Athrotaxis*, is southern. The others are northern. Four species are fully deciduous. Most of the others have hard, spined leaves, some scale-like, but Sciadopitys has long leathery leaves. The cones are globular, not large; some often spiny, some fragile. The one common feature is a stringy, fibrous red-brown bark. All species are best raised from seed, though cuttings of most will root.

COAST REDWOOD *Sequoia sempervirens* (evergreen – no great oddity in a conifer, but this was at first classed as a Swamp Cypress, hence its great distinction was in not being deciduous). This grows among low hills behind the coast from central California to the Oregon border, a narrow belt 800km long, bathed in the sea-fogs of summer. Those on the valley bottoms can grow 100m tall without their tops drying out and many are around 110m high – the tallest trees in the world. The biggest in Europe are in the rainy west and north of Britain; in drier warmer areas they tend to be thin and may scorch in winter. Cuttings root slowly but seedlings grow fast. The crushed foliage has a distinct scent of grapefruit. 10–20–40m. II.

GIANT SEQUOIA *Sequoiadendron giganteum*; Wellingtonia; Sierra Redwood. This is found only in 72 groves, mostly small, on the west flanks of the southern Sierra Nevada in California and 'Sierra Redwood' distinguishes it best by name from the other Californian redwood along the coast. It was found in 1852 as a result of the 1849 goldrush. One of them, 'General Sherman' 87m tall, 24.3m round, is the world's biggest tree. Within 90 years of coming to Britain, this was the biggest tree in every county of the British Isles. In E England lightning rounds the tops of many exposed trees but they are rarely if ever blown down. Even more than the Coast Redwoods,' the bark is very spongy – thick and yielding. The crushed foliage has a strong smell of aniseed. Neither redwood likes town air. Coast Redwood grows thin and miserable; Giant Sequoia keeps its admirable shape but grows slowly. 8–13–50m. I.

JAPANESE RED CEDAR *Cryptomeria japonica* grows also in China and the first seed came from there in 1842 so the oldest trees have a looser more pendulous habit than the more bunched foliage of the Japanese form which, after 1861 became the more usual. This tree is quite frequent in all parts but more common and luxuriant in the west. Many trees flower profusely with the males prominent from autumn until shedding pollen in February. Old cones may adhere to the shoots in great numbers. Coning will begin on trees only 5–6 years old. It is the most important timber tree in Japan, but is not grown for timber here. 8–15–38m. II.

'Lobbii' (William Lobb, Cornish collector brought it) is a Japanese form with more densely bunched foliage in upright tufts is quite frequent.

'Elegans' with fluffy foliage turning purple-red in winter is common, usually bushy and often on many stems splaying out and bending over with age. 3–6–20m. III.

fl. 2–3 ♂

seeds

×½

unripe cone

fl. 2–3 ♂ ♀

summer 'Elegans'

winter

35m
COAST REDWOOD

40m
GIANT SEQUOIA

30m
JAPANESE
RED CEDAR

bark at 70cm

bark at 90cm

bark at 50cm

DECIDUOUS CYPRESSES *Taxodium*. Three Redwood species, from N America; two are truly deciduous and one semi-evergreen and too tender to grow in N Europe (*T. mucronatum*).

autumn

25m

'knee'

cone *8*
×⅓

♂ fl. *4–5*

shoot with leaves

SWAMP CYPRESS *Taxodium distichum* (in two rows from the leaf arrangement), more usually called Bald Cypress in America, grows by tidal creeks from Delaware to Texas and flooding riverside swamps inland and for 2000km up the Mississippi River. In Britain it is customarily planted beside lakes and rivers and even on concrete-sided islands in town park lakes, but not by brackish water. It needs hot summers more than wet roots and the best are in London and the south, often in suburban gardens and parks far from water, and it becomes scarce towards the north and west. It needs standing water or regular flooding to grow the woody 'knees', which possibly help the aeration of the roots. The timber, although weak, withstands frequent wetting and drying, so is used in greenhouses. 5–11–35m. I.

DECICUOUS REDWOODS

POND CYPRESS *Taxodium ascendens* (new shoots ascend vertically from the branch) grows among southern Swamp Cypresses and is hardy only S England. The leaves are held close to the shoot which thus looks like a slender  cord. The ends of the branches usually curve sharply down, the cords spraying out and hanging from the end: the form 'Nutans' (nodding) hardly distinct in the wild. The bark is grey, coarsely ridged. Autumn colours are orange and brown. 3–6–18m. l.

16m

autumn

16m DAWN REDWOOD

POND CYPRESS

DAWN REDWOOD *Metasequoia glyptostroboides* (like *Glyptostrobus*, another deciduous Chinese redwood). Long known as a widespread fossil, this was discovered living in C China in 1941 and seed arrived here in 1948. It ▷ has been planted in almost every large garden and in many small ones and in a damp, sheltered site it grows fast. It differs from Swamp Cypress in having shoots and leaves in opposite pairs, and comes into leaf two months earlier. It shares the autumn shedding of the whole shoot plus leaves. Cones are long-stalked, rather cylindrical, and numerous after a hot summer, but male flowers need a hotter climate than Britain. Until 1979 there was no more seed from China and trees were raised from cuttings, softwood in early July or hardwood in January. 9–15–?35m. l.

bark at 40cm

TASMANIAN CEDARS *Athrotaxis* (crowded arrangement – the leaves) are a group of three redwoods from the hills of W Tasmania, similar in cone, slow growth, stringy bark and small size. The first two mentioned have hard foliage and differ only in that of the Summit Cedar being held close around the shoot.

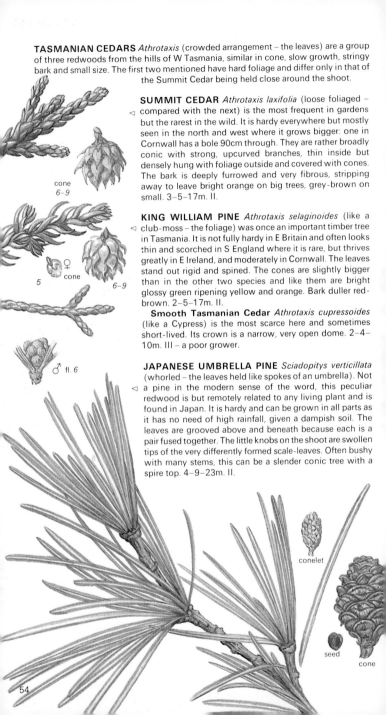

cone
6–9

♀ cone

5

6–9

♂ fl. 6

SUMMIT CEDAR *Athrotaxis laxifolia* (loose foliaged – compared with the next) is the most frequent in gardens but the rarest in the wild. It is hardy everywhere but mostly seen in the north and west where it grows bigger: one in Cornwall has a bole 90cm through. They are rather broadly conic with strong, upcurved branches, thin inside but densely hung with foliage outside and covered with cones. The bark is deeply furrowed and very fibrous, stripping away to leave bright orange on big trees, grey-brown on small. 3–5–17m. II.

KING WILLIAM PINE *Athrotaxis selaginoides* (like a club-moss – the foliage) was once an important timber tree in Tasmania. It is not fully hardy in E Britain and often looks thin and scorched in S England where it is rare, but thrives greatly in E Ireland, and moderately in Cornwall. The leaves stand out rigid and spined. The cones are slightly bigger than in the other two species and like them are bright glossy green ripening yellow and orange. Bark duller red-brown. 2–5–17m. II.

  Smooth Tasmanian Cedar *Athrotaxis cupressoides* (like a Cypress) is the most scarce here and sometimes short-lived. Its crown is a narrow, very open dome. 2–4–10m. III – a poor grower.

JAPANESE UMBRELLA PINE *Sciadopitys verticillata* (whorled – the leaves held like spokes of an umbrella). Not a pine in the modern sense of the word, this peculiar redwood is but remotely related to any living plant and is found in Japan. It is hardy and can be grown in all parts as it has no need of high rainfall, given a dampish soil. The leaves are grooved above and beneath because each is a pair fused together. The little knobs on the shoot are swollen tips of the very differently formed scale-leaves. Often bushy with many stems, this can be a slender conic tree with a spire top. 4–9–23m. II.

conelet

seed

cone

54

KING WILLIAM
PINE

7m

m

JAPANESE UMBRELLA PINE

♂
fl. 5

ripe cone

CHINESE FIR 16m

bark at 30cm

CHINESE FIR *Cunninghamia lanceolata* (spear-shaped, curved sides to a slender point – the leaf) is a redwood ▷ which has the typical bark and cones but the foliage slightly resembles a Monkey-puzzle's although brighter green and with orange dead foliage inside the crown. It is biggest and least uncommon in the south and west in sheltered gardens. It may have two or more stems. Old trees almost cease upward growth and their tops become dense, flattened domes. 6–10–26m. II.

underside

55

● **PINE FAMILY** Pinaceae has 200 species in ten genera, all in the northern hemisphere. They are the most highly developed of the conifers. Their woody cones are of spirally arranged scales each bearing two seeds; the leaves are linear or needle-like. Propagation of all the species is by seed; of the cultivars by grafting.

SILVER FIRS *Abies* (classical name for Common Silver Fir). About 50 species, usually the tallest trees in their region, with symmetrical growth from a single bole, erect cones, often large and leathery leaves rarely spined, attached by sucker-like bases.

core ot
old
cone

cone,
10
×¼

♀ 5

♂ 5

30m

CAUCASIAN FIR *Abies nordmanniana* (Nordmann; German botanist) is frequent everywhere in gardens except in East Anglia, often planted to replace Common Silver Fir where that suffered from disease. It is healthier and more luxuriant in foliage and more slender and shapely in crown. The bark is dull grey, cracked into small squares. Like all silver firs it is raised from seed. At first it makes a broad little plant before starting rapid growth in height, and benefits from light shade in the early years. Cones are borne only around the top of the tree after some 50 years of growth so are seldom within 30m of the ground, and break up on the tree. 8–15–42m. II.

BEAUTIFUL FIR *Abies amabilis* (beautiful) earns its name in the wild in Washington state with a silvery bark and dark, spire-like crown to 60m but varies widely in Britain. In the north and west it is usually of rapid growth, especially in stoutness of bole, and luxuriant in leaf; but in warmer, drier ▷ parts it can be thin. Crushed foliage gives a strong scent of tangerines. Leading shoots on vigorous plants, 1m long, bear small, erect side-shoots, rare in silver firs, around the middle. The shoots are covered with pale brown hairs. 6–15–32m. I – a very attractive tree.

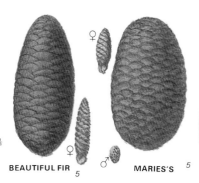

BEAUTIFUL FIR ⚥ ⅓ 5 ♀ ♂ **MARIES'S** 5 ♀ ♂ **VEITCH'S** ▷

bark at 40cm

VEITCH'S SILVER FIR *Abies veitchii* (John Gould Veitch discovered it) is a typical tree of the small mixed groups of conifers frequent in large gardens everywhere. Except in N Scotland, where it flourishes greatly, it is unlikely to survive ▷ 70 years and for years before that it will have ceased growth in height and begun to die back. A hallmark of this tree is a deeply fluted, pocketed and ribbed trunk. Outer shoots usually curve up to show their silvered undersides. 7–14–28m. II.

MARIES'S FIR *Abies mariesii* (Charles Maries collected it in Japan) is rare and has foliage like the Beautiful Fir except that the shoot has dense orange hairs and the leaves are only 2cm long instead of 3–4cm. Also the aroma from ▷ crushed leaves is gingery. The bark is pale grey with many darker freckles and, where branches have been shed, whorls of scars surrounded by a few black rings. 6–12–23m. I.

BORNMÜLLER'S FIR *Abies bornmuellerana* makes fine forests in a small area in NW Asia Minor and is in a few collections in Britain. It is to some extent intermediate between Caucasian and Grecian firs and has a shoot like ▷ the latter, smooth red-brown but unlike either, the leaves are densely set and nearly erect from the shoot and have prominent white patches near the tip on the upper side. The bark is smooth and purplish-black. 8–15–28m. I – a robust tree with bold foliage.

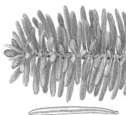

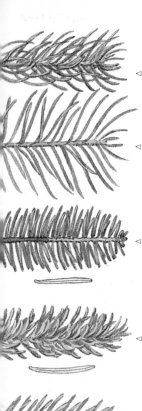

COLORADO WHITE FIR *Abies concolor* (same colour; the leaf is as blue above as beneath). This White Fire is uncommon, mainly in eastern and northern counties. It comes from the eastern Rocky Mountain system from Idaho to Arizona. The 5–6cm long leaves stand vertically from the shoot and the bark is blackish and lightly ridged. These are the chief differences from the western form below.

Low's White Fir *A.c.* var. *lowiana* (Low's Nurseries of Clapton introduced it), is much more common and a superbly shapely conic tree to 50m tall. This has either a deeply brown-fissured corky grey bark and leaves parted and upcurved with some blue-white above, or blackish bark and leaves spread flat, green above. These forms indicate a gradation from White Fir to Grand Fir. 8–15–50m. II.

SUTCHUEN FIR *Abies fargesii* (Père Farges, a botanically active French priest in China around the turn of the century) is a narrow-crowned tree in some of the gardens special-ising in conifers particularly in the north. It is often named '*Abies sutchuenensis*'. The gloss on the deep green leaves and the purple and mahogany brown shoots are marked features. 6–12–20m. II.

ALPINE FIR *Abies lasiocarpa* (with rough cones) is a beautiful and extraordinarily slender spire of a tree at 2500 to 3000m altitude in most parts of the Rocky Mountains but is not so fine in Britain. In a few Scottish gardens it is shapely and of moderate size but elsewhere it suffers from a disease causing swellings on the shoot and it grows very slowly with an irregular crown. 4–8–16m. X.

The **Cork Fir** *A.l.* var. *arizonica*, is rare but better, very blue, with thick corky bark. 4–9–20m. II.

CILICIAN FIR *Abies cilicica* (from Cilicia, Asia Minor) is a scarce but usually luxuriantly foliaged tree related to the Caucasian Fir and differing in longer, curved leaves but more notably in the bark, where shed branches leave cir-cular systems of black rings. The leaves are very variable as to the amount of white they show on the upper side to-wards the tip. 7–12–32m. II.

×¼

♀ 5

Colorado

♀ 5

Alpine

bark at 40cm

Cilician

5m
White Fir

COLORADO
WHITE FIR

young tree

old
tree
50m ▷

GRAND FIR 30m ×½

GRAND FIR *Abies grandis* (the biggest Silver Fir in many parts of its range) occurs near the coast from Vancouver I. to N California and inland to Montana and has been found about 100m tall. It is planted in some forests on a small scale and is common in large gardens, more in the west and north than in drier easterly parts. It can grow remarkably rapidly; the best are 40m tall in 40 years. Above that the top ▷ may blow out then new shoots replace it and grow as fast again. Like the Beautiful Fir's, its crushed leaves have a strong scent of tangerines. Cones are rarely seen closely as they are borne only around the top of trees some 50 years old and break up on the tree in autumn. 11–18–55m. I – exceptional vigour with good shape and foliage.

59

40m

NOBLE FIR

40m

RED FIR

×¼

bark at 60cm

bark at 60cm

♀ 5

◁

♂ 5

NOBLE FIR *Abies procera* (lofty) grows wild along the Cascades and in small areas of the Coast Range in Washington and Oregon only. In the British Isles, it has been commonly planted since 1850. The biggest trees are mostly in Perthshire and Argyll and only in East Anglia is it uncommon. The blue-grey crown distinguishes the tree among big conifers. The splendid pint-mug sized cones break up on the tree by November. They may be borne on trees only 9m high and their weight can cause damage to the tops of tall trees. Seedlings arise in quantity in damp woods, especially in NE Scotland, often on logs nearly decayed away, in dense lines. 8–15–47m. II.

RED FIR *Abies magnifica* (splendid; trees in the wild 70m tall are often still very shapely). With few exceptions, the big Red Firs are growing in Perthshire and Northumberland, for they are short-lived in dry and warm places. The bole often appears to swell out like a barrel and may actually do so a little near the base. The red bark which gives it the name is seen only in the higher parts of its range in California, and Oregon, not yet in Britain. It preserves a much more regular, symmetrical crown than Noble Firs of the same age. 6–15–38m. l – a marvellous shape.

FORREST'S FIR *Abies forrestii* (George Forrest discovered and introduced it in 1910) is one of several Chinese silver firs related to Delavay's Fir and distinguished by its bright orange hairless shoot and flat leaf. Young plants have whorls of rising branches widely spaced up the stem as they grow fast but they maintain this growth only in the cool, damp north and west. Elsewhere they tend to slow down severely then die. 6–14–24m. ll.

The variety *georgei* (George Forrest), a high altitude form, has shorter, greyer foliage with hairy shoots and cones with prominent bracts.

HIMALAYAN FIR *Abies spectabilis* (showy; foliage) has leaves to 6cm long banded beneath brilliantly white, in dense ranks each side of the shoot. The buds are 1cm long, white with resin on stout shoots of pale brown with deep furrows full of reddish hairs. The trees are gaunt with sparse level branches even where well foliaged in mountainous country and are thinly crowned and short-lived in dry lowland areas. The bark is dark grey with loosely scaled ridges. 5–12–30m. l – for its stout foliage, wonderfully silvered underneath.

PINDROW FIR *Abies pindrow* (the Indian name) grows at lower levels in the Himalayas than Himalayan Fir with which it may hybridise but is very distinct in Britain. The shoot is even stouter and is smooth pale pink or grey and the leaves, to 7cm have greenish-grey bands beneath. It is short-lived except in cool mountainous areas and the best trees are in Cumbria and N Scotland. They have a narrowly spired, level-branched crown and dark grey bark rather smoothly ridged. 5–11–32m. l – a very shapely tree with bold foliage.

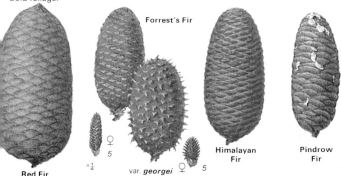

Forrest's Fir

♀ 5

×¼

var. *georgei* ♀ 5

Himalayan Fir

Pindrow Fir

Red Fir

EAST SIBERIAN FIR *Abies nephrolepis* (kidney-shaped scale; cone) is the related species replacing Siberian Fir in Manchuria, Korea and N China. It is grown in some collections, like the small group of conifers behind Balmoral Castle. In foliage it is between Veitch's and Sakhalin firs, the leaves in denser rows than in Veitch's and only greenish-white banded beneath. The bole is smoothly rounded. Crushed foliage is sticky and gives a smell like paint. 4–7–15m. III.

KING BORIS'S FIR *Abies borisii-regis* grows in Bulgaria and Greece and is possibly a natural hybrid between Common Silver Fir and Grecian Fir. It is a vigorous, often coarse tree in a number of gardens with dark grey roughly scaling bark and strong branches. The shoot is densely covered in pale brown hairs. The leaves are longer, more slender and sharper than in Common Silver Fir and more densely set. 6–15–32m. II.

East Siberian Fir ♀ ♂ 5

King Boris's Fir

Sakhalin Fir

Siberian Fir

Silver Fir

× ¼

SAKHALIN FIR *Abies sachalinensis* (from Sakhalin, the long, thin island off Russia north of Japan) also grows on Hokkaido, the northern island of Japan and in the Kurile Islands. Seed from Japan gives very small plants, bushy and slender-shooted for years but is no doubt the best for British conditions and will be the origin of the reasonably fine trees found in a few collections. They have purplish-brown smooth bark lined horizontally and with red-brown blisters full of resin, and neat regular crowns. The grey-brown shoot has fine hairy grooves and bears singularly dense sprays of grass-green slender leaves. When crushed these are sticky and give a scent of cedarwood oil. 1–4–20m. II.

SIBERIAN FIR *Abies sibirica* has a vast range from the Urals eastward and south into the high mountains of C Asia, but none of it likely to give plants suitable for Britain. A few may be found true to label but usually the tree grown as Siberian Fir is Sakhalin Fir. The true one has smoothly rounded shoots covered in soft white hairs and creamy buds but is otherwise similar. The bark is blistered like Sakhalin Fir. 5–7–12m. III.

30m

KING BORIS'S FIR

40m

COMMON SILVER FIR

COMMON SILVER FIR *Abies alba* (white; pale bark on branches of old trees) occurs from the Pyrenees through the mountains of C Europe. It was introduced in 1603 and from 1700 was much planted as a timber tree. It grows much faster and to a bigger size than any conifer known until the western American trees were discovered, and one or other specimen was the tallest tree in Britain until 1960 when the American trees began to exceed the oldest, which by then were failing. There was little planting of Common Silver Fir after 1850 because a greenfly became a serious pest and the American trees escaped it. Now there are big trees commonly only in Perthshire, Argyll and Ireland. The shoot has scattered fine blackish hairs. The soft, light wood may be used in indoor work and for boxes. 3–12–47m. III.

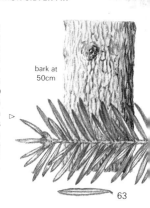

bark at 50cm

SPANISH FIR

20m
GRECIAN FIR

27m
NIKKO FIR

♀
5
×¼
♂

27m
ALGERIAN FIR

GRECIAN FIR *Abies cephalonica* (Cephalonia, an island in Greece) is one of the very few silver firs to grow to a huge tree in dry eastern areas like East Anglia or on limestones. It grows even bigger in wet areas. Big trees are rugged with wide-spreading high branches, often loaded with cones and liable to be broken. The leaves are stiff and sharply pointed, radiating all round the shiny dark red-brown shoots. The finely scaly orange-tinged grey bark of young trees matures to dull grey small squared raised plates. The buds are among the first on a conifer to shoot in spring and can be damaged by a late frost; so young trees do best grown under light shade for protection. 5–11–36m. III.

Nikko ×¼ ♀ 5 Spanish ♀ 5

♂ 5 △ 5 ♂ Algerian

NIKKO FIR *Abies homolepis* (with scales similar; cone structure) is a Japanese tree present in most gardens which grow conifers in variety, in all parts. Even near towns it grows quite well, and with the Algerian Fir is the only silver fir that will. Young trees are sturdy and have well marked layers of somewhat raised straight branches. The distinctive features are the hairless pale pink or white shoots grooved into plates and broad leaves brightly striped white beneath. 5–11–28. II.

SPANISH FIR *Abies pinsapo* (short for 'Pinus saponis', soap pine; twigs crushed in water yield a kind of soap) survives in the Sierra Nevada in southern Spain in only a few small groves around Ronda. It will grow on limestone and in dry places but often lives for less than 100 years and is thin and twiggy in the crown before it dies. It is a shapely young tree and the leaves can be grey-blue. They are stiff and blunt and radiate all round the shoot giving the tree its other name, 'Hedgehog Fir'. 3–9–25m. III.

ALGERIAN FIR *Abies numidica* (Numidia, old name for Algeria) is one of the best silver firs for dry or chalky soils or near towns and grows as well in wet, cool areas, but is not common. It is a shapely, dark foliaged tree with level branches and dense foliage with close rows of short very broad leaves crowding above the shiny green-brown shoot. The bark of young trees is smooth, grey with pink tinges, and begins to crack around the base. On old trees the cracks form a regular network of thin, rounded scales. 5–12–30m. I – a handsome, sturdy fir, growing where others fail.

Grecian 40cm   Nikko 40cm   Spanish 40cm   Algerian 40cm

× ½

Korean Fir

9m

26m

SANTA LUCIA FIR

KOREAN FIR

♀
♂
5
◁
underside

KOREAN FIR *Abies koreana* is the only conifer to be grown as, in effect, a flowering shrub. In the form first found and introduced, which grows on Quelpaert Island, S Korea, it begins to flower when about 1m high and soon bears rows of pink, greenish or purple erect female flowers and crowded golden globules of males. The cones are dark violet-blue but the colour is largely obscured by brown, downcurved bracts. This form stays as a dense small tree but those raised from wild trees on the mainland of S Korea grow much faster into more slender, taller, less densely twigged trees. The bark is smooth, almost shiny and black with white spots. 1–3–9m or 3–6–14m. I – for flowers and cones alone.

MOMI FIR *Abies firma* (the leaves are thick and firm) comes from Japan and is grown in many western and southern gardens. Young trees can be very strong growing with tiers of raised branches from a stout stem but on old trees the branches are level. The rather smooth bark has areas with a pale orange tint and is finally flaky and mostly dark grey. 8–14–35m. II.

MIN FIR *Abies recurvata* (curved back; leaves on 2nd year growth, pronounced on trees of some origins, negligible on others). This tree from W China is usually seen only in conifer collections in big gardens. Rather like a smaller leafed version of Momi fir, it similarly has the bands on the underside of the leaf only pale green, not silver as in most silver firs. The bark is brown and finely flaked and the bole may bear sprouts. It is a conic tree, narrow, with small, level branches. 5–10–20m. II.

Momi Fir   Min Fir

Santa Lucia Fir

Manchurian Fir

SANTA LUCIA FIR *Abies bracteata* (long-whiskered bracts project from the cone) comes from the Coast Range of S California with rainless summers but in Britain it grows best and lives longest in areas of moderately high rainfall. It is the only silver fir with a slender, pointed bud and one of the few with hard and sharply spined leaves. The bark is black, finely roughened and marked with rings of scars from fallen branches. Cones can be borne by trees 40 years old and are bright green through the summer. Very few Silver Firs seed themselves in Britain, and a seedling arising in a shrubbery between two big old Santa Lucia Firs at Exeter University is a remarkable occurrence. 5–12–38m. I – for its bold foliage, fine slender crown, and unique cones.

MANCHURIAN FIR *Abies holophylla* (complete-leafed; not notched at the tip, unlike most Asian species) is quite rare but grows well in Britain and usually has luxuriant foliage of long bright green upswept leaves, banded grey beneath. The shoot is stout, smooth corky-pink, faintly ribbed and the bud globular and red-brown. The pinkish-grey bark is finely flaky. 5–11–20m. I – good foliage and crown.

CEDARS *Cedrus* (classical name for Cedar of Lebanon). There are only four true Cedars and they are confined to the Old World. Many different New World and Australasian conifers with aromatic wood have been called 'cedar', but are not related to the true Cedars. Cedars flower in autumn and are raised by seed.

DEODAR *Cedrus deodara* (native name) is the Cedar of the W Himalayas where it has been known to be nearly 70m tall. Introduced to Britain in 1831 it was soon growing in many estates and gardens, popular for churchyards and for shelter and screening for gardens on the outskirts of towns, now suburbs. The leading shoot and the shoots at the ends of branches all droop; old trees may have some drooping branches but also often some turning erect. Young trees are usually pale grey, very weeping and attractive but darken and become twiggy with age. Cones are borne only on fairly mature trees and only on some of the branches but these can be near the ground. The bark becomes black with age, fissured into small ashen grey plates. 8–12–36m. II.

ATLAS CEDAR *Cedrus atlantica* (of the Atlas Mountains) grows in Algeria and Morocco and is common throughout the British Isles in parks, churchyards and large gardens. It is a good tree for dry or limey soils and grows fast into a large spreading tree. The leading shoot of a young tree nods perceptibly at the tip and shoots at the ends of branches rise at a shallow angle. Foliage colour varies from deep green through blue-greens to the whitish-blue of selected forms.

The **Blue Atlas Cedar** *C.a.* var. *glauca*, which is now the commonest form, planted everywhere but quite unsuited to small gardens as it grows so fast. Big trees are narrower than the green form and have a pale grey bark. 8–15–36m. I.

CEDAR OF LEBANON *Cedrus libani* was planted first in Britain around 1640 but the enormous trees on many mansion lawns mostly date from 1760 or later, growth being very rapid and most of the earlier trees being killed by the winter of 1740. It has been hardy since that time but young trees are sometimes killed by hard frosts. Young trees are slender and conic like a Deodar but are not common. The needles are 3cm long compared with 2.5cm in Atlas Cedar but old trees becoming senile may bear them less than 2cm and shed them in autumn. 5–11–40m. I.

CYPRUS CEDAR *Cedrus brevifolia* (short-leafed) has needles half the length of the shortest of the other Cedars and a more open crown. It is grown in a few collections or large gardens, sometimes with the mistaken idea that it is always a dwarf. The new shoots arch rather stiffly at the ends of the level branches and may be tinged yellowish. The bark is dark purplish-grey and smooth until rectangular cracks open in it and become numerous. 4–8–21m. I.

Atlas 40cm

28m

DEODAR

24m

ATLAS

old cone

×⅓

29m

CEDAR OF LEBANON

LARCHES *Larix* (classical name). The entire circumpolar plains tree-belt has vast areas of just three of the ten larches in the world – Tamarack, Siberian Larch and Dahurian Larch. The other seven are in small relict populations scattered widely in some of the mountains to the south. All larches are deciduous and have leaves set spirally on new extension shoots and in short dense whorls on spurs on older wood. The cones ripen in the first year but may remain on the tree for many years, having shed their seeds. The drying foliage of cut branches has the sweet scent of hay. Raised from seed.

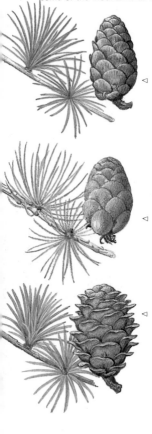

EUROPEAN LARCH *Larix decidua* (first classed as a Pine, it differed by being deciduous). Is native through the Alps to the Tatra Mountains and since 1780 has been an important tree for strong timber, especially in boat building, and is a good tree for shelterbelts and game-coverts. Early growth is rapid everywhere except near cities. The times of leafing out and shedding and its good leaf-litter are right for bluebells and other flowers of oakwoods to flourish and redpolls, siskins, tits and goldcrests are among the birds attracted by larchwoods. With the early bright greens and late gold and orange, larch is an excellent garden tree. 8–15–43m. l.

SIBERIAN LARCH *Larix sibirica* ranges from N Russia east to the Yenisei River where it meets and hybridises with the Dahurian Larch. It needs a hard and constant winter and is brought into leaf by mild spells in January and damaged by any hard frosts coming later. It is thus rare and usually short-lived with us but makes a shapely tree in N Europe. The shoot and cone are softly hairy. X (in Britain).

JAPANESE LARCH *Larix kaempferi* (Engelbert Kaempfer, German doctor, studied plants in Japan) began to be planted in British forestry in 1900 and by 1930 replaced European Larch over large areas of bracken land and poor soil because it grows faster there. It has a more twiggy dense crown and heavier leaf-fall which allow only grasses and woodsorrel to thrive beneath it. Old trees have broad crowns of level branches often laden with cones but without the hanging shoots of old European larches. Seedlings are easily raised, and if planted out when two years old they will soon grow 1–1.3m shoots. 10–16–36m. ll.

HYBRID LARCH *Larix × eurolepis* (a combination from the names of the parent larches, 'europaea' and 'leptolepis' – both now superseded). This hybrid between the European and Japanese larches was first raised at Dunkeld, on the Atholl Estates, Perthshire around 1900. By 1910 it was being planted extensively in the Tay Valley and as seed became available, in forests elsewhere. It grows faster than either parent tree on the poorer, higher sites. The best seed is from grafted plants of selected superior trees of each parent species grown together in 'seed orchards'. Many gardens have one or two Hybrid Larch rapidly becoming big trees. 11–18–32m. l.

$\times \frac{1}{2}$

25m

EUROPEAN LARCH

♀ fl.

2–3

23m

bark at 40cm

♀ 3–4

♂ 2–3

Japanese

♂ 3–4

European

bark at 40cm

3–4 ♀

Hybrid

♂ 3–4

71

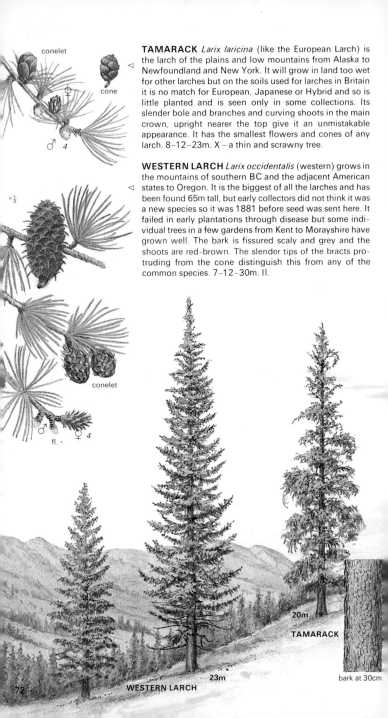

TAMARACK *Larix laricina* (like the European Larch) is the larch of the plains and low mountains from Alaska to Newfoundland and New York. It will grow in land too wet for other larches but on the soils used for larches in Britain it is no match for European, Japanese or Hybrid and so is little planted and is seen only in some collections. Its slender bole and branches and curving shoots in the main crown, upright nearer the top give it an unmistakable appearance. It has the smallest flowers and cones of any larch. 8–12–23m. X – a thin and scrawny tree.

WESTERN LARCH *Larix occidentalis* (western) grows in the mountains of southern BC and the adjacent American states to Oregon. It is the biggest of all the larches and has been found 65m tall, but early collectors did not think it was a new species so it was 1881 before seed was sent here. It failed in early plantations through disease but some individual trees in a few gardens from Kent to Morayshire have grown well. The bark is fissured scaly and grey and the shoots are red-brown. The slender tips of the bracts protruding from the cone distinguish this from any of the common species. 7–12–30m. II.

conelet

cone

♂ 4

×½

conelet

fl. ♂ ♀ 4

20m

TAMARACK

23m

WESTERN LARCH

bark at 30cm

DAHURIAN LARCH *Larix gmelinii* (Johann Gmelin, German naturalist who worked in Siberia) extends from the Yenisei River across the E Siberian plains to the Pacific where there are three forms. One, Prince Rupert's Larch with large cones and late leafing out is the only one suited to our winters. The others come into leaf in January when their low crowns become a mass of grassy green but they suffer in later frosts and remain stunted, except in a few northern plots at high altitude where they are shapely and 25m tall. 2–4–12m. X.

SIKKIM LARCH *Larix griffithii* (discovered by Dr William Griffiths, British botanist). The southernmost isolated larch species have big cones with protruding bracts and this, the most southerly of all, has the extreme of both features. The cones, standing erect from hanging shoots can be 10cm long and the bracts arch out 1cm clear from them. A tree of the eastern Himalayas, it is rare and usually short-lived with us, but one from the first seed, sent in 1848, survives in Devon. 5–8–20m. II.

autumn

GOLDEN LARCH

15m

GOLDEN LARCH *Pseudolarix amabilis* (beautiful) comes from a small area of S China and while similar to other larches in its deciduous foliage it is quite different in flower and cone. Male flowers replace the leaves on some spurs, about 20 in a bunch, and are on separate branches from female flowers. The cones have thick, leathery scales. They remain green until late autumn before disintegrating on the tree. It is tender as a small plant and transplants badly but becomes hardy with age. It is mainly confined to the south and west. Seed is obtained commercially from Italy, much of it coming from a single tree, and plants are not always available. Autumn colour changes from yellow through orange to foxy-brown over a long period. 2.5–4–23m. I.

bark at 30cm

73

SPRUCES *Picea*. A large group of some 50 species right across the northern hemisphere, on the plains in the north and confined to mountains in the south. They are all similar, differing only in details; all harsh and rough from scaly, never ridged bark, pegs left on the shoots from the bases of fallen leaves, and hard, usually spined leaves. The cones are all pendulous when ripening, which takes one season, and are shed whole. Many are important timber trees. Raised from seed.

TIGER-TAIL SPRUCE *Picea polita* (polished, presumably referring to the leaves) is the most savagely prickly of a largely spiny group. This Japanese tree tends to live for only 50 years with us although two survive from the first seed, sent in 1861. It has brown bark rough with papery scales, level branches and a narrow crown usually dense with dead twigs inside, and is the brightest green of any spruce. The leaves are rigid and have stout but very sharp spines which, in any but the lightest grasp will penetrate the skin. It is rare outside the largest gardens. 4–7–22m. III.

SCHRENK'S SPRUCE *Picea schrenkiana* (discovered by Schrenk in 1840). This tree has an extensive range in the interior of Asia and is not well adapted to the mild winters and variable springs of Britain. In its native Siberia, the cold winter keeps the buds from unfolding until the frosts have gone. A few are seen in collections from Sussex to Deeside, Aberdeen, slender trees with rather bunched but thin crowns. The foliage is like the Morinda Spruce but not hanging; each leaf straighter and more abruptly pointed. 5–8–20m. X – a straggly, poor tree here.

MORINDA SPRUCE *Picea smithiana* (commemorating an early botanist) from the central and western Himalayas is seen in many gardens in all parts. It is the only fully weeping spruce reaching 25–35m tall (Brewer Spruce may join it one day but is as yet seldom 15m) and many of the oldest and tallest are becoming very thin around the top or have died back. These are mostly around 130 years old, yet the two original trees of 1818 are in good shape. They benefit from shelter and cool damp summers, so the best tend to be in the north and west. 6–15–38m. II.

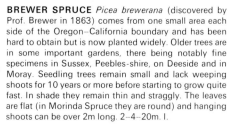

BREWER SPRUCE *Picea brewerana* (discovered by Prof. Brewer in 1863) comes from one small area each side of the Oregon–California boundary and has been hard to obtain but is now planted widely. Older trees are in some important gardens, there being notably fine specimens in Sussex, Peebles-shire, on Deeside and in Moray. Seedling trees remain small and lack weeping shoots for 10 years or more before starting to grow quite fast. In shade they remain thin and straggly. The leaves are flat (in Morinda Spruce they are round) and hanging shoots can be over 2m long. 2–4–20m. I.

×¼

SPRUCES

♂ fl.
of Brewer Spruce
5–6

20m

MORINDA SPRUCE

18m

BREWER SPRUCE

Brewer   35cm

SIKKIM SPRUCE *Picea spinulosa* (the leaves are tipped by small spines). This eastern Himalayan tree is found in a few of the larger gardens in all parts and can be recognised by the pale grey very scaly bark and the very open light crown. The shoots near the ends of the branches spray out but those behind hang down. The slender leaves point forwards so their very white undersides are best seen by looking along the shoot from the bud. The cones are 8cm long with numerous rounded scales ripening shiny brown. 8–12–25m. II.

♂

♀ 5

×⅓

75

20m

23m

SARGENT SPRUCE

SERBIAN SPRUCE

bark at 30cm

×⅓

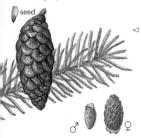

♂

fl. 5

seed

♂   ♀

SARGENT SPRUCE *Picea brachytyla* (short swollen lump or knot) comes from W and C China and was collected in several different areas between 1901 and 1910. These early trees in the gardens which received seed from the expeditions of Ernest Wilson show several variant forms, one bushy and short, but most of the trees are more open with rising branches. The silvery white beneath the leaf often extends across the midrib. The minor shoots hang and new shoots are pure white fading to cream. 6–14–26m. l.

SERBIAN SPRUCE *Picea omorika* (local name) astonished botanists when it was discovered in 1875 because all the other flat-leafed spruces inhabit only the Pacific region and E Himalayas. It is one of the most useful of all conifers for ornamental planting, for its neat shape, and ability to grow fast on both chalky and very acid soils. Opening its buds late it escapes damage from late frosts. It is easily raised from seed from groups of trees here and is the best spruce in or near towns. Most trees are slender-conic but a few are dense very narrow columns. 8–15–30m. l.

5

k at 35cm

30m

25m

SITKA SPRUCE

23m

HONDO SPRUCE

ORIENTAL SPRUCE

ORIENTAL SPRUCE *Picea orientalis* (more easterly than the Common Spruce) from the Caucasus Mountains and E Turkey has the shortest leaves of any spruce. They are glossy with bevelled tips and point along the shoot rather than spread from it, encasing it and giving each shoot a rather spiky appearance. It also has very regular whorls of level branches and young trees would be highly superior Christmas trees. 8–15–32m. I.

SITKA SPRUCE *Picea sitchensis* (from Sitka Island, Alaska) extends from Kodiak I, Alaska, all the way round the coast to mid-California, rarely out of sight of the sea. It is by far the biggest spruce and many are 80m tall. It will grow 1m a year in wet areas on the poorest peaty soils well up the hillsides by our west coasts and faster than any other tree on high moors. Hence it is the chief forest tree in the west and is planted by the hundred million every year. The timber is light and strong. The foliage is sharply spined and hard. 9–18–52m. III.

HONDO SPRUCE *Picea jezoensis* var. *hondoensis* (from Honshu, Japan, *jezoensis* is from Yeddo, now Hokkaido, the northern island). This is a sturdy tree with stout *white* shoots (not, as often described, yellow) and broad leaves strongly coated with white beneath. It is uncommon, with the biggest trees in the west from Cornwall north to NE Scotland. 4–11–28m. II.

♀ 5

77

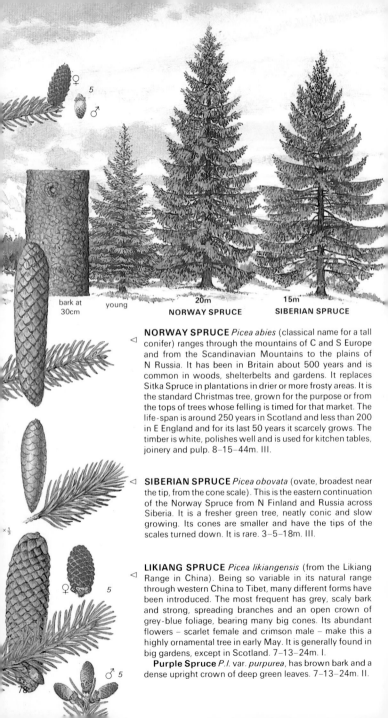

bark at 30cm | young | **20m** | **15m**
NORWAY SPRUCE | **SIBERIAN SPRUCE**

NORWAY SPRUCE *Picea abies* (classical name for a tall conifer) ranges through the mountains of C and S Europe and from the Scandinavian Mountains to the plains of N Russia. It has been in Britain about 500 years and is common in woods, shelterbelts and gardens. It replaces Sitka Spruce in plantations in drier or more frosty areas. It is the standard Christmas tree, grown for the purpose or from the tops of trees whose felling is timed for that market. The life-span is around 250 years in Scotland and less than 200 in E England and for its last 50 years it scarcely grows. The timber is white, polishes well and is used for kitchen tables, joinery and pulp. 8–15–44m. III.

SIBERIAN SPRUCE *Picea obovata* (ovate, broadest near the tip, from the cone scale). This is the eastern continuation of the Norway Spruce from N Finland and Russia across Siberia. It is a fresher green tree, neatly conic and slow growing. Its cones are smaller and have the tips of the scales turned down. It is rare. 3–5–18m. III.

LIKIANG SPRUCE *Picea likiangensis* (from the Likiang Range in China). Being so variable in its natural range through western China to Tibet, many different forms have been introduced. The most frequent has grey, scaly bark and strong, spreading branches and an open crown of grey-blue foliage, bearing many big cones. Its abundant flowers – scarlet female and crimson male – make this a highly ornamental tree in early May. It is generally found in big gardens, except in Scotland. 7–13–24m. I.

Purple Spruce *P.l.* var. *purpurea*, has brown bark and a dense upright crown of deep green leaves. 7–13–24m. II.

COLORADO BLUE SPRUCE *Picea pungens* var. *glauca* ('pungens' from the pungent [stiff, spined] leaves). This tree in the wild along the eastern ranges of the Rocky Mountains is variably green or blue. A few blue-white forms have been selected and are among the commonest conifers in gardens. The shoots are stout and either orange-brown or purple, rough where the leaves have been shed, from the large pegs left behind. The scales of buds at shoot ends bend out as in Dragon Spruce. Bark purple-brown, coarsely scaly. 3–6–23m. II.

'**Hoopesii**' is a strikingly ice-blue-white, probably semi-dwarf form now planted. I.

♂ 5

15m

ENGELMANN SPRUCE

18m

COLORADO BLUE SPRUCE

×⅓

ENGELMANN SPRUCE *Picea engelmannii* (first described by Georg Engelmann, a St Louis doctor) is found at moderate elevations in the eastern Rocky Mountain ranges from Jasper, Alberta to the Mexican border and in the western ranges south to Oregon. It is scarce in Britain; a slender tree grown mainly in the north. 5–9–30m. III.

The form '**Glauca**' is more widespread here and like a good Colorado Blue Spruce but with soft, flexible leaves, orange-brown bark with fine papery scales and small copper-brown cones. Crushed leaves smell of menthol. 4–7–25m. I.

♂ 5

BLACK SPRUCE *Picea mariana* (of Maryland, in a broad sense; it is not native there) is native to almost all of Canada and extends to the USA only around the Great Lakes. It has the shortest leaves of any spruce except the Oriental in which they are bevelled and blunt and in Black Spruce they are finely pointed. The trees are slender and blue-grey with bark pinkish-grey at first then dark purplish with grey flakes not yet here as black as in Canada. Tiny cones cluster densely around the crown tops. It is sometimes seen in more or less suburban gardens. 3–6–19m. III.

RED SPRUCE *Picea rubens* (growing red, from the cones) comes from SE Canada and the high Allegheny Mountains to Tennessee. It is closely related to the Black Spruce but grows faster and bigger here, and is more scarce. The bark is purple-brown flaking finely until the tree is old and big and has smooth rounded scales. The slender leaves usually rise abruptly above the shoot, but share with Black Spruce a strong menthol scent when crushed. 5–14–28m. II.

WHITE SPRUCE *Picea glauca* (glaucous, blue-white bloomed foliage) grows right across Canada and round the Great Lakes. It was sent to Britain nearly 300 years ago but has never been much planted, although in Denmark it has been very successful behind sand-dunes and may be more planted in Britain soon. It is a slender tree which grows quite fast when young but slowly with advancing age. The shoot is smooth, and white or pink. Crushed leaves give a scent of grapefruit or currants but some find it mousey. Old trees have purple-grey bark with circular plates. 8–15–24m. II.

DRAGON SPRUCE *Picea asperata* (rough, harsh; from the stiff, spined leaves). This Chinese tree has been sent in various forms since 1910 varying only in detail. The dark brown or purplish-grey bark flakes untidily on the bole and lower branches, which are big and spreading while upper ones may curve over and hang heavy with foliage. The end buds have pale brown papery scales curving out. The leaves radiate from all round the stout, grooved shoot. 5–10–24m. III.

ALCOCK'S SPRUCE *Picea bicolor* (two-coloured; almost the only square-leafed spruce with the undersides much whiter than the top sides). This Japanese spruce can be known at a distance by its crown of long, low branches gently curving up, each with its dense canopy of foliage. A group well spaced is a striking feature, and like Likiang Spruce, the flowering in early May can be spectacular. Young trees have a dull grey bark tinged pink and roughly scaly becoming on older trees more purplish with smoother square plates. 3–7–20m. II.

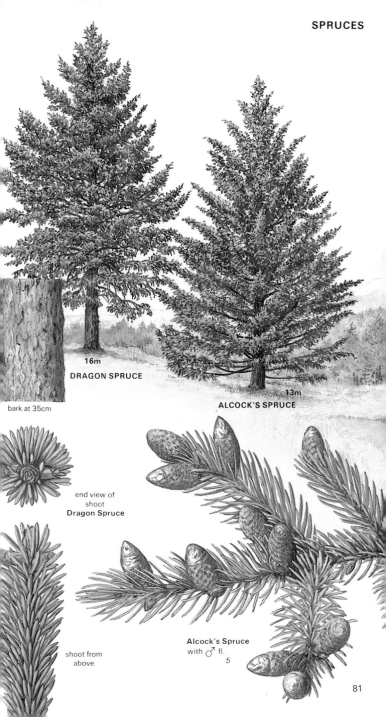

bark at 35cm

16m
DRAGON SPRUCE

13m
ALCOCK'S SPRUCE

end view of
shoot
Dragon Spruce

shoot from
above

Alcock's Spruce
with ♂ fl.
5

81

HEMLOCKS *Tsuga* (the Japanese name). Nine or ten species and one natural hybrid, with two species in each of eastern and western N America, the Himalayas and Japan, and two or three in China. Hemlocks are closely related to spruces and their timber is largely used for paper-pulp. All are raised from seed.

♀ 5

4

♂

underside

36m

bark at 40cm

cone

×½

WESTERN HEMLOCK *Tsuga heterophylla* (with other leaves, leaves of mixed size on the same shoot). This is the giant among the Hemlocks, with trees to 70m tall in the middle parts of its great range from Alaska to N California. It is also by far the biggest in W Europe where it grows at great speed on soils as different as light sands and clay or shallow peat, but not on chalk. It grows fastest in its early years under light shade and thrives on a heavy rainfall but will grow in dry areas, although, in exposure there its top becomes thin and may die back. Elsewhere it is remarkably constant in its elegant, narrow-spired conic crown and its long, *drooping* leading shoot. 8–17–45m. I.

EASTERN HEMLOCK *Tsuga canadensis* was the first of the genus known to Europeans. The scent from its bruised leaves was thought similar to that of the poisonous herb, hemlock. In the Appalachian Mountains it is a pale, slender and graceful tree to 45m but in Britain where it is frequent though far less so than the Western Hemlock, it is a dark, broad-topped, heavily branched shapeless tree with coarse blackish bark. As a hedge it is inferior to the Western, which clips beautifully. A mark of this species is the line of reversed leaves along the shoot. 6–9–30m. X.

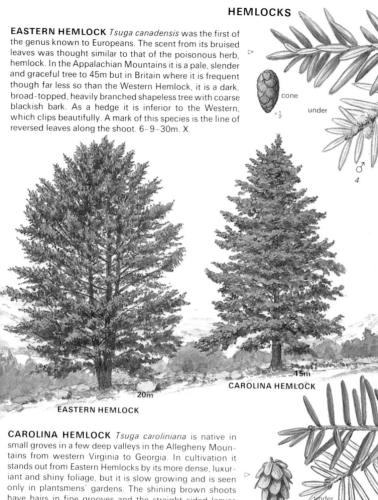

CAROLINA HEMLOCK

EASTERN HEMLOCK

CAROLINA HEMLOCK *Tsuga caroliniana* is native in small groves in a few deep valleys in the Allegheny Mountains from western Virginia to Georgia. In cultivation it stands out from Eastern Hemlocks by its more dense, luxuriant and shiny foliage, but it is slow growing and is seen only in plantsmens' gardens. The shining brown shoots have hairs in fine grooves and the straight-sided leaves stand out from the shoot. The bright rosy purple female flowers are numerous in some years. 2–5–12m. I.

CHINESE HEMLOCK *Tsuga chinensis* was discovered and sent here in 1900 but has never been freely available and grows only in some conifer collections. The crown is strongly branched broad and bushy like the two Japanese Hemlocks (p.84) but it differs at a distance by the pale green foliage with arching shoots. The foliage is like the Western Hemlock but yellower above and the bands beneath are green, not silver. The dark brown bark is coarsely scaly then fissured. 4–6–17m. III.

83

SOUTHERN JAPANESE HEMLOCK *Tsuga sieboldii*
(Philip von Siebold, German eye-surgeon who brought
many kinds of plants back from Japan when it was closed
to foreign travellers) is grown in a number of collections
and sometimes in other gardens. It is always bushy and
often has many stems but some of the taller trees have a
single bole. The foliage varies somewhat towards that of
Southern Japanese Hemlock but the quite hairless shoot is
usually paler and often shining buff or white, and the leaves
may point forwards in irregular rows. 3–6–19m. III.

NORTHERN JAPANESE HEMLOCK *Tsuga diversifolia*
(leaves of varying form) seen only in collections, less often
than the Southern species although it has prettier foliage.
The shoot is bright orange or chestnut-brown and it needs
a lens to see that it has a thin cover of fine hairs. The short,
broad and blunt leaves are hard and project at right angles
and, are very broadly banded bright white beneath. It is a
dense and bushy tree, usually growing more than one
stem. 2–5–15m. II.

HIMALAYAN HEMLOCK *Tsuga dumosa* (shrubby, a
slur on a good tree) is too tender to thrive in eastern parts
and the few big trees are in Cornwall and Ireland. It is
shrubby when young; egg-shaped and pendulous, but in
the right place it makes a broad tree on one or two sinuous
boles. The bark is dull pink, heavily ridged and flaky with
shallow fissures, like an old larch. The leaf at 3cm is longer
than in any other hemlock, and is rigid. The pale pink-
brown shoot is finely hairy. 3–5–23m. II.

♀5

MOUNTAIN HEMLOCK *Tsuga mertensiana* (discovered
by Karl Mertens, German naturalist) grows near the snow-
line and on bleak high lavas from Alaska to C California and
is very tough. It grows best in Britain in Perthshire and
further north, a highly attractive pendulous bluish tree but
uncommon. The leaves radiate all round the shoot and
where the shoots are short they look like the spurs of a blue
cedar, but are so.. with rounded tips. 2–5–31m. I.

×½

JEFFREY'S HEMLOCK *Tsuga ×jeffreyi*. John Jeffrey
sent the seed from which the tree was named, but had
collected it from a Mountain Hemlock. Others turned up
among mixed seedlings from Vancouver Island and among
rhododendron seedlings from the Selkirk Mountains. This
hybrid between Mountain and Western Hemlocks was not
discovered growing wild until 1968. It is in a few collections, where it has a very scaly blackish bark. Young trees
are rounded, upswept bushes, olive-grey in colour. The
leaves are thinner, more sparse and flatter than Mountain
Hemlock. 2–5–15m. II.

Northern
Japanese
Hemlock

bark at 20cm

10m

**SOUTHERN JAPANESE
HEMLOCK**

8m

**NORTHERN
JAPANESE
HEMLOCK** bark at 20cm

♀5

MOUNTAIN HEMLOCK

♂5

20m

DOUGLAS FIRS *Pseudotsuga* (false hemlock; a name devised when the genus was separated from spruces, to show its affinities). 7 species, 4 in China, 2 in western N America; 1 in Japan. Unique cone with projecting 3-pronged bract. Differ from Spruces in soft foliage and fissured bark; from Silver Firs in hanging cone shed complete. Raised from seed.

♀ 4

var. *glauca*

♀ 4

48m

bark at 45cm

×½

Douglas Fir

Blue Douglas Fir

DOUGLAS FIR *Pseudotsuga menziesii* (discovered by Archibald Menzies in 1793, though introduced later by David Douglas). Common everywhere, in plantations, shelterbelts, and gardens. It grows very fast and very tall; nearly every tree in Britain above 55m is a Douglas, most of them in the deep narrow valleys of N Scotland. The strong, heavy red timber has many uses. Crushed foliage has a sweet, fruity scent. 9–17–59m. II.

Blue Douglas Fir var. *glauca* from the eastern Rockies is more a southern garden tree but uncommon. The foliage has little scent. 6–12–26m. I – a good blue form is a remarkably attractive fir tree.

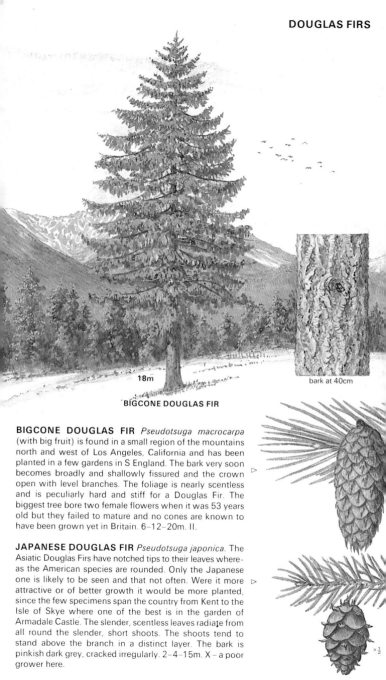

18m

BIGCONE DOUGLAS FIR

bark at 40cm

BIGCONE DOUGLAS FIR *Pseudotsuga macrocarpa* (with big fruit) is found in a small region of the mountains north and west of Los Angeles, California and has been planted in a few gardens in S England. The bark very soon becomes broadly and shallowly fissured and the crown open with level branches. The foliage is nearly scentless and is peculiarly hard and stiff for a Douglas Fir. The biggest tree bore two female flowers when it was 53 years old but they failed to mature and no cones are known to have been grown yet in Britain. 6–12–20m. II.

JAPANESE DOUGLAS FIR *Pseudotsuga japonica.* The Asiatic Douglas Firs have notched tips to their leaves where-as the American species are rounded. Only the Japanese one is likely to be seen and that not often. Were it more attractive or of better growth it would be more planted, since the few specimens span the country from Kent to the Isle of Skye where one of the best is in the garden of Armadale Castle. The slender, scentless leaves radiate from all round the slender, short shoots. The shoots tend to stand above the branch in a distinct layer. The bark is pinkish dark grey, cracked irregularly. 2–4–15m. X – a poor grower here.

×½

87

PINES Pinus (classical Latin name) are the largest and most widespread genus of conifer with over 100 species in all the temperate and subtropical areas of the Northern Hemisphere. They are the most important source of softwood timber. All are raised from seed.

TWO-NEEDLE PINES. Pines differ from all other conifers by their leaves being borne in bundles of 2, 3 or 5. Northern species are nearly all 2-needled.

conelet 6

SCOTS PINE *Pinus sylvestris* (of the woods or forests). This is the most far ranging pine, extending from Spain to E Siberia and is the only one native to Britain. There are fine stands of natural origin, as in Glen Affric and as far south as the Black Wood of Rannoch but south of this and throughout England, Wales and Ireland all the woods were planted. Re-introduced to N Hampshire in 1660 and to the New Forest in 1770 Scots Pine has run wild over the southern heaths. But in commerial forestry it is being replaced (except in N Scotland) by the faster growing Corsican Pine. The timber is 'deal', widely used in buildings. It grows fast for some years on any well-drained soil except chalk, often making shoots 1m long, but soon becomes slow. 8–12–36m. III.

RED PINE *Pinus resinosa* (resinous) is the American equivalent of the Scots Pine from around the Great Lakes and has a similar 'red' bark, particularly on the branches. It is a more handsome tree with longer, more lax leaves which are very slender and have the feature of snapping cleanly when bent in a sharp curve, which those of other 2-needle pines do not. It is rarely seen outside pine collections. 6–12–20m. I – a good-looking tree.

JAPANESE RED PINE *Pinus densiflora* (with flowers closely set) is the Scots Pine of SE Asia, growing in China, Japan and Korea. Young plants are attractive and may be seen in a number of gardens. They are neatly conic, quite vigorous, and have slender shoots of bright pale green conspicuous between the sparsely set slender leaves. Unfortunately they lose their vigour early in life, flatten at the top and become twiggy and many die. Flowers are borne by trees only a few years old, the small brownish males crowded on the basal 10cm of new shoots. 5–10–15m. II.

BISHOP PINE *Pinus muricata* (rough with sharp points; the cones) was discovered near San Luis Obispo (town of Bishop St Louis) in S California and occurs in other small groves scattered along that coast. Southern groves yield trees with heavy branches, broad crowned and green, but seed from a few northern groves is preferred for its more slender blue-grey trees which grow exceedingly fast on the poorest soils. Both forms resist the worst seawinds. Cones can be tightly held on the branches for 60 years with good seed inside. 10–18–30m. II.

2-NEEDLE PINES

♀ 6

BISHOP

27m

SCOTS

20m

RED

20m

conelet

×½

Scots

Red

×½

Japanese
Red

×½

×¼

Bishop

Scots 30cm

Red 30cm

Japanese Red
30cm

Bishop 50cm

89

25m
AUSTRIAN PINE
bark at 60cm
× ½

35m
CRIMEAN PINE

35m
CORSICAN PINE
bark at 60cm

♂ 6

♀ 6

♂ 6

♀

90

AUSTRIAN PINE *Pinus nigra* var. *nigra* (black). This Central European form of the Black Pine is usually broad and heavily branched but may have a narrow crown and a single bole. The timber is too rough and knotty for use but the tree gives valuable shelter on exposed ridges, even if of chalk, and is often on railway embankments and around the gardens of large Victorian houses. 5–11–35m. X – a dark, scruffy tree.

CRIMEAN PINE *Pinus nigra* var. *caramanica* (from Crimea) is the Black Pine also of Asia Minor and is the strongest growing form. The bole breaks into many close vertical stems. 8–15–40m. II.

CORSICAN PINE *Pinus nigra* var. *maritima* (by the sea) comes also from S Italy and Sicily and is uniformly shapely with short, level branches until very old, and an open crown of slender greyish leaves. It is the forest tree of southern heaths giving rapid yields of mining and pulp timber. It is one of the few pines to grow well in clay and on chalk and to resist polluted air quite well. The leaves of young plants are green and twisted and may arise in 3s or 4s near the shoot-tips. 8–15–43m. II.

20m

**LODGEPOLE
PINE**

bark at 30cm   ×⅓

18m

SHORE PINE

♂ 3–4

♀ 3–4

SHORE PINE *Pinus contorta* var. *contorta* (twisted, from the branches in windswept stands by the sea). In the last 30 years large tracts of high moors have been planted with this tree in the west for its very rapid early growth on wet peats at high altitudes, but it is quite rare in gardens. The boles tend to be swept in a curve from the long shoot of the young plants being bent by the wind. It grows by the coast from Alaska to California. 8–15–30m. II.

LODGEPOLE PINE *Pinus contorta* var. *latifolia* (broad-leafed) grows inland from the Shore Pine in the Rocky Mountains from Alaska to Colorado. In Britain it is a less vigorous, narrower, more open-crowned tree, often much forked but straighter than the Shore Pine. There are plantations on some inland, drier peaty moors and some trees in a few gardens. The bark has fine scales and is rarely fissured. 6–11–23m. X – a thin grower.

91

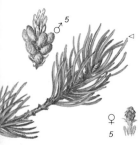

JACK PINE *Pinus banksiana* (Joseph Banks, botanist with Capt. Cook; Director of Kew). No pine grows further north than does this in Canada and few can grow as well on poor boggy soil. Even on good garden soil however, it remains a twiggy tree of poor shape, so it is little planted. Young trees make quite vigorous but slender shoots and start bearing cones when 3–4 years old. Bark dull orange-brown, with grey ridges. The cones remain fixed as the shoot becomes a branch and are partly embedded in it. They point towards the tip of the shoot and are smooth, unlike the short-spined, downward pointing cones of the similar Lodgepole Pine. 6–11–20m. X – a scrawny tree.

MOUNTAIN PINE *Pinus uncinata* (with hooked tip; cone-scales) occurs in the Pyrenees and the Alps and is the tree form of the Dwarf Mountain Pine, *Pinus mugo*, which is a 1m bush, used rarely here but often in the USA in city shrub-borders where it resists exhaust fumes. The tree form is sometimes planted for shelter at the top of exposed, high, forest plantations. In gardens it is like a sturdy Lodgepole Pine but with dark grey bark and unique cone-scales. 4–8–17m. X – a tree with little character.

JACK PINE

12m

♂ 5

♀ 5

MOUNTAIN PINE

12m

♀ 5

×⅓

young cones on shoot

young cones

2nd year cone

×⅓

ripe cone

BOSNIAN PINE

18m

JAPANESE BLACK PINE

20m

♂ 6

♀ 6

BOSNIAN PINE *Pinus leucodermis* (white-skinned, from the white bark of old native trees). This is a pine of great merit, but still uncommon. Shapely, tough and healthy, it thrives on any well-drained soil. The bark is a clean pale grey evenly cracked into small plates, becoming paler with age, and if the foliage is rather black, it is embellished in summer by deep blue cones. Young plants are upright with shoots bloomed blue-grey on pale brown. Once male flowers are borne, the foliage is in dense whorls separated by the bare length of shoot which bore them. 4–10–23m. I.

JAPANESE BLACK PINE *Pinus thunbergii* (Carl Thunberg, one of the first botanists to study Japanese plants) is found infrequently as an old tree, recognisable by its wandering slender branches of whorled foliage and dark bark. Young trees are attractively upright and dense with stout golden brown shoots and the buds conspicuously white with long, loose, fringed scales. Very dark grey bark, deeply fissured. Female flowers often too crowded, without room for cones to develop properly. Normal cones have loose scales and are fragile. 4–6–23m. II.

♂ 6

♀ 6

93

Maritime 40cm

Aleppo 35cm

ALEPPO PINE

10m

Calabrian
Pine   ×⅓

15m

♂ 5

ALEPPO PINE *Pinus halepensis* (from Aleppo, Syria). In slightly warmer, drier countries than Britain this is a familiar sight with its light grey-green hazy crown, far beyond its natural range from Spain to Asia Minor and Syria. Young trees are tender even in S England and although three big trees grow at Kew unharmed by the coldest winters, very few others are known in Britain. Cones are often brought back by Mediterranean holidaymakers attracted by the purple colour. 4–9–15m. X – a good pine, but not in N Europe.

CALABRIAN PINE *Pinus brutia* (old name for Calabria). Although this Mediterranean species was first described from Calabria it no longer grows there. A sturdy old tree of 13m at Kew is the only large one known in England, but there are two good specimens at Glasnevin. The crown is markedly darker and denser than Aleppo's.

Calabrian
Pine,
cones
straight

×⅛

Aleppo Pine,
cones
down-curved

Stone Pine
35cm

94

MARITIME PINE   30m

STONE PINE   18m

×⅓

STONE PINE *Pinus pinea* (relating to the pine) is the 'Umbrella Pine' prominent in Spain and Italy but is hardy north to SE Scotland, although nowhere common. Young trees are upright with silvery blue, juvenile, flat, solitary leaves until 1.3m tall, then bush out to a globular shape. Juvenile leaves appear again in sprouts when a shoot is grazed or cut. The heavy cones, borne after 20 years, hold plump seeds which in Italy are ground up and used in the sauce 'al pesto', and whole in confectionery. 3–5–20m. II.

MARITIME PINE *Pinus pinaster* (like a pine) has the stoutest and longest leaves of any 2-needle pine. A few plantations on southern dunes and other sandy coastal areas are known by the very open crowns and the lower boles being curved all in the same direction. Seedlings spend 3 years as upright plants with silver-blue juvenile leaves before growing away very fast on the poorest soils. This is an uncommon garden tree of southern counties. 9–15–32m. III.

×⅓

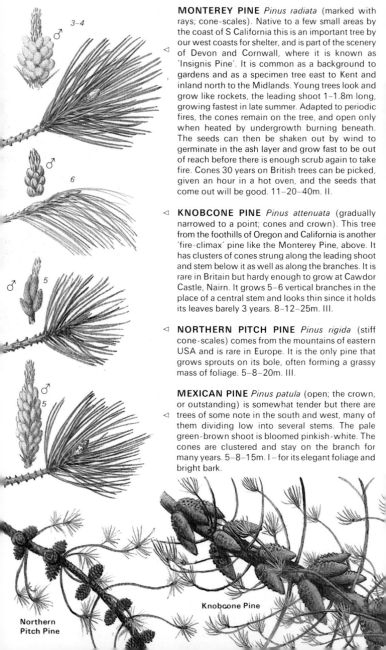

THREE-NEEDLE PINES are confined to the Himalayas and China, the Canary Isles, and N America – where they dominate in the south-eastern states and are common in the south-western. The timber is hard and strong. Many have massive woody cones.

MONTEREY PINE *Pinus radiata* (marked with rays; cone-scales). Native to a few small areas by the coast of S California this is an important tree by our west coasts for shelter, and is part of the scenery of Devon and Cornwall, where it is known as 'Insignis Pine'. It is common as a background to gardens and as a specimen tree east to Kent and inland north to the Midlands. Young trees look and grow like rockets, the leading shoot 1–1.8m long, growing fastest in late summer. Adapted to periodic fires, the cones remain on the tree, and open only when heated by undergrowth burning beneath. The seeds can then be shaken out by wind to germinate in the ash layer and grow fast to be out of reach before there is enough scrub again to take fire. Cones 30 years on British trees can be picked, given an hour in a hot oven, and the seeds that come out will be good. 11–20–40m. II.

KNOBCONE PINE *Pinus attenuata* (gradually narrowed to a point; cones and crown). This tree from the foothills of Oregon and California is another 'fire-climax' pine like the Monterey Pine, above. It has clusters of cones strung along the leading shoot and stem below it as well as along the branches. It is rare in Britain but hardy enough to grow at Cawdor Castle, Nairn. It grows 5–6 vertical branches in the place of a central stem and looks thin since it holds its leaves barely 3 years. 8–12–25m. III.

NORTHERN PITCH PINE *Pinus rigida* (stiff cone-scales) comes from the mountains of eastern USA and is rare in Europe. It is the only pine that grows sprouts on its bole, often forming a grassy mass of foliage. 5–8–20m. III.

MEXICAN PINE *Pinus patula* (open; the crown, or outstanding) is somewhat tender but there are trees of some note in the south and west, many of them dividing low into several stems. The pale green-brown shoot is bloomed pinkish-white. The cones are clustered and stay on the branch for many years. 5–8–15m. I – for its elegant foliage and bright bark.

Knobcone Pine

Northern Pitch Pine

25m

Monterey

20m

an

k at 30cm

bark at 50cm

bark at 40cm

CAN PINE

×¼

MONTEREY PINE

♀ 5

♀ 3-4

♀

5

NORTHERN
PITCH
PINE

NOBCONE
PINE

97

JEFFREY PINE *Pinus jeffreyi* (discovered by John Jeffrey, Scottish collector for the Oregon Association) replaces the Ponderosa Pine everywhere above 2000m in California and Oregon. It quickly makes a fine shapely tree in all parts of Britain, narrowly conic until mature. It differs from Ponderosa Pine by larger cones, blue-bloomed shoots and leaves and blackish bark, so is more like Bigcone Pine but with unridged bark and fragile cones of thin scales, not massively woody. Shed cones leave some basal scales on the tree. 6–15–35m. I.

Jeffrey
young cone

×¼

Ponderosa

25m   bark at 80cm
JEFFREY PINE

35m   bark at 80cm
PONDEROSA PINE

PONDEROSA PINE *Pinus ponderosa* (heavy – the timber) ranges over the whole Rocky Mountain system south from BC with one variety in eastern parts and one in southern parts of its range. Good specimens grow in all parts of Britain, where they can be confused only with Jeffrey Pine, except for their scaly pink-brown bark, shiny brown shoot and smaller cones. Many specimens have evenly tapering conic crowns although 30m tall. Old trees may have long slender shoots dangling from the crown and abruptly upcurved to the tip which is crowned with leaves. The first seed arrived in 1827. 6–15–40m. I.

98

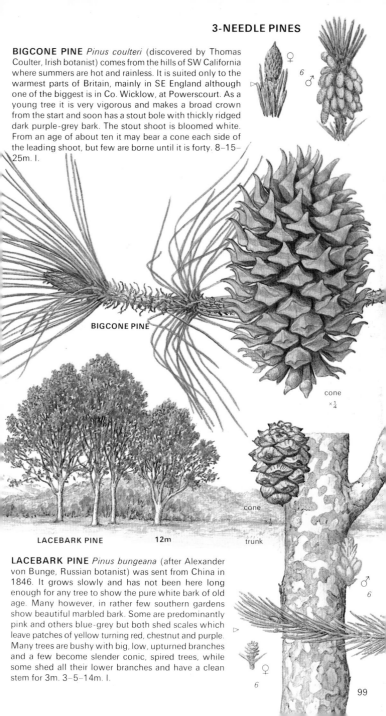

3-NEEDLE PINES

BIGCONE PINE *Pinus coulteri* (discovered by Thomas Coulter, Irish botanist) comes from the hills of SW California where summers are hot and rainless. It is suited only to the warmest parts of Britain, mainly in SE England although one of the biggest is in Co. Wicklow, at Powerscourt. As a young tree it is very vigorous and makes a broad crown from the start and soon has a stout bole with thickly ridged dark purple-grey bark. The stout shoot is bloomed white. From an age of about ten it may bear a cone each side of the leading shoot, but few are borne until it is forty. 8–15–25m. I.

BIGCONE PINE

cone ×¼

LACEBARK PINE 12m

cone

trunk

LACEBARK PINE *Pinus bungeana* (after Alexander von Bunge, Russian botanist) was sent from China in 1846. It grows slowly and has not been here long enough for any tree to show the pure white bark of old age. Many however, in rather few southern gardens show beautiful marbled bark. Some are predominantly pink and others blue-grey but both shed scales which leave patches of yellow turning red, chestnut and purple. Many trees are bushy with big, low, upturned branches and a few become slender conic, spired trees, while some shed all their lower branches and have a clean stem for 3m. 3–5–14m. I.

99

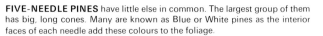

FIVE-NEEDLE PINES have little else in common. The largest group of them has big, long cones. Many are known as Blue or White pines as the interior faces of each needle add these colours to the foliage.

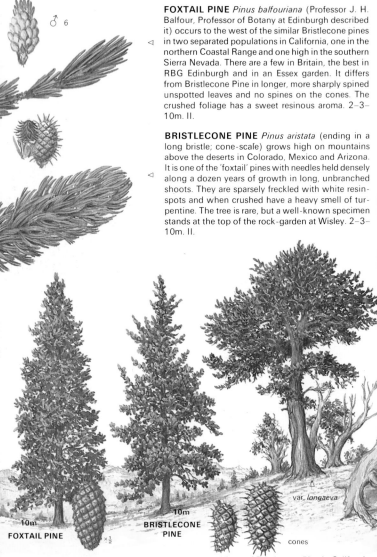

♂ 6

FOXTAIL PINE *Pinus balfouriana* (Professor J. H. Balfour, Professor of Botany at Edinburgh described it) occurs to the west of the similar Bristlecone pines in two separated populations in California, one in the northern Coastal Range and one high in the southern Sierra Nevada. There are a few in Britain, the best in RBG Edinburgh and in an Essex garden. It differs from Bristlecone Pine in longer, more sharply spined unspotted leaves and no spines on the cones. The crushed foliage has a sweet resinous aroma. 2–3–10m. II.

BRISTLECONE PINE *Pinus aristata* (ending in a long bristle; cone-scale) grows high on mountains above the deserts in Colorado, Mexico and Arizona. It is one of the 'foxtail' pines with needles held densely along a dozen years of growth in long, unbranched shoots. They are sparsely freckled with white resin-spots and when crushed have a heavy smell of turpentine. The tree is rare, but a well-known specimen stands at the top of the rock-garden at Wisley. 2–3–10m. II.

var. *longaeva*

10m
FOXTAIL PINE
× ½

10m
BRISTLECONE PINE

cones

Pinus aristata var. *longaeva* is an unspotted form of Bristlecone Pine in California and Nevada, which is known to have lived for 5000 years in the White and Inyo Mountains – longer than any other tree. The Giant Sequoia has not yet exceeded 3500 years. The tree shown here could be 4000 years old.

Hartweg's Pine

6

20m

MONTEZUMA PINE

bark at 50cm

×⅓

▷

MONTEZUMA PINE *Pinus montezumae* (Montezuma II was the last Aztec emperor) is a complex of Mexican pines divisible into dozens of species or varieties but, the form typical in Britain with straight, radiating grey leaves is not known in the wild now. There are fine broad-crowned trees like this in many western gardens and at Sheffield Park, Sussex and for 50 years or so they grow very fast. The shoots are upcurved, stout, ribbed, and shiny orange-brown. 6–14–27m. I.

Hartweg's Pine var. *hartwegii* is narrower with dull green needles often in 3s and 4s on violet-bloomed shoots. 8–12–25m. II.

101

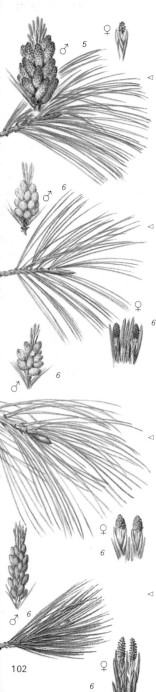

BHUTAN PINE *Pinus wallichiana* (Nathaniel Wallich, Danish botanist who worked in India) from the Himalayas grows in all parts of Britain and is the only 5-needle pine likely to be found in town parks and large suburban gardens. An attractive young tree, narrow with hanging bluish foliage, it grows fast for some 20 years, then tends to lose shape. Old trees have heavy spreading branches very liable to breakage and their leading shoots die back, but cones are still numerous at the tips of lower branches. The shoot is stout, hairless and bloomed blue-grey, in contrast to the slender pale brown-green shoot of Weymouth Pine and the finely hairy shoot of Holford Pine, the two species most like Bhutan Pine. 8–18–35m. II.

HOLFORD PINE *Pinus × holfordiana* (raised by Sir George Holford of Westonbirt) is the hybrid between Mexican White Pine and Bhutan Pine and is a good mixture of features from each. Some trees raised from seed of the hybrid tend to be more like one or other parent, and were sent to many gardens from Westonbirt. The true hybrid has the orange-brown bark of the Bhutan but downy shoot of the Mexican White Pine and a cone bigger than either, broad and blunt. It grows rapidly with spreading branches making a broad crown and the bole often slightly curved at base. The first groups were planted in 1908 and grew the first cone in 1933. 9–17–29m. II.

MEXICAN WHITE PINE *Pinus ayacahuite* (Mexican name) is grown in some southern gardens. The broad conic crown has long, level branches with slender 15cm needles hanging from finely downy, pale green shoots. The bark cracks early into scales, then square plates, dark purplish-brown. Small pale green male flowers are well spaced along the basal half of the shoot. Bright red females are erect on 2cm stalks at the shoot-tip. They ripen into pendulous orange-brown cones on stout 2cm stalks. The cones are variable in size but usually big, up to 40cm long, heavy, leathery and with the tips of the basal scales spreading and turned back sharply. The scales of the middle of the cone are often out-turned too. 8–15–25m. II.

WEYMOUTH PINE *Pinus strobus* (pine-cone – the ancient name for some pine). Native to wide expanses of plains around the Great Lakes and mountains south to Georgia. Formerly in most large gardens, but the fungus blister-rust has left few of the big old trees with black scaly bark and wide, broken tops. It is infrequent as a young, conic tree with layers of level branches and dark grey shallowly fissured bark. The slender shoot has a patch of fine hairs just below each bundle of 10cm needles. The timber is remarkably even, working in all directions and taking intricate shapes well; e.g. for mouldings and in musical instruments. 8–14–32m. III.

20m
XICAN WHITE PINE

BHUTAN PINE

bark at 40cm

25m

WEYMOUTH
PINE

pe
ne

Weymouth Pine

bark at 40cm

Mexican White Pine

×⅕

Holford Pine

Bhutan Pine

60m
SUGAR PINE

cone   ×⅙

unripe   ×⅓

25m

bark at 40cm

MACEDONIAN PINE

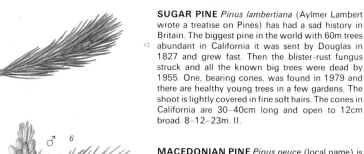

♂   6

♀   6

SUGAR PINE *Pinus lambertiana* (Aylmer Lambert wrote a treatise on Pines) has had a sad history in Britain. The biggest pine in the world with 60m trees abundant in California it was sent by Douglas in 1827 and grew fast. Then the blister-rust fungus struck and all the known big trees were dead by 1955. One, bearing cones, was found in 1979 and there are healthy young trees in a few gardens. The shoot is lightly covered in fine soft hairs. The cones in California are 30–40cm long and open to 12cm broad. 8–12–23m. II.

MACEDONIAN PINE *Pinus peuce* (local name) is a 5-needle pine which grows steadily but not usually at a great rate, on any soil and at any altitude in all parts, and is remarkably healthy. European and Asiatic pines resist the blister-rust fungus to which the American species are so susceptible. This pine makes a sturdy columnar tree, densely foliaged, with apple green smooth shoots and curved cones. The bark may be pale grey or purplish-brown small shallow plates. Good trees are in many gardens but it is not common. 5–11–30m. I.

bark at 40cm

20m

young bark
at 40cm
WESTERN WHITE PINE

×⅕

CHINESE WHITE PINE

25m

WESTERN WHITE PINE *Pinus monticola* (mountain-dweller) grows from BC to California, often a slender spire 55m or more tall with short, level branches and on older trees ornamental bark of smooth, regular small black or red-brown round plates. One or two are on the same lines in Britain but blister-rust disease deforms and kills most of the older trees. Young trees, with long shoots are less rare and soon bear bunches of long cones at the branch-tips. The copper-brown shoots are densely and finely hairy. 8–15–35m. II.

CHINESE WHITE PINE; DAVID'S PINE *Pinus armandii* (discovered by Armand David, French missionary-naturalist in China in the 1880s) resembles a rather impoverished form of Bhutan Pine (p.102), except for its cones. It has a hairless smooth shoot, green, and marked by resin-blisters. Some bundles of needles are crimped or bent at the base, hanging often limply and sparsely set. They fall in their second year making for an open crown. Two trees from the first seed, sent in 1897, grow at Kew and it is in similar collections that this tree is likely to be seen. 7–11–23m. III.

105

young cone

ripe cone

AROLLA PINE

20m

bark at 40cm

×¼

♂ 6

♀ 6

AROLLA PINE *Pinus cembra* (Italian name for the tree). This is the tree planted above its natural stands in the Swiss Alps to stabilise the snow in avalanche areas, where it has to resist erosion by driven snowflakes above the surface and fungal attack beneath it. It is grown in our gardens, some-times in suburbs, mainly in the north and west. It forms a sturdy, columnar tree until opening out at the top with considerable age and is densely crowned. It is some 40 years old before a cone is borne. It falls unopened and the seed are released when the cone rots on the ground. Usually the seeds are eaten out by rodents before that and the core of the cone remains with about 100 ivory white cup-shaped half seed-shells. 3–7–29m. II.

JAPANESE WHITE PINE *Pinus parviflora* (small flowered) is frequent in rock gardens and Japanese style gardens as a low-growing, spreading tree with blue and white leaves. This was the form sent first and is a selection raised for small gardens in Japan. The wild form is less seen and is a tall tree with nearly green leaves. The bark of both forms is grey-purple with patches of lifting flakes. The garden form bears numerous cones from an early age, usually 3 at each whorl of shoots, bright green until ripe. 3–5–18m. II.

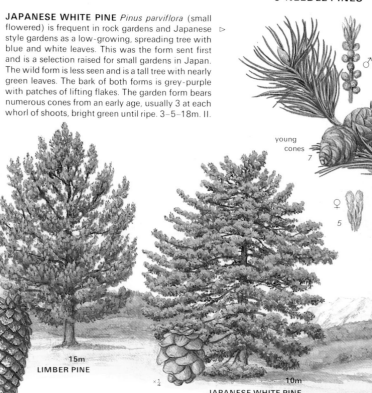

young cones

15m
LIMBER PINE

10m
JAPANESE WHITE PINE

LIMBER PINE *Pinus flexilis* (flexible; shoots can be twisted and knotted without snapping; hence also 'Limber Pine'). The candelabra crown of this tree is a familiar sight by most of the high passes in the Rocky Mountains and is beginning to show on the older trees in Britain. The tree is, however susceptible to blister-rust fungus and old trees are scarce. A good group in Windsor Great Park now 47 years old has lost a tree or two in this way. The shoot is pale green, lightly covered with fine brown hairs. 6–9–20m. II.

KOREAN PINE *Pinus koraiensis* is widespread in E Asia and makes a hardy attractive young tree in Britain but few are to be seen. Older trees tend to fail in England and are thin in the crown and yellowish and only in N Wales and in Scotland do they remain a healthy deep blue-green in the leaf and bear cones. During their first summer these are splendid objects, 15cm long, rich glossy green. The tree is most like an Arolla Pine and has the same woolly red-brown hairs on the shoot, but it has longer leaves and a noticeably more open crown. 4–7–18m. II.

WILLOW FAMILY

WILLOW FAMILY Salicaceae. Poplars and Willows. Fast growing trees in damp soils, sexes usually separate, seeds covered in wool. Tending to hybridise freely.

POPLARS *Populus*. About 30 northern species, mostly of rapid growth to great size. Only White, Grey and Aspen need to be raised from seed rather than cuttings or root-suckers. Sexes separate.

bark at 60cm

25m
BLACK POPLAR

26m
LOMBARDY POPLAR

4

Lombardy

BLACK POPLAR *Populus nigra* var. *betulifolia* (birch-leafed) is native to SE and C England. It is becoming scarce as a big tree, being short-lived and seldom planted now in the countryside. But it is resistant to smoky air and has long been planted in northern cities as 'Manchester Poplar', maturing into a broad-headed tree with black bark. In good soils, deep and damp, it grows very fast and much bigger than among paving-stones. The trunk is heavily burred. 10–17–32m. II.

Lombardy Poplar *P.n.* 'Italica' was brought from Turin to St Osyth, Essex, in 1758. Cuttings from it were soon growing fast in all parts of the British Isles, all too often in lines which jar on the landscape and are liable to be ruined by the loss of one or more trees. But they make splendid tight groups. This narrow tree with its tapered top is a male. The female, 'Gigantea', is less common and has bigger branches fanning out slightly to a broad top. 10–17–36m. II.

BERLIN POPLAR *Populus* ×*berolinensis* (arising in Berlin) is a cross between an Asiatic balsam poplar and the Lombardy Poplar, and inherits something of the latter's narrow crown. It has occurred several times, usually as a female tree though there are male forms. It withstands more heat and cold than most poplars, so is valued in places with climates more extreme than Britain's, and is uncommon here. The young shoots are slightly winged and at first downy. The narrowly tapered base of most leaves and the whitened underside distinguish this from Black poplars. The top of the crown flattens with age. 10–18–27m. III.

HYBRID BLACK POPLARS *Populus × canadensis*. A number of hybrids of the N American Eastern Cottonwood, *P. deltoides*, and the European *P. nigra*. Commonly planted in England for their very fast growth, but less good in the cooler north and west. The wood, strong and shock-resistant but rough, is used for boxes and crates.

Black Italian Poplar *P.* 'Serotina' is one of the oldest and commonest, often a big tree in broad valleys and town parks, but its heavy branches break off in early senility. It is male, and very late into leaf. 10–18–45m. III. **Golden Poplar** *P.* 'Serotina Aurea' is slower growing, with a dense crown, frequent in town parks. **'Robusta'** (of strong growth). The poplar common in S England in roadside shelterbelts and small plantations. It is conspicuous with its big red male catkins and a flush of orange-red leaves in April. It remains conic and shapely, with regular branching until over 30m tall, a more leafy handsome tree than other hybrid Black Poplars. It arose in France, a cross between the Lombardy Poplar and the Eastern Cottonwood of America, in 1895. 14–25–40m. I. **'Eugenei'** has Lombardy Poplar as one parent, and a narrower crown than the others and smaller leaves. 11–18–37m. I. **'Regenerata'** is no longer much planted but is still common in London parks, by railways and for screening. It is female. The bole is lined with long deep fissures and high ridges. In contrast to the Black Italian, its branches arch out and slender pendulous twigs are early into leaf. 10–17–32m. III.

♂ 4

Black Italian

♂

3–4

'Robusta'

'Eugenei'

♀

'Regenerata' 4

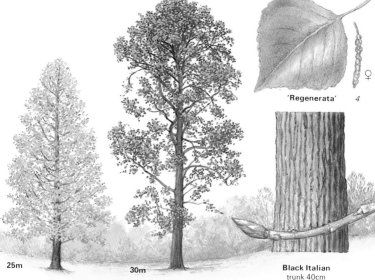

25m

'Robusta' new leaves, April

30m

'Eugenei'

Black Italian
trunk 40cm
and twig

109

leaf spray

WHITE POPLAR 15m

young bark at 30cm

under

bark at 30cm

WHITE POPLAR *Populus alba* (white under leaf, shoot and bark), is native to S Europe but was brought to Britain by some of the first settlers after the Ice Ages who will have valued its rapid growth in great exposure and on the poorest loose soils. It suckers strongly in blown sand, and is common near coasts but elsewhere it is less seen than the much bigger-growing Grey Poplar, with which it is easily confused. Towards autumn the white felting of the shoots wears thin. Before being shed rather early, the leaves may briefly turn bright yellow. 9–15–20m. III.

GREY POPLAR *Populus canescens* (grey-white; hoary) is halfway between Aspen and White Poplar except in size: it grows to twice the size of either of them. It was probably brought here with the White Poplar and, like it, suckers widely, but it can be a huge, massively boled tree. The finest specimens tend to be in chalkland valleys in S England and limestone country in Ireland but it resists sea-winds well and can grow in sand and in the far north. A big tree stands on the beach at Dunrobin Castle, Sutherland. Female trees are rare; males take on a purplish tint in February as the catkins swell. Bark similar to White Poplar's. New foliage makes the crown silver-white but less snowy and flashing than White Poplar and by summer it is dark grey-green as the slightly greyed white felt is largely shed. 10–15–37m. II.

ASPEN *Populus tremula* (quivering – the long, slender, flattened stalks allow the leaves to flutter in the slightest breeze) was an early arrival among our native trees and is common only in the north by streamsides. In the south it is local but each tree tends to sucker widely and make a copse, which will all be of the same sex. Rooted suckers do not transplant well but fresh seed germinates within a day of sowing and the seedlings grow very fast. The bark is very smooth and grey-green until old, then brownish and ridged. The leaves on late summer shoots are coppery red, and in autumn the trees in Scottish glens turn luminous gold, but in the south the colour is variable. Being both absorbent and strong, its wood is the best for matches. 8–12–18m. II.

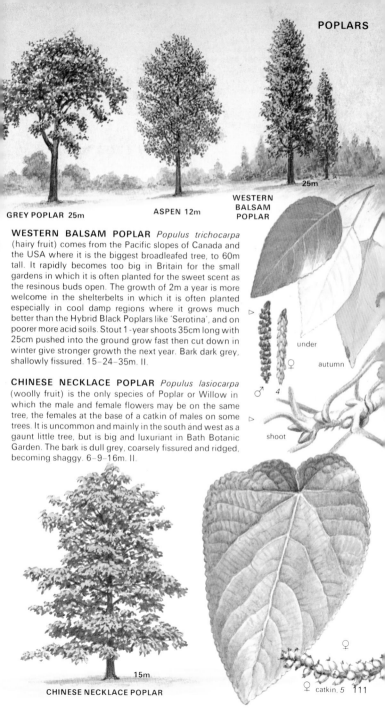

GREY POPLAR 25m

ASPEN 12m

WESTERN BALSAM POPLAR 25m

under

autumn

♀

♂ 4

shoot

WESTERN BALSAM POPLAR *Populus trichocarpa* (hairy fruit) comes from the Pacific slopes of Canada and the USA where it is the biggest broadleafed tree, to 60m tall. It rapidly becomes too big in Britain for the small gardens in which it is often planted for the sweet scent as the resinous buds open. The growth of 2m a year is more welcome in the shelterbelts in which it is often planted especially in cool damp regions where it grows much better than the Hybrid Black Poplars like 'Serotina', and on poorer more acid soils. Stout 1-year shoots 35cm long with 25cm pushed into the ground grow fast then cut down in winter give stronger growth the next year. Bark dark grey, shallowly fissured. 15–24–35m. II.

CHINESE NECKLACE POPLAR *Populus lasiocarpa* (woolly fruit) is the only species of Poplar or Willow in which the male and female flowers may be on the same tree, the females at the base of a catkin of males on some trees. It is uncommon and mainly in the south and west as a gaunt little tree, but is big and luxuriant in Bath Botanic Garden. The bark is dull grey, coarsely fissured and ridged, becoming shaggy. 6–9–16m. II.

CHINESE NECKLACE POPLAR 15m

♀

♀ catkin, 5   111

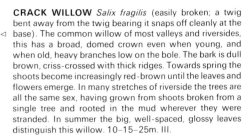

WILLOWS *Salix* (the classical name). A widespread group of 300 species and many hybrids, mainly shrubby. In most the leaves are alternate, slender and long-pointed. Only the Goat and Grey Willows fail to strike cuttings. Sexes on separate trees.

CRACK WILLOW *Salix fragilis* (easily broken; a twig bent away from the twig bearing it snaps off cleanly at the base). The common willow of most valleys and riversides, this has a broad, domed crown even when young, and when old, heavy branches low on the bole. The bark is dull brown, criss-crossed with thick ridges. Towards spring the shoots become increasingly red-brown until the leaves and flowers emerge. In many stretches of riverside the trees are all the same sex, having grown from shoots broken from a single tree and rooted in the mud wherever they were stranded. In summer the big, well-spaced, glossy leaves distinguish this willow. 10–15–25m. III.

BAY WILLOW *Salix pentandra* (having five stamens) was an early arrival amongst our native trees and grows by streamsides from N Wales northwards. It is seldom planted. This is a great pity as it is a splendid tree with glossy olive-green shoots and deep green glossy leaves, slightly bluish-white beneath. Its bright yellow male catkins open amongst fully grown leaves, unlike our other willows where the leaves are still expanding. The crown is a broad, low dome in the open but tall and narrow in woods. 3–6–18m. I.

GOAT WILLOW or SALLOW *Salix caprea* (of the goat; the earliest known engraving showing this tree pictured a goat eating the foliage). Native everywhere in Britain except the Outer Hebrides, this will spring up rapidly on disturbed soil from seeds blown far with their fluffy coats. In the open they grow into upright shrubs but in woodland clearings and on the edges they may be rather crooked stemmed trees, 15m tall. The golden catkins of the male plants are 'pussy willow'. A few in sheltered corners open at the turn of the year but the main flowering is through March and April. 8–10–18m. III.

GREY WILLOW *Salix cinerea* (soft grey hairs on the shoots) is native everywhere and is very similar to the Goat Willow; the two are equally 'sallow' or 'pussy willow' when in flower, but Grey Willow is never more than a very small tree and usually a shrub. The hairy shoots, narrower leaf and little leafy stipules remaining at the base of each leaf also separate these two species. 3–4–6m. III.

VIOLET WILLOW *Salix daphnoides* (like a Laurel, foliage). This tree grows across Europe and in various forms east into Asia, but it failed to make the crossing to Britain while the land-bridge was there. It was not introduced until 1829 and although admired when seen it is rarely planted. It is probably very short-lived and only young trees are seen. Gardeners sometimes cut them back every year or two to make them grow 2m shoots with brightly blue-violet bloom on the bark. 8–10–12m. II.

20m

CRACK WILLOW

GOAT WILLOW   12m

♂ flowers
opening
1–4

Violet
illow twig,
winter

Grey
Willow

Goat Willow
shoot

113

WILLOWS

15m

SILVER WILLOW

25m

WHITE WILLOW

♂

♀ 4

WHITE WILLOW *Salix alba* (white) is a probable native, scarce in the north and also less common in southern valleys than the Crack Willow from which it is easily distinguished by its small, grey-blue leaves and more dense, higher domed crown. This, and all the forms below are easily raised by inserting 30cm lengths of strong shoot into good moist soil and leaving only one or two buds above ground. 12–16–25m. III.

Silver Willow *S.a.* 'Argentea' is locally frequent by rivers and lakes in town parks and in leaf is a soft silvery grey. It is slower than the normal form and does not become so big.

Weeping Willow *S.* ×*chrysocoma* (golden locks) is probably a hybrid with the Babylon Willow of China (tender here) and is the common Weeping Willow. There are other willows that weep, but they are very rare. 6–13–20m. II.

Bat Willow *S.a.* 'Coerulea' is an extra fast growing, more upright form first found in East Anglia and is planted in rich wet soils in SE England for cricket bats. 16–20–30m. III.

Coralbark Willow *S.a.* 'Britzensis' is often seen around village ponds, gardens pools and by riversides planted to give winter colour. I.

twig,
winter

114

25m

BAT WILLOW

WEEPING WILLOW   18m

CORKSCREW WILLOW *Salix matsudana* 'Tortuosa', a
strange form of the Pekin Willow, is now planted commonly
in parks and gardens. It is very early into fresh, bright green
leaf and holds them still green but darker into early winter.
The shoots are very sinuous and as they thicken with age,
the sharp curves smooth out gradually but are still visible
faintly in the bole, as the trees are raised from cuttings. It
grows rapidly even in dry soils. 8–13–18m. I.

10m   **CORKSCREW WILLOW**   shoot

● WALNUT FAMILY Juglandaceae. Walnuts, Wingnuts, Hickories. The first two have distinctively chambered pith, well seen by slicing diagonally across a twig.

WINGNUTS *Pterocarya* (wing and nut). Handsome, vigorous and usually strongly suckering trees. Winter buds have no scales; they are two unexpanded leaves pressed together and covered in short brown hairs. Five species in China; one in Japan and one in mountains by the south of the Caspian Sea.

bark at 50cm

♂

♀

4

fruits

5–9

CAUCASIAN WINGNUT *Pterocarya fraxinifolia* (ash-like leaves) is grown usually beside water in some parks and large gardens in the southern half of the British Isles. ◁ Unless mown or grazed around it soon becomes a thicket and very quickly a high copse, for its suckering is rampant and many trees are partly hidden by outworks 20m tall. Others, as at Cambridge Botanic Garden become a group of dozens of equal trees, but the three biggest and finest, all in Dorset, at Abbotsbury and Melbury, are single boles with no suckers around. The leaves turn a rich yellow in autumn. The side-buds in the angles between shoots are often on 2cm stalks. 10–15–35m. II.

CHINESE WINGNUT *Pterocarya stenoptera* (narrow wing). This tree is much less frequent than the Caucasian or the hybrid between the two and is more southerly than ◁ either. It does not sucker so strongly but a few plants are grafts on to the Caucasian and that suckers as usual. It tends to have a narrower crown for the same height as the other two and the leaves are smaller with generally fewer leaflets. The wings on the central stalk of the leaf open widely between leaflets and are toothed; an easy distinction. The fruit are pinkish in summer then soon ripen pink and brown, looking highly attractive among the rich green leaves. 6–12–25m. l.

♂

♀ 4

5–9

20m

HYBRID WINGNUT *Pterocarya × rehderana* (Alfred Rehder, botanist at the Arnold Arboretum, Mass.) is one of the most vigorous trees that we can grow. In 20 years it can have a bole nearly 60cm through which is more than either parent can do – a fine example of 'hybrid vigour', but in other respects it is intermediate between them. It occurred in 1879 when seed of Chinese Wingnut was sent to the Arnold Arboretum near Boston, Mass., and Caucasian Wingnut was near the seed-tree. It suckers strongly and as in the other wingnuts, taken with fibrous roots these will grow; but good plants are easily raised from cuttings taken in June and planted in the autumn when they will have grown some 30cm. 11–17–27m. II.

♂ ♀ 4

fruit

5–9

CHINESE WINGNUT

bark at 50cm

WALNUTS *Juglans* (Jupiter's nut) are 15 species from N and S America and from S to NE Asia with edible nuts and high quality timber. As in Wingnuts, the pith or hollow centre to the shoot is closely divided into tiny chambers by transverse plates. Only the Wingnuts share this feature. Walnuts are raised from seed, except selected fruiting varieties, which are grafted.

COMMON WALNUT *Juglans regia* (royal) is probably a native from SE Europe to China but ancient cultivation spread it widely and it may have been brought to Britain by the Romans. It grows in all parts but is uncommon to the north of Yorkshire. Big trees are most frequent from Lincolnshire to Somerset. The aromatic leaves emerge late and red-brown fading slowly and still tinged pale brown in summer. The timber is very stable after it has been worked, which makes it valuable for gun-stocks, and it has a good figure and takes high polish so is used in high quality furniture. A straight bole suitable for veneering can be worth thousands of pounds. 5–12–30m. II.

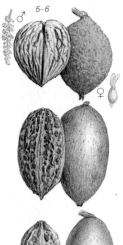

BLACK WALNUT *Juglans nigra* (black; bark) from eastern N America is a far finer tree than the Common Walnut. It grows a straight, long bole and has a tall domed crown of hanging bright green leaves. It grows fast in deep rich soils in warm areas, all but a few of the best trees being S and E of a line from Dorset to York. The fruit is scarcely edible but like the Common Walnut, the green husk yields a singularly persistent dye, and when bruised has a sweet fruity scent. Fresh moist nuts give seedlings 60–80cm tall first season, which should be planted out and cut to the base. 8–15–32m. I.

BUTTERNUT *Juglans cinerea* (grey; bark contrasts in native woods with Black Walnut) from eastern N America grows fast and is hardy but is very scarce in gardens. It differs at once from the Black Walnut in having bark like Common Walnut and bigger leaves with fewer, more widely spaced leaflets, decreasing in length towards the base of the leaf and on a central stalk which is densely hairy. It also bears up to 12 edible fruit on each catkin. 8–12–26m. II.

MANCHURIAN WALNUT *Juglans mandschurica* is rare and only in S England. It is a spreading heavily branched tree with pale grey widely fissured bark and leaves to 70cm long. The shoot and leaf-stalk are matted with sticky red-brown hairs and the leaflets taper to a fine point. 3–6–12m. III.

JAPANESE WALNUT *Juglans ailantifolia* (leaves like Tree of Heaven) is less scarce than the Manchurian Walnut and grows in Scotland and Ireland but is not often seen. Its leaf can be even bigger, to 1m long and the leaflet tips taper abruptly. The shoot and leaf-stalk have the same sticky hairy covering. Female flowers on a 10cm erect spike are decorative as the styles are bright red. The fruit is also covered in sticky down. 4–12–18m. II.

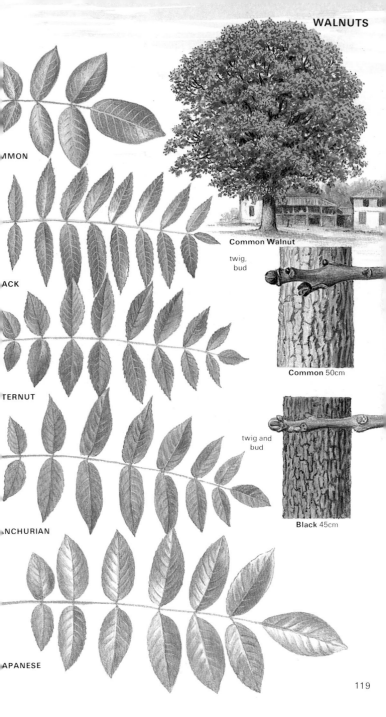

MMON

ACK

TERNUT

NCHURIAN

APANESE

Common Walnut

twig,
bud

Common 50cm

twig and
bud

Black 45cm

119

HICKORIES *Carya* (caryon, Greek for a nut). Of the 20 species of hickory, 19 are native to N America, one to SW China. They differ from other trees in the Family, walnuts and wingnuts, in having solid pith and 3-pronged male catkins.

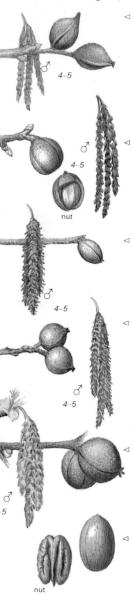

BITTERNUT *Carya cordiformis* (heart-shaped; base of the fruit) ranges from Texas and Florida to SE Canada so there should be sources of hardy trees. A few are grown in the north but the need for hot summers means that it grows well only in the south, but is not common there either. It differs from the others we grow, except for the very rare Pecan, in its slender bright yellow-spangled bud and in having more than 7 leaflets. The end leaflet tapers right down to the base of the top pair. 4–6–26m. I – a most elegant tree with fine autumn colour.

SHAGBARK HICKORY *Carya ovata* (egg-shaped; fruit) makes a broader tree than other hickories, with big low branches level and covered in bark nearly as shaggy as the bole. Mostly the leaves are leathery and oily to the touch but a few are darker and hard. It is the only hickory with big leaves uniformly with 5 leaflets. There is often a ring of pale brown hairs round the shoot just below a bud-scar. Like other hickories, this should be planted out finally in its first year from seed to grow the taproot it needs. 4–8–20m. II.

PIGNUT *Carya glabra* (smooth; the least hairy hickory) is undeservedly rare even in the rather few gardens with hickory collections. Its leaves are so much smaller than the other hickories that it seems more like an ash. In autumn, however, it is a striking blaze of gold and orange and the big tree at Kew has smooth dark purple bark. 3–5–20m. I.

SHELLBARK HICKORY *Carya laciniosa* (with folds or flaps; from the bark). Confined to S. England and far from common there, this elegant tree has a narrow crown of raised, slender long branches arching out towards the top. Its usually 7-parted leaves can be 75cm long and are similar to those of the Mockernut, which are seldom more than 50cm. They also differ from Mockernut in the soft hairs on the main stalk and the short stalk (0–1cm) on the end leaflet. The bark of young trees has long, gently curved narrow raised strips. With age it is shaggy like the Shagbark. 5–9–23m. II.

MOCKERNUT *Carya tomentosa* (thickly hairy, from the foliage) is only occasional in S England and SE Ireland. Unlike the other big-leafed hickories it has a smooth bark. The leaves are usually hard and dark with the veins beneath and the stalk densely covered with hard hairs. In autumn, like the others, it becomes a tower of pure gold. Crushed leaflets give an aroma of paint or mown grass. The slender stalk of the end leaflet is 2–4cm long. 5–8–23m. II.

PECAN *Carya illinoensis* (from the State of Illinois) is the only hickory we grow with more than 9 leaflets. It has 11–15 and they are slender, long-pointed and often curved back. It has a slender yellow bud like the Butternut and flaky grey bark. It hardly survives in Britain but there is one of 15m at both Cambridge Botanic Garden and at Wisley and two smaller ones at Bedgebury, Kent. 3–5–20m. II.

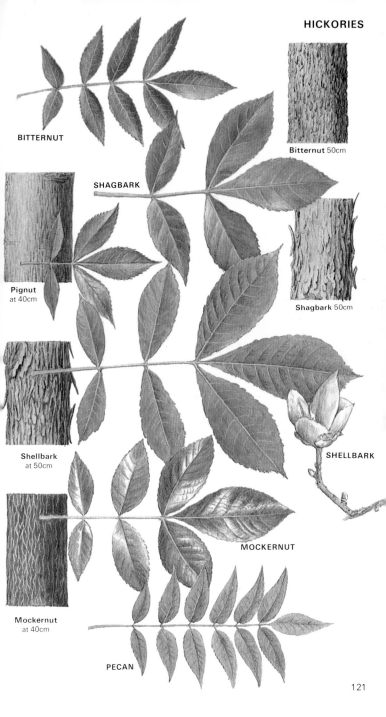

HICKORIES

BITTERNUT

Bitternut 50cm

SHAGBARK

Pignut
at 40cm

Shagbark 50cm

Shellbark
at 50cm

SHELLBARK

Mockernut
at 40cm

MOCKERNUT

PECAN

121

● BIRCH FAMILY Betulaceae. Birches, Alders.

BIRCHES *Betula* (the classical name). A group of 40 species across the northern hemisphere, reaching further north than any other trees. Most are trees of middle size with tough, hard timber much used in plywood, rarely big enough for beams. They spread by their light seed in a tiny winged nut blowing far, and grow best when these land on bare soil. Very fast growth when young. Raised from seed.

♂ ♀
3–4

fruit

Swedish Birch

♂ ♀
3–4

♂ 3–4

♂ 3–4

fruit

◁ **SILVER BIRCH** *Betula pendula* (weeping crown) is the birch of the light sandy soils of commons and heaths and on mountainsides. Dense tracts of birch on heaths show the extent of fires many years before, as this tree seeds in before others. It fruits prolifically every year which attracts winter flocks of redpolls, siskins and other small birds, even into outer suburbs. It is of great value in new, open gardens to give shelter and light shade quickly, but old trees, often incorporated in new gardens, on light ground will rob the soil of food and water for plants beneath. They also drop bunches of dead twigs for much of the year and bud-scales, male catkins and empty fruit in season. 8–18–26m. II.

◁ **Swedish Birch** 'Dalecarlica (found in Dalecarlia in Sweden, 1767) is a fine town tree with a smoothly rounded bole of whiter bark and flimsy leaves which rot rapidly on the ground. 8–15–25m. I.

'**Fastigiata**' is narrow but opens out with age. 8–15–25m. II.

'**Tristis**' is scarce and very pendulous.

'**Youngii**' is an umbrella of small foliage grafted at 2m on a stem. X – except sometimes by a small pool.

◁ **WHITE BIRCH** *Betula pubescens* (finely hairy; shoots and leafstalks) is local on heaths and commons, growing in the wet hollows and is common in the valley bottoms in hill country. Its crown is an irregular fuzz of twigs and its bark has horizontal banding but no black diamonds, which are the sign of a Silver Birch only. The soft white hairs on the shoots are most dense on young trees and new shoots. 6–9–23m. III.

◁ **SZECHUAN BIRCH** *Betula platyphylla* var. *szechuanica* (from Szechuan, now Sichuan, Province of China) has been planted in recent years in gardens where the less usual plants are prized. Older trees are mainly in gardens which grow the plants from Ernest Wilson's seeds sent in 1908. The leaves are thick and leathery and have translucent spots beneath. The chalky white bark leaves a dusty white trace on the hand when rubbed. 6–10–12m. II.

◁ **PAPER BIRCH** *Betula papyrifera* (paper bearing; bark) ranges in various minor forms from Labrador to Alaska with pure but dull white bark freckled with grey. In cultivation here it is variable too and the bark is tinged orange or pink or can be brown and purple. It is uncommon but can be known by the large leaf with only 5–10 pairs of veins, on a hairy stalk and a warty shoot. The bark was used by Canadian Indians to make canoes giving the alternative name, Canoe-bark Birch. 6–12–23m. II.

BIRCHES

20m

SILVER BIRCHES

Silver Birch twig

White Birch twig

old Silver Birch

Silver 35cm

White 35cm

Szechuan 35cm

Paper 35cm

123

ERMAN'S BIRCH *Betula ermanii* ranges widely in E Asia but probably only the Japanese seed, received first in 1890, yields trees suited to our climate. Old trees are in a few gardens and their bark is dull pink liberally hung with slender papery shreds. Young trees are more widespread and have very white bark and as the bole becomes pink the branches become prominently pure white. Prolific fruit remain all winter and help to identify the tree. The tapered base and closely set parallel veins on the leaf are features. It hybridises readily with the Silver Birch so seed raised here is seldom true. 8–12–24m. l.

♀   ♂

4

CHINESE RED-BARK BIRCH *Betula albosinensis* (white and Chinese; perhaps when Silver Birch was *Betula 'alba'* to imply 'the Chinese Silver Birch') has 7cm leaves soon free of hairs. The form so prominent in some gardens, like Branklyn, Perth, has widely spaced dark leaves to 17cm long with silky hairs on the veins beneath and tufts of hairs in the vein-angles. This is the variety *septentrionalis* (northern) in the best forms of which the outer bark rolls away in strips to leave large smooth areas of reddish purple faintly bloomed violet or white, or dark red without bloom. Young trees have rich, mahogany-red, shining bark banded horizontally with raised pores. Many trees are grafted at the base on Silver Birch since seedlings raised from garden trees do not come true, being a mixture of hybrids with Silver Birch. 8–12–18m. l.

var. *septentrionalis*

HIMALAYAN BIRCH *Betula utilis* (useful) ranges from W China through Nepal and grades into Jacquemont's Birch in Kashmir. A few grown in Britain have the bark variously brown marbled with black (as illustrated here) but the majority of the stronger growing trees have white bark and substantial leaves with slight lobing and often red stalks, and 10–14 pairs of parallel veins. They turn bright gold in autumn. The shoot and leaf-stalk are thinly covered in soft hairs. 8–14–20m. l.

♂
4

JACQUEMONT'S BIRCH *Betula jacquemontii* (Victor Jacquemont, French botanist who worked in India) occurs from Kashmir eastwards towards Nepal turning into Himalayan Birch on the way. It has been planted of late in numerous parks and gardens for its shining, smooth clear white bark. In Kashmir this is usually cream or orange and these white barked trees come from the eastern end of the range. Indeed many of the best have leaves with more than 9 pairs of veins and are thus nearer to Himalayan Birch, for the true Jacquemont's has only 7–9 pairs. It is also less hairy on veins and leaf-stalks and has only minute tufts beneath. 8–12–18m. l.

♂
4

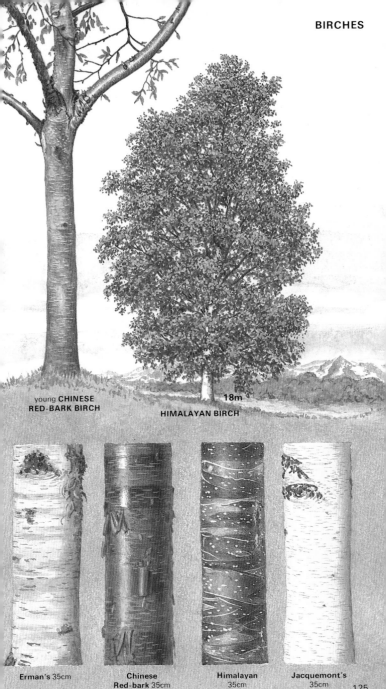

young **CHINESE RED-BARK BIRCH**

18m

HIMALAYAN BIRCH

Erman's 35cm

Chinese Red-bark 35cm

Himalayan 35cm

Jacquemont's 35cm

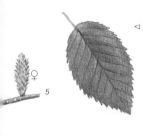
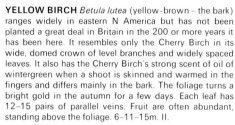

YELLOW BIRCH *Betula lutea* (yellow-brown – the bark) ranges widely in eastern N America but has not been planted a great deal in Britain in the 200 or more years it has been here. It resembles only the Cherry Birch in its wide, domed crown of level branches and widely spaced leaves. It also has the Cherry Birch's strong scent of oil of wintergreen when a shoot is skinned and warmed in the fingers and differs mainly in the bark. The foliage turns a bright gold in the autumn for a few days. Each leaf has 12–15 pairs of parallel veins. Fruit are often abundant, standing above the foliage. 6–11–15m. II.

CHERRY BIRCH *Betula lenta* (flexible, the twigs) resembles the Yellow Birch. They can be distinguished by the bark, and by the Yellow Birch's usually bigger, flatter leaf. This is very evident in American woods, but in gardens here they are seldom found together. The leaf is more regularly toothed and has usually fewer veins. The buds are conic, acutely pointed, yellow-green. By summer, the shoot is glossy dark chocolate-brown and when skinned at any time emits a strong scent of oil of wintergreen. 8–12–16m. II.

RIVER BIRCH *Betula nigra* (black, bark on old trees) is found in the eastern USA beside rocky streams in the foothills and around swamps in the plains. In England the best of the few seen are on dry sands – although one at Wisley Gardens is beside a lake. Hot summers are more important here than wet soil, and restrict good growth to the south-east. The leaves are variably silvered or whitish beneath and hairy, at least on the veins. The bark is at first cream-brown with dark flaking ridges and darkens until it is blackish red-purple, hung with tattered peelings. 4–6–18m. II.

TRANSCAUCASIAN BIRCH *Betula medwediewii* (Medwedieff, a Russian botanist). This interesting little tree from the mountains of the southern Caspian shores is seen mainly in the gardens of plantsmen who value its unusual shape and fine autumn colours. It branches from low on the bole into a broad, erect, bushy tree, dense from bearing leaves on dwarf shoots well back along the branches. The dark, alder-like leaves, with stipules persisting, turn bright gold in autumn. The grey-brown pale bark has flaky ridges like a hazel. 2–5–8m. I.

MONARCH BIRCH *Betula maximowicziana* (Carl Maximowicz, Russian botanist who studied plants in E Asia). This fine Japanese tree has not yet been planted widely but can grow in all parts. Its leaves are more like a lime than a birch, heart-shaped at base and broader than any other, up to 14×11cm. No other birch has female flowers and fruit in clusters of 2–5. The branches are strong and rise at 45° making a fairly broad crown and rather open. The new foliage on some young trees is covered at first in soft purplish-brown hairs. The bark is dark brown on young trees, then white, tinged pink and orange in patches as it grows. 7–12–20m. I.

YELLOW BIRCH 20m

RIVER BIRCH 20m

Yellow
35cm

Cherry
35cm

River
35cm

Monarch
35cm

ALDERS *Alnus* (the classical name) are a group of 30 trees and shrubs adapted to grow in cold wet places. Their roots have nodules, as in the Pea family, in which nitrogen-fixing bacteria grow, so they are useful trees on infertile soils. The wood withstands constant wetting and drying so was used for mill-clogs and lock-gates, and it makes the best charcoal for gunpowder. Raised from seed.

COMMON ALDER *Alnus glutinosa* (sticky; new shoots and leaves) is native everywhere in Britain growing beside water from lowland lakes to mountain streams at 500m and in damp woods along a spring-line. Dark red bunches of hard roots from waterside trees line the banks and make a good protection against erosion. Male catkins give a purple tinge to the crowns in January and open dull yellow-brown from February to April. The leaves, as in all alders, show no autumn colours at all and fall dark green in November. 8–15–25m. II.

GREY ALDER *Alnus incana* (hoary, grey) was brought from Europe to Britain 200 years ago but is seldom seen in gardens. It is a fast-growing tree even on dry soils and is valuable in planting derelict land and old spoil-heaps. Small groups may be found in town parks, the smooth dark grey bark conspicuous. Shoots and new leaves are densely covered with soft pale grey hairs, which remain on the underside of the leaf and together with the more acute point and the margin not curling under distinguish this from Red Alder leaves which are also big and lobed. 9–17–25m. II.

RED ALDER *Alnus rubra* (red – the wood) abounds in the hills from Alaska to California but is scarce in this country. Small plantations have grown with great rapidity at first, sometimes 1.5m a year but in W Scotland at least, they soon begin to fail and bigger trees are in only a few gardens. The leaves may be 20 ×12cm and are at once known by their margins being minutely but sharply rolled under. 12–15–25m. II.

ITALIAN ALDER *Alnus cordata* (heart-shaped; leaf) is in most ways the finest of the group. It grows into the biggest and much the most shapely trees with the most prolific and longest catkins, the biggest fruit and the most elegant, glossy foliage. It is occasional in parks, gardens and by roadsides and is now being planted much more widely. It needs a fairly retentive good soil but does not need a wet site, and grows very fast. The underside of the leaf has small tufts of straight orange hairs at intervals along the midrib. 9–16–29m. I.

GREEN ALDER *Alnus viridis* (green) is the alder of the Alpine woods and streams. Scarce in Britain, it is often shrubby but may be found as a small tree. It is the only alder without stalked buds likely to be found. It has large male catkins and many-scaled fruit, 2cm long in bunches of 5–8. They remain on the tree until spring (as in other alders) but turn nearly black. 3–5–12m. III.

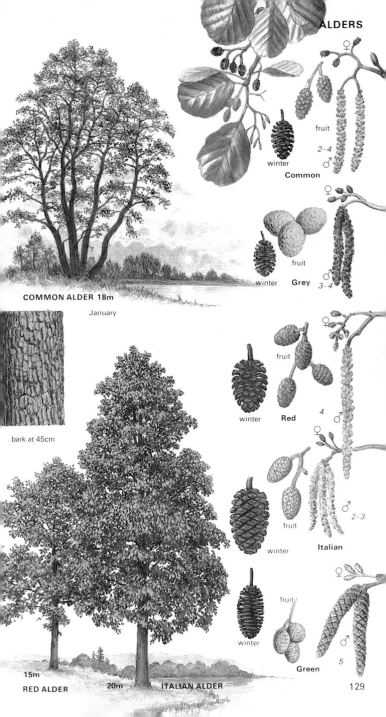

ALDERS

Common

fruit

winter

2–4

♀

♂

Grey

fruit

winter

3–4

♀

♂

COMMON ALDER 18m

January

bark at 45cm

Red

fruit

winter

4

♀

♂

Italian

fruit

winter

2–3

♀

♂

Green

fruit

winter

5

♀

♂

15m

RED ALDER   20m   ITALIAN ALDER

129

● HORNBEAM FAMILY Carpinaceae.

HORNBEAMS *Carpinus* (classical name) are 45 medium and small sized trees of the northern hemisphere related to birches and alders but with their male catkins enclosed in winter buds. The sharply toothed leaves have prominent parallel veins. Raised from seed.

HORNBEAM 20m

'Fastigiata' 12m

HORNBEAM *Carpinus betulus* (like a birch) is native to SE England and dominant over some areas of Epping and Hainault Forests in Essex. It is local and planted far into N Scotland mostly in parkland and gardens. It makes a good hedge, holding its leaves rich brown through the winter. It grows well on clays too heavy for most trees and in autumn the leaves turn yellow, orange and russet. The timber is one of the hardest and strongest of all, the only one that could be used for mill-cogs and the hubs of cartwheels, and is still used for hammers in pianos and for the centres of chopping-blocks. 6–11–30m. II.

'Fastigiata' is so neat and dense that it almost looks its best in winter. Grown with the trunk cleaned of shoots for 2m it makes a splendid tree for limited spaces and is popular for planting along bypasses, in streets, parks and formal gardens. Very young trees are narrowly columnar. 7–11–20m. I.

JAPANESE HORNBEAM *Carpinus japonica* is found only in a few southern collections and two of the older specimens have recently died. The 10cm leaf has 20 or more pairs of veins ending in up-curved whiskers and the big fruit have 2cm bracts with 4–5 coarse teeth. 2–4–10m. II.

ORIENTAL HORNBEAM *Carpinus orientalis* comes from SE Europe and Asia Minor and is grown in some gardens in S England. It is a broad, bushy little tree with notably small ▷ leaves on slender shoots with long silky hairs. The leaves are folded in the bud, concertina-fashion, at each vein and remain partly so when expanded. The unlobed bract of the fruit is distinctive as is its colour being the same as the leaves. 2–3–11m. II.

Hornbeam 20cm   **Japanese** 20cm   **Oriental** 20cm   **15m**

HOP-HORNBEAM

♂

fruit 5

♂

5

♂

4

3 4

fruit

fruit

fruit
6–8

HOP-HORNBEAMS *Ostrya* (Greek name for a tree with very hard wood, probably the Hornbeam) are 7 northern species with male catkins exposed in winter.

EUROPEAN HOP-HORNBEAM *Ostrya carpinifolia* ▷ (with a leaf like the Hornbeam) ranges from SE France to the Caucasus Mountains. It is scarce in Britain but occasional in any size of garden as far north at least as Aberdeen. In the open as usually grown it makes a very broad tree with low, long level branches with age but among other trees it would no doubt have a respectable bole like its very similar relative in E America, and young trees are conic with a good central stem to the tip. The large hanging fruit are prominent in summer, white against the dark green leaves. 5–9–19m. II.

bark at 35cm

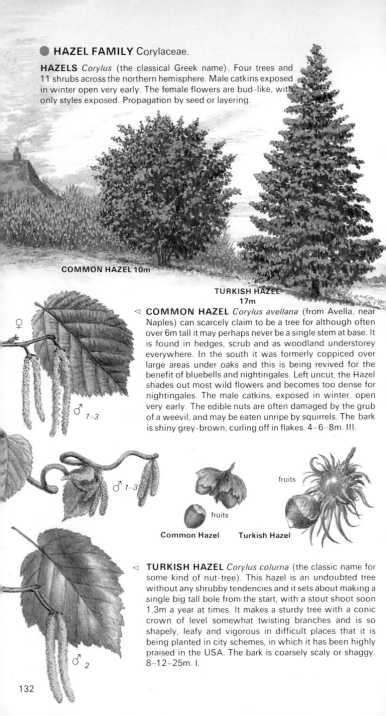

● HAZEL FAMILY Corylaceae.

HAZELS *Corylus* (the classical Greek name). Four trees and 11 shrubs across the northern hemisphere. Male catkins exposed in winter open very early. The female flowers are bud-like, with only styles exposed. Propagation by seed or layering.

COMMON HAZEL 10m

TURKISH HAZEL
17m

◁ **COMMON HAZEL** *Corylus avellana* (from Avella, near Naples) can scarcely claim to be a tree for although often over 6m tall it may perhaps never be a single stem at base. It is found in hedges, scrub and as woodland understorey everywhere. In the south it was formerly coppiced over large areas under oaks and this is being revived for the benefit of bluebells and nightingales. Left uncut, the Hazel shades out most wild flowers and becomes too dense for nightingales. The male catkins, exposed in winter, open very early. The edible nuts are often damaged by the grub of a weevil, and may be eaten unripe by squirrels. The bark is shiny grey-brown, curling off in flakes. 4–6–8m. III.

♀

♂ 1–3

♂ 1–3

fruits

Common Hazel   Turkish Hazel

fruits

◁ **TURKISH HAZEL** *Corylus colurna* (the classic name for some kind of nut-tree). This hazel is an undoubted tree without any shrubby tendencies and it sets about making a single big tall bole from the start, with a stout shoot soon 1.3m a year at times. It makes a sturdy tree with a conic crown of level somewhat twisting branches and is so shapely, leafy and vigorous in difficult places that it is being planted in city schemes, in which it has been highly praised in the USA. The bark is coarsely scaly or shaggy. 8–12–25m. I.

♂ 2

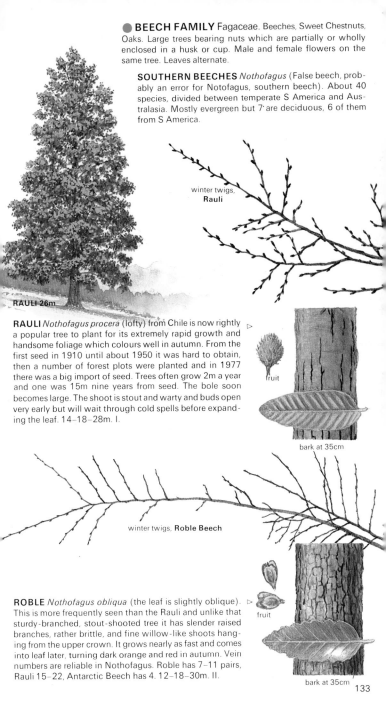

● **BEECH FAMILY** Fagaceae. Beeches, Sweet Chestnuts, Oaks. Large trees bearing nuts which are partially or wholly enclosed in a husk or cup. Male and female flowers on the same tree. Leaves alternate.

SOUTHERN BEECHES *Nothofagus* (False beech, probably an error for Notofagus, southern beech). About 40 species, divided between temperate S America and Australasia. Mostly evergreen but 7˙ are deciduous, 6 of them from S America.

winter twigs,
Rauli

RAULI 26m

RAULI *Nothofagus procera* (lofty) from Chile is now rightly a popular tree to plant for its extremely rapid growth and handsome foliage which colours well in autumn. From the first seed in 1910 until about 1950 it was hard to obtain, then a number of forest plots were planted and in 1977 there was a big import of seed. Trees often grow 2m a year and one was 15m nine years from seed. The bole soon becomes large. The shoot is stout and warty and buds open very early but will wait through cold spells before expanding the leaf. 14–18–28m. I.

fruit

bark at 35cm

winter twigs, **Roble Beech**

ROBLE *Nothofagus obliqua* (the leaf is slightly oblique). This is more frequently seen than the Rauli and unlike that sturdy-branched, stout-shooted tree it has slender raised branches, rather brittle, and fine willow-like shoots hanging from the upper crown. It grows nearly as fast and comes into leaf later, turning dark orange and red in autumn. Vein numbers are reliable in Nothofagus. Roble has 7–11 pairs, Rauli 15–22, Antarctic Beech has 4. 12–18–30m. II.

fruit

bark at 35cm

133

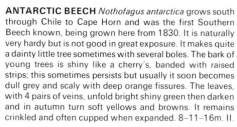

ANTARCTIC BEECH *Nothofagus antarctica* grows south through Chile to Cape Horn and was the first Southern Beech known, being grown here from 1830. It is naturally very hardy but is not good in great exposure. It makes quite a dainty little tree sometimes with several boles. The bark of young trees is shiny like a cherry's, banded with raised strips; this sometimes persists but usually it soon becomes dull grey with deep orange fissures. The leaves, with 4 pairs of veins, unfold bright shiny green then darken and in autumn turn soft yellows and browns. It remains crinkled and often cupped when expanded. 8–11–16m. II.

fruit

DOMBEY'S SOUTHERN BEECH *Nothofagus dombeyi* (Joseph Dombey, French botanist who worked in Chile) is an evergreen tree which can be tender when young but once established it grows with great vigour in all but the coldest areas. It is nearly confined to the largest gardens but is now being planted a little more widely. The bark is at first very smooth except for wrinkles and is nearly black but it becomes scaly then rich brown stripping to leave dark red patches. 6–12–28m. I.

fruit

SILVER BEECH *Nothofagus menziesii* (Archibald Menzies, botanist with Vancouver) has a white bark when young in its native New Zealand but in Britain, where it is seen in a few western and southern gardens, the bark is like a cherry-tree from the start. It remains dark and shiny closely banded by raised pale ridges. The angles of the basal veins beneath contain tiny hair-filled pits. Young trees often have blue-grey foliage. 5–9–17m. III.

RED BEECH *Nothofagus fusca* (dusky brown) is evergreen yet will often show autumn colours at any time of year and may shed a good proportion of its leaves in a hard winter. The older leaves turn yellow, orange and dark red before falling. The common name in its native New Zealand refers to hillsides of the tree looking quite red in autumn. It is hardier than its frail, papery leaves and slender growth suggest and is growing fast in Edinburgh. The only really big tree, however, with a bole 1m through is at Nymans Garden in Sussex. 8–12–26m. II.

BLACK BEECH *Nothofagus solandri* (Daniel Solander sailed with Captain Cook) from New Zealand has the smallest leaves of any broad-leaved tree we grow. They are borne on short bunches of wiry little shoots close along the upper sides of the few, long, wandering branches in a gaunt open crown. The tiny bright red male flowers are numerous on older trees. 8–15–25m. II.

Mountain Beech *N.s.* var. *cliffortioides* (George Clifford, creator of a famous garden in Holland) is similar except that its leaves are curiously buckled.

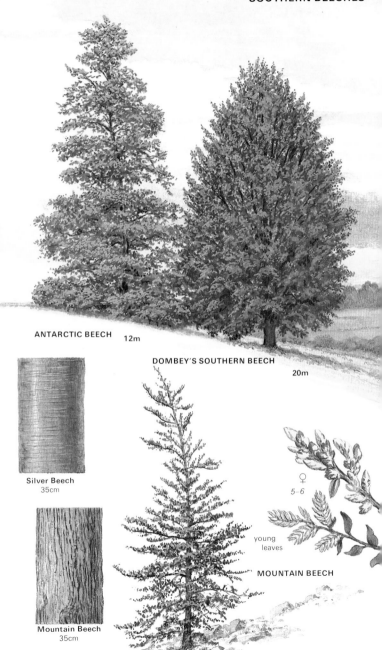

ANTARCTIC BEECH 12m

DOMBEY'S SOUTHERN BEECH 20m

Silver Beech
35cm

Mountain Beech
35cm

♀
5–6

young
leaves

MOUNTAIN BEECH

15m

135

BEECH *Fagus* (Classical name implying edible [nut]). Ten northern hemisphere species, 2 European, 1 N American, 7 E Asiatic, very similar in stature, foliage and smooth grey bark. Male flowers clustered in little long-stalked globes; 1–2 nuts in woody husks.

new growth

autumn

5

♀

♂

fruit

seeds

37m

bark at 60cm

COMMON BEECH *Fagus sylvatica* (of the woods). Not extending as a true native in Britain beyond England, but planted widely everywhere, the Beech grows only on freely draining soils whether over chalk or on acid sands. It needs abundant water and can send its roots far and deep in open soils to find it. The crown is so efficient at trapping light that Beech can grow up under other trees but none can grow under Beech, so woods on light soils eventually become beechwoods with sparse undergrowth. The timber is strong and hard-wearing but not durable out of doors, so it is used for furniture, stairs and turnery. It is finely flecked red-brown. 6–10–40m.

bud

'Pendula' 15m

'Copper' 25m

'Dawyck' 23m

FORMS OF BEECH

Dawyck Beech 'Dawyck' was found in a plantation at Dawyck, Peebles and brought down to the garden in about 1860. A few well-known gardens received grafts in 1907 but the first public planting was done in 1937 on the Basingstoke bypass. Some outer shoots loosely curving down out of the crown of big trees distinguish them in winter from Lombardy Poplars. 8–12–29m. I.

Weeping Beech 'Pendula' is grafted at 1 or 2m and sends vertical branches with hanging shoots rapidly to a good height. In some, the shoot-tips root when they reach the ground and send up more branches, one tree thus eventually making a complete copse. 3–10–29m. II.

Copper Beech 'Purpurea' includes one with leaves almost a good dark red and this must be grafted. Many others are seedlings of various murky shades of muddy purple after a brief flush of pink. 6–10–35m. X.

Fernleaf Beech 'Asplenifolia' can be told in winter by its dense array of fine twigs sprouting from the branches. It is frequent around public buildings and in parks and notable for outbreaks of normal leaves amongst the slender deeply cut ones, and some more like an oak. 5–9–25m. II.

ORIENTAL BEECH *Fagus orientalis* is a handsome and vigorous tree from The Balkan area, Asia Minor and the Caucasus Mountains but it is rare. The leaves are bigger than Common Beech, more widely spaced and have 7 or more pairs of veins instead of 7 or less normal in the green Common Beech. The husks have leafy projections not spines. 8–15–23m.

CHINESE BEECH *Fagus englerana* (Engler, a German botanist) is seen in a few gardens and is an elegant small tree sometimes with two stems. Its leaves turn gold and orange in the autumn. 4–7–16m. I.

new growth

Copper

Fernleaf

fruit

bud

SWEET CHESTNUTS *Castanea*.

Ten species across the southern parts of the northern temperate world: two shrubs and eight large trees but with similar foliage.

♀   ♂ 7

♂ 6–7

fruit   seeds

bark at 90cm

28m

SWEET CHESTNUT *Castanea sativa* (cultivated) is native to S Europe and was probably brought to Britain by the Romans. It is thoroughly at home here and the oldest dated tree, planted in 1550, is north of Inverness. It sows itself, often helped by jays, on well-drained non-limy soils and grows rapidly. The bark of young trees is silvery and the first fissures are vertical. With increasing age they lean into an ever flatter spiral. The female flowers are at the base of smaller catkins beyond the big male ones. These are also male but only open in some years, and then weeks later. In a good summer the nuts ripen and are edible. Some woods are coppiced – cut down to regrow many stems, which are split to make fencing. 8–14–35m. III.

SWEET CHESTNUTS

FORMS OF SWEET CHESTNUT

'Laciniata' is sometimes met with and may be 15m tall. It may revert to normal foliage on some branches and then return to the cut leaf and always has some less deeply cut and long whiskered than others. II.

Variegated Sweet Chestnut, **'Albomarginata'** and **'Aureomarginata'**. Perhaps these often revert to normal colouring for large trees are quite rare but small ones much less so. II.

'Laciniata'

'Albomarginata'

CHINKAPINS *Chrysolepis* (golden scale, in which the foliage is covered) is a group of 2 shrubs and one tree in the western USA. They are a link between the sweet chestnuts and oaks.

15m

Golden Chestnut

♂ 7

leaf spray with fruit

GOLDEN CHESTNUT *Chrysolepis chrysophylla* (with golden leaves) is an evergreen with hard and rigid leaves and with the shoot covered like the underside of the leaf, in tiny yellow scales. It is common over huge tracts of the lower mountains of Oregon and California and although hardy in probably all of Britain it is seldom seen outside botanic gardens. In our northern parts the plants are fairly tall bushes and the few tall, shapely trees are confined to the south but this may be due to our seed coming from the warmer parts of the range. The flowers are often not out in Britain until after midsummer. Male flowers are borne both on the long catkins and on smaller partly erect catkins near the shoot-tip. These small ones, which bear female flowers at the base, open a few weeks later, and in some years not at all. 3–5–15m. II.

under

bark at 25cm

139

Cypress oak   **COMMON OAK 25m**

bark at 50cm

OAKS Quercus (Latin for the Common Oak). One of the biggest of all groups, with at least 500 species across the northern hemisphere, 125 in Mexico alone, and with another 86 natural hybrids recognised in the USA. About half are evergreen. All bear recognisable acorns; they are the best means of propagation.

5

COMMON OAK *Quercus robur* (rugged or strong). Ranges across Europe and invaded Britain later than the Sessile Oak. Generally in southern and eastern Britain on heavy clays. The nearly stalkless leaves are soon being eaten by insects and spangled with galls, though without discernible harm to this long-lived tree, which provides for so much wildlife. A recent addition is the wasp which causes the knopper gall, grossly distorting the acorn, rampant since 1979 in many areas. 4–9–36m. III.

Cypress Oak 'Fastigiata' is usually a graft of a tree found in S Germany, but may be raised from acorns and is then variable in shape. 6–11–26m. I.

SESSILE OAK *Quercus petraea* (of the rocks; the hillside oak as opposed to the valley oak). The acorns of this early native tree are sessile – without stalks – but the leaves have good yellow stalks and are altogether more shapely, firm, healthy and handsome than those of the Common Oak. It is a finer tree too, faster growing, with a longer bole and straighter branches on which the foliage is evenly spread, not bunched. It is the oak of the Welsh and Scottish hillsides where pied flycatchers breed, as in Cumbria and Yorkshire too. The timber is like the Common Oak, strong and very durable. 6–12–43m. I.

140

DOWNY OAK *Quercus pubescens* (with short, soft hairs).
The 'Green Oak' of southern France where it is common on
dry hillsides. It has never become frequent in our gardens.
When found it has usually grown quite fast into a big ▷
rugged tree. In some ways it is like a Common Oak with the
foliage of Sessile Oak but densely hairy on the shoot and
leafstalk. The acorns are stalkless or nearly so, too, but the
leaf is smaller and less substantial, also less regularly shaped
than that of Sessile Oak. 5–10–24m. III.

under

DOWNY OAK
20m

bark at 50cm

TURKEY OAK 30m

TURKEY OAK *Quercus cerris* (the classical name). This
tree from S Europe behaves like a native now, but was first
planted by an Exeter nurseryman, J. Lucombe, as late as
1735. It is also called Mossy Cup Oak. It grows very fast ▷
and straight and makes a monumental specimen in the
open and a fine long bole in woods but the timber cracks
and shatters easily so is of no value. The side buds as well
as the end ones are surrounded by persistent whiskers, a
feature only of this and the Chestnut-leafed Oak. In clipped
hedges, some leaves are longer than normal and elaborately
cut into deep lobes. 8–15–38m. III – but useful in city
parks, being indifferent to soil or atmosphere.

♂ 6

new growth
5

141

CHESTNUT-LEAFED 20m
OAK

25m
MIRBECK'S
OAK

5

5-6

♂

♂

bark at 60cm

CHESTNUT-LEAFED OAK *Quercus castaneifolia*
(leaves like the Sweet Chestnut). This Caucasian tree
is one of the most handsome and fastest growing trees
we have. The first tree planted in Britain is the superb
specimen at Kew dating from 1846 and a seedling from it
near the Main Gate has grown in 25 years to 15m tall and
55cm diameter of bole. The whiskered side-buds are
found only in this oak and the Turkey Oak. The leaves of
the Kew trees are 20cm long but on some others are
12–15cm. They differ from the leaves of the Sawtooth
and Lebanon Oaks by lacking whiskers at the lobe tips.
8–12–32m. I.

MIRBECK'S OAK *Quercus canariensis* (from the Canary
Isles, where it is not, in fact, native). This vigorous and
very shapely tree is semi-evergreen. About half the leaves
turn yellow in autumn and fall while the other half remain
dark green through the winter. The leaves are hard and
often hooded but may be very flat on other trees. New
shoots are covered in soft orange wool which soon rubs
off. The tree is native to S Spain and to N Africa but is
completely hardy with us although not seen and planted
as much as it deserves. 6–11–30m. I.

142

LUCOMBE OAK 25m

TURNER'S OAK 20m

♂ 6

♂ 6

bark at 50cm

TURNER'S OAK *Quercus × turneri* (raised by Spencer
Turner, nurseryman in Essex) is a hybrid between the
Common Oak and the Holm Oak arising before 1780 and
propagated entirely by grafting. It is nearly evergreen but
sheds the old leaves not many weeks before the new
ones open, and gives a handsome appearance in mid-
winter. It inherits from the Holm Oak the short, dense
white down on the shoots and on the 7cm spike which
carries the female flowers. It seems to need to be 60 years
old before it bears acorns. There are two forms; one has
leaves tapering smoothly to the stalk from above halfway.
2–5–23m. I – for its interesting evergreen foliage.

LUCOMBE OAK *Quercus × hispanica* 'Lucombeana'.
The Turkey and Cork oaks cross where they overlap in
Spain but the forms of this hybrid that we grow originated
in Lucombe's nursery, Exeter in 1763 and 1830. They
stand out as large-leafed, tall evergreen oaks in many
country, and some town gardens and parks. Some have
thick, corky bark, some not so thick, and some normal
and blackish. The first cross trees, most seen in Devon,
keep in the winter a thin fringe of large shiny leaves; the
later trees keep all their leaves except in the hardest
winters. 4–10–35m. II.

143

PYRENEAN OAK *Quercus pyrenaica* from Iberia and Morocco is occasionally an open crowned rather erect tree but is more seen with long pendulous shoots, grafted at 2m on Common Oak. It is in either case easily recognised by the craggy bark and the deeply cut, long leaves covered in soft grey down. It is the last oak to flower, in late June to early July but the most spectacular. The male catkins are profuse, long and a good yellow. 3–5–15m. II.

HUNGARIAN OAK *Quercus frainetto* (an error for 'farnetto', the Italian name for the tree). This is a magnificent tree growing rapidly to make a noble specimen whose great domed crown carries large, boldly cut leaves. The edge of the crown against the sky shows sprays of jagged edged leaves unlike any other oak. The pale grey bark is finely divided into small smooth plates. The oldest trees are grafted at the base on to Common Oak from which sprouts may emerge. 8–15–30m. I – perhaps the noblest of all oaks.

CAUCASIAN OAK *Quercus macranthera* (having large anthers). This fine tree is found in some of the major gardens as quite big specimens and a little more widely as young trees but is not yet at all common. In leaf it resembles Mirbeck's Oak but with dense short hairs persisting on the shoot and leafstalk, and all the leaves shed in autumn. Like Mirbeck's Oak, the leaves are hard and often hooded, but they retain the soft hairs on the underside. The bark is dull grey, sometimes purplish, and flakes coarsely. The buds are large, bright shiny red with a hairy tip. 5–10–28m. I – a very handsome tree.

DAIMYO OAK *Quercus dentata* (with teeth; some Japanese oaks have entire leaves). A scrubby little tree on the hills of Japan, this is often little better here but there are some which make respectable small trees. Those which are struggling have most of their growth killed each winter but have grown enough to have stout branches from which bunches of feeble shoots arise each year. It is striking for its immense leaves, up to 40cm long and 20cm across. Many of these will remain brown on the tree during much of the winter. The very stout shoots of healthy trees are densely covered in fine hairs as are the very short leafstalks. The bark is dark grey, thick and corky, coarsely fissured. The acorn cups are stalkless and have slender downy scales. 2–3–15m. III – worth growing only for the size of its leaves.

♂ 6

Hungarian
Oak

18m
PYRENEAN OAK

26m
HUNGARIAN OAK

bark at 40cm

▷

Hungarian
Oak

♂ 6

Caucasian Oak

♂ 6

Daimyo
Oak

145

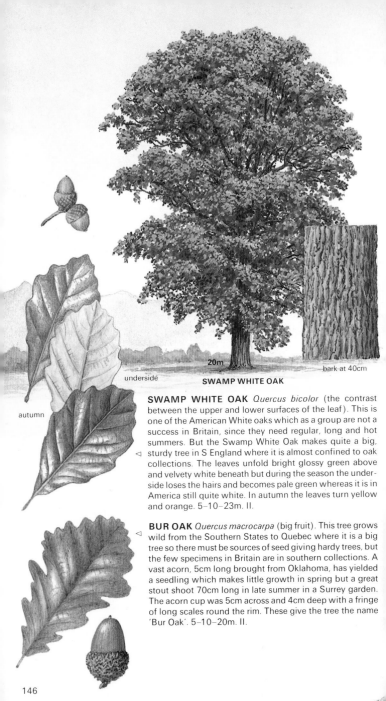

20m

underside

SWAMP WHITE OAK

autumn

bark at 40cm

SWAMP WHITE OAK *Quercus bicolor* (the contrast between the upper and lower surfaces of the leaf). This is one of the American White oaks which as a group are not a success in Britain, since they need regular, long and hot summers. But the Swamp White Oak makes quite a big, sturdy tree in S England where it is almost confined to oak collections. The leaves unfold bright glossy green above and velvety white beneath but during the season the underside loses the hairs and becomes pale green whereas it is in America still quite white. In autumn the leaves turn yellow and orange. 5–10–23m. II.

BUR OAK *Quercus macrocarpa* (big fruit). This tree grows wild from the Southern States to Quebec where it is a big tree so there must be sources of seed giving hardy trees, but the few specimens in Britain are in southern collections. A vast acorn, 5cm long brought from Oklahoma, has yielded a seedling which makes little growth in spring but a great stout shoot 70cm long in late summer in a Surrey garden. The acorn cup was 5cm across and 4cm deep with a fringe of long scales round the rim. These give the tree the name 'Bur Oak'. 5–10–20m. II.

WATER OAK *Quercus nigra* (black, presumably from the bark but that is grey as seen in the wild). This oak is related closely to the Willow Oak and comes from the south-eastern USA where it grows fast and is often planted in city streets. In Britain it is rare and confined to a few places in southern England. The leaves are always narrowly tapered to the stalk and broadest near the tip but very variable in toothing. They remain on the tree quite green until the end of the year. 3–5–18m. III.

BLACKJACK OAK *Quercus marilandica* (from Maryland), is found in some southern gardens occasionally and should be planted more for its fine foliage. The bright glossy green leaves are hard and thick and may be 17cm each way and variably rusty hairy beneath. It ranges from New York to Texas where it covers hundreds of miles of low, dry rocky hills, as a branchy shrub. The olive green shoot is covered in short, curly pale brown hairs. The acorns are nearly globular, borne in pairs or singly on stout 5mm stalks. 3–5–15m. II.

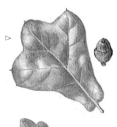

WHITE OAK *Quercus alba* (white, from the bark of old trees) ranges wild from S Canada to the Gulf of Mexico, all of which area has summers hotter and longer than ours. This restricts it to southern England. The leaves differ according to the light they receive and those on the outer crown are elegantly and deeply cut while the interior leaves are more like Common Oak but with tapered bases. In America autumn colours are orange, scarlet and deep red and highly spectacular. In Britiain they tend to be purple. 4–9–17m. II.

bark at 40cm

autumn

BLACKJACK OAK

12m

WHITE OAK 15m

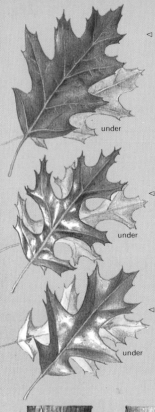

RED OAK *Quercus rubra* (red; autumn colour) is the most common and much the largest growing of this American group in Britain and seeds itself in some areas of sandy soils. All of this group have acorns which remain minute for one season and ripen in the second year and have leaves with whisker-tipped teeth and, in many, deeply cut broad lobes. It is the fastest-growing oak from N America, and the best one for cool areas. The leaves on young trees and sprouts can be 25–30cm long with much shallower lobing. The underside is always pale matt green. In autumn young trees may be bright then deep red but big ones are more usually yellow, orange and brown. 10–15–32m. II.

SCARLET OAK *Quercus coccinea* (scarlet; autumn colour) is much less common than the Red Oak and a smaller tree but is quite frequent in gardens. It differs from the Red Oak in the smaller, more deeply and evenly lobed leaf, glossy above and beneath, turning scarlet one branch at a time then deep red, and dead leaves staying on lower branches until the end of the year. The crown, however, is more open and irregular. It ranges from Maine to Georgia. 7–12–28m. I – for its foliage.

PIN OAK *Quercus palustris* (of the marshes) is a little less frequent here than the Scarlet Oak by roadsides, in parks and gardens and is more likely to be planted in wet soils. Young trees have distinctive crowns with clean boles for 3m and a dense ring of slender shoots spraying down like a skirt. The main vein angles beneath hold tufts of pale brown hairs. 7–12–26m. I – in the south only.

Red 40cm   Scarlet 40cm   Pin 40cm   Black 40cm

BLACK OAK *Quercus velutina* (velvety; young leaves) is rare in comparison with the other three red oaks above and comes from the same regions of eastern USA. The orange fissures in the dark, knobbly grey bark identify it as well as the velvety haired shoot, leafstalk and young leaf. Also the big leaf, to 25cm, is hard and crinkled, often hooded and equally often mis-shapen by the midrib dividing halfway making big lobes each side but no central lobe. It grows rapidly into a broadly domed tree. 9–14–30m. II.

autumn leaf with forked midrib

30m
RED OAK autumn

22m
SCARLET OAK

PIN OAK 22m

Scarlet Oak
autumn

acorn
♂ 6
Red Oak

♂ 6
Scarlet

♂ 6
Pin

♂ 6–7
Black

12m

**CALIFORNIAN
LIVE OAK**

22m

HOLM OAK

young

6
♂

bark at 40cm

mature

under

HOLM OAK *Quercus ilex* (the classical name for this tree, later used for the Holly) comes from the western Mediterranean but has been grown in Britain for some 400 years. By far our commonest evergreen oak, it is particularly valued as a shelterbelt tree against sea winds. It slowly grows a densely twiggy, bushy crown with spine-edged, holly-like leaves. The young shoots, leaf-stalks and leaf undersides are closely white-felted. With age it becomes less of a bush and more of a tree and the leaves become smooth-edged. The bark is almost black, breaking into small, shallow squares. Its heavy dark mass can be oppressive. In early summer masses of slender male catkins hang gold among silver-haired new leaves and the tree is briefly much less dreary. 3–5–28m. III.

CALIFORNIA LIVE OAK *Quercus agrifolia* (literally 'field-leafed' probably intended to be 'aquifolia', like the Holly) is abundant in low hills and by gulches full in winter but dry in the hot, rainless summer. The trees in a few collections in the British Isles show that it can adapt to rainy summers and grow quite well in the warmer areas. Prominent distinctions from the Holm Oak are the smooth black bark striped brown and the smooth underside of the leaf with hairs only in tufts in the main vein-angles. 3–5–15m. II.

CHINESE CORK OAK trunk

CORK OAK 11m

Cork Oak

under

cork

CORK OAK *Quercus suber* (cork) is a Mediterranean tree that grows happily to the far north in Scotland but only in the southwest of England is it at all frequent. Even there good trees are few as it is a slow, ungainly tree and may rest some branches on the ground. With its dull foliage and gloomy aspect as well, the curious bark is the only excuse for growing it. The cork of everyday use is stripped from trees in Spain and Portugal, leaving them dark red before it regrows, with the inner layers and cambium unharmed. 2–3–18m. III.

CHINESE CORK OAK *Quercus variabilis* (variable; probably in size of leaf) yields commercial cork in China and although it may not be as good for this as the European tree it is an altogether finer plant with usually big, handsome leaves silvered on the under surface. It grows slowly but it is not long before the bark is craggy and pink-brown with very deep wavy fissures. It is seen in only a few southern gardens; one in Cornwall has a grove of tall specimens. The acorn is nearly hidden in a cup of long, curled scales. 4–6–18m. I.

ARMENIAN OAK *Quercus pontica* (from the south shore of the Black Sea). This is a very splendid oak for foliage but does not make much of a tree, being more a broad bush on a very short stem. It is gaunt in winter, handsome in summer and beautiful in autumn golds. The shoot is very stout, ribbed and hairless, tipped by a big bud with brown-edged hairy scales. The leaves are up to 18cm long, thick, pale green underneath, and with hooked teeth. Male catkins are only 1–3 in a bunch, but may be 20cm long. Female flowers are 4–5, crowded on a 3cm stalk. They ripen to acorns 3–4cm long, tapered at each end and turning deep mahogany red. 2–4–9m. I.

151

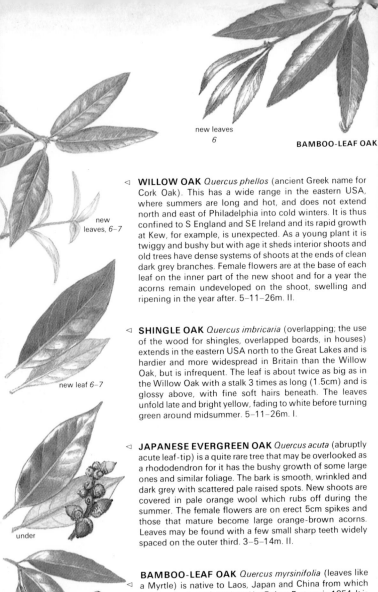

new leaves
6

BAMBOO-LEAF OAK

new
leaves, 6–7

new leaf 6–7

under

◁ **WILLOW OAK** *Quercus phellos* (ancient Greek name for Cork Oak). This has a wide range in the eastern USA, where summers are long and hot, and does not extend north and east of Philadelphia into cold winters. It is thus confined to S England and SE Ireland and its rapid growth at Kew, for example, is unexpected. As a young plant it is twiggy and bushy but with age it sheds interior shoots and old trees have dense systems of shoots at the ends of clean dark grey branches. Female flowers are at the base of each leaf on the inner part of the new shoot and for a year the acorns remain undeveloped on the shoot, swelling and ripening in the year after. 5–11–26m. II.

◁ **SHINGLE OAK** *Quercus imbricaria* (overlapping; the use of the wood for shingles, overlapped boards, in houses) extends in the eastern USA north to the Great Lakes and is hardier and more widespread in Britain than the Willow Oak, but is infrequent. The leaf is about twice as big as in the Willow Oak with a stalk 3 times as long (1.5cm) and is glossy above, with fine soft hairs beneath. The leaves unfold late and bright yellow, fading to white before turning green around midsummer. 5–11–26m. I.

◁ **JAPANESE EVERGREEN OAK** *Quercus acuta* (abruptly acute leaf-tip) is a quite rare tree that may be overlooked as a rhododendron for it has the bushy growth of some large ones and similar foliage. The bark is smooth, wrinkled and dark grey with scattered pale raised spots. New shoots are covered in pale orange wool which rubs off during the summer. The female flowers are on erect 5cm spikes and those that mature become large orange-brown acorns. Leaves may be found with a few small sharp teeth widely spaced on the outer third. 3–5–14m. II.

BAMBOO-LEAF OAK *Quercus myrsinifolia* (leaves like
◁ a Myrtle) is native to Laos, Japan and China from which last country it was introduced by Robert Fortune in 1854. It is seen only in botanic and plantsmen's gardens in S England, the most elegant of the evergreen oaks. It may be a small tree on a single bole or with a number of slender stems, with slender, raised branches from which the well-spaced leaves mostly point at a downward angle but do not hang since they are hard. Female flowers and acorns are on a slender, erect 4cm spike. 3–5–12m. I.

20m
WILLOW OAK

18m
SHINGLE OAK

bark at 30cm

1st year acorn

SAWTOOTH OAK *Quercus acutissima* (very sharply pointed; leaves and the teeth on them). This deciduous oak ranges from the Himalayas to Korea and Japan and is planted in a few southern gardens in England and Ireland. The bark is dark grey, coarsely fissured and flaky and the crown roughly conic with level branches. The shoot is downy at first, soon smooth pale green and the buds are pale green and slender pointed. The leaves are 20cm long and have little tufts of hairs in the angles of the veins beneath. The acorns have not been seen in Britain but in the USA where it is more commonly planted they are almost hidden in the long curving scales of the cup. 4–7–15m. I.

LEBANON OAK *Quercus libani* grows from Syria to Asia Minor among mountains and is hardy at least as far north as Edinburgh but has been planted very rarely. Two of the best specimens are in the National Pinetum in Kent. The bark is dark grey with orange fissures and may be somewhat corky. The crown rather open on a straight bole. The acorns are on very short, thick stalks and enlarge and ripen fully only in some years and then are nearly all fertile but the seedlings appear to be hybrids with Turkey Oak. The Lebanon Oak differs from the similar Sawtooth Oak (above) in its olive-brown shoot, orange-brown bud and shorter spined teeth. 6–11–20m. I.

153

● **ELM FAMILY** Ulmaceae. Eighteen species of Elm (*Ulmus*, the classical name) occur north of the Himalayas and east of the Rockies. In most the flowers open before the leaves, making the whole tree look dark red, but a few flower in the autumn. The leaves of all species are to some extent asymmetric at the base. Raised from seed, cuttings or root-suckers.

fls *3*

5

fruits *7*

WYCH ELM *Ulmus glabra* (smooth – the bark of young trees, unlike other elms where it is soon fissured) grows across N and C Europe into W Asia and is the only elm certainly native in Britain. It is most abundant by streams from N Wales and Yorkshire to the far north of Scotland and in Ireland. In S England it was more local, planted in parkland, but all except a few trees have been killed by Elm disease and, spreading by seed, not suckers, it will be a long time returning. It is much planted in Scottish city squares. The leaves and the stout red-brown shoots are harsh all over with short stiff hairs. 8–15–38m. III.

Camperdown Elm 'Camperdown' was found as a seedling at the castle of that name in Angus. Grafted on to normal Wych Elm it makes a head of furiously twisting branches then weeps to the ground with leaves to 20cm long.

'Lutescens' usually has a broad bushy crown but can be tall. I.

'Horizontalis' is taller with straight branches not fully weeping. 6–9–15m. II.

Camperdown

'Lutescens'

'Horizontalis'

WYCH ELM

'Camperdown'

Elm Disease is a fungus, *Ceratocystis ulmi*, which is carried by an Elm-bark beetle when it hatches from its pupa in dead elm wood and flies to shoots high in the crown of a healthy elm where the beetle feeds. A mild form was common 1920–1945 but a virulent form was brought here from N America in the mid-1960s. The name 'Dutch Elm Disease' is used because the Dutch studied it to breed resistant trees, before the 154 worse form arose.

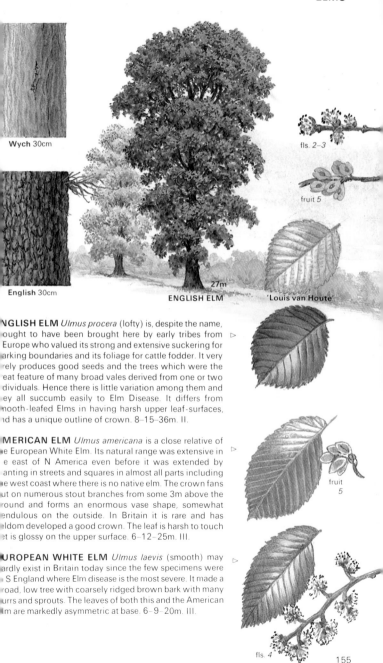

Wych 30cm

fls. 2–3

fruit 5

English 30cm

27m

ENGLISH ELM

'Louis van Houte'

fruit 5

fls. 4

ENGLISH ELM *Ulmus procera* (lofty) is, despite the name, thought to have been brought here by early tribes from Europe who valued its strong and extensive suckering for marking boundaries and its foliage for cattle fodder. It very rarely produces good seeds and the trees which were the great feature of many broad vales derived from one or two individuals. Hence there is little variation among them and they all succumb easily to Elm Disease. It differs from smooth-leafed Elms in having harsh upper leaf-surfaces, and has a unique outline of crown. 8–15–36m. II.

AMERICAN ELM *Ulmus americana* is a close relative of the European White Elm. Its natural range was extensive in the east of N America even before it was extended by planting in streets and squares in almost all parts including the west coast where there is no native elm. The crown fans out on numerous stout branches from some 3m above the ground and forms an enormous vase shape, somewhat pendulous on the outside. In Britain it is rare and has seldom developed a good crown. The leaf is harsh to touch yet is glossy on the upper surface. 6–12–25m. III.

EUROPEAN WHITE ELM *Ulmus laevis* (smooth) may hardly exist in Britain today since the few specimens were in S England where Elm disease is the most severe. It made a broad, low tree with coarsely ridged brown bark with many burrs and sprouts. The leaves of both this and the American Elm are markedly asymmetric at base. 6–9–20m. III.

fl. 3

fruit 6

bark at 40cm

SMOOTH-LEAFED ELM 30m

SMOOTH-LEAFED ELM *Ulmus carpinifolia* (hornbeam-leafed; similar parallel veins) was brought in by pre-Roman tribes and was the countryside elm of East Kent and much of East Anglia and an uncommon parkland tree over much of England. By 1980 there were a few isolated large trees surviving in Essex and in the NE Midlands but Elm Disease has killed nearly all in SE England. The leaf is leathery and smooth on the upper surface and has tufts of white hairs in the vein angles beneath. Commonly with hanging masses of twisting shoots and small leaves, but non-pendulous forms with bigger, darker leaves to 12cm long, were frequent around the Hertfordshire-Cambridge area. 9–15–32m. l.

◁ **Wheatley Elm** 'Sarniensis' (from Guernsey, anciently Sarnia) is a form of the elm common on Guernsey and Jersey sold from 1836. Its formal shape and lack of heavy branches make it popular for avenues, bypasses, streets and parks particularly in the north Midlands and N England. 8–14–36m. l.

◁ **Cornish Elm** *U.c.* var. *cornubiensis* replaces English Elm west of Barnstaple and Okehampton and overlaps it from Plymouth to Ivybridge. A few large plantings further east have now died. It is common from Waterford to Cork in Ireland. 8–12–36m. l.

156

fl. 4

fruit 6

25m

Huntington Elm

27m   30m

Wheatley Elm   Cornish Elm

DUTCH ELM *Ulmus × hollandica*. 'Hollandica' is one of
the hybrids between Wych and Smooth-leafed Elm which
arose in Europe. Its timber works well and was keenly
sought but since it was frequent only from Hampshire to
the S Midlands, where disease struck early and hard, there
are few, if any left. The crown is odd; a slightly sinuous bole
bearing a few nearly erect branches holding a thin, flat
umbrella of stout shoots. Suckers will grow 2m a year. The
bark is smoothly scaly. 9–15–32m. III.

Huntington Elm 'Vegeta' (vigorous) is another cross
between Wych and Smooth-leafed elms, raised in Huntington in 1760. Its straight, radiating branches make a fine
domed crown. The bark is of regularly interwoven ridges.
The flowers and fruit are large and conspicuous. 8–15–
32m. I.

CHINESE ELM *Ulmus parvifolia* (small leafed) flowers in
October and holds its leaves green until the end of the year.
The bark changes from its early brown with orange scales
to blue-white with orange scales. It is now in demand as an
excellent city tree resisting Elm Disease, but old trees are
rare. 5–10–15m. I.

fruit   6

SIBERIAN ELM *Ulmus pumila* (dwarf) is the universal
shade-tree from Winnipeg to New Mexico so it can grow in
greater extremes of hot and cold than we have, but the few
seen are mostly in the south. It grows very fast to make a
broad, open, loose crown, very unlike that of Chinese Elm
and differs also in flowering in spring, grey then brown
bark and bigger less neatly toothed, nearly symmetrical
leaves. 8–12–20m. III.

26m
CAUCASIAN ELM

trunk

ZELKOVA. Five species related to the Elms, occurring in Cyprus, the Caucasus Mountains, China and Japan. One is a big tree, one is medium-sized and the others small. Two are too rare to include. Zelkovas can be killed by Elm disease but normally the beetle carrying it feeds only on elms. Raised from seed and suckers.

fruit

CAUCASIAN ELM *Zelkova carpinifolia* (leaves like Horn-beam). This fine tree is uncommon in parkland and big gardens in all parts. The brush-like crown of a hundred or so stems is normal here but a few trees are shaped like other trees, as they are in the wild. It suckers freely and can make a hedge like the elm. Young trees are slender and for some years grow slowly but then the bole expands rapidly. Autumn colours are yellow, orange and russet. It is a splendid city-park tree. 5–12–31m. I.

CUTLEAF ZELKOVA *Zelkova* 'Verschaffeltii' (Ambrose Verschaffelt, Belgian nurseryman) is of obscure origin but probably a garden form of Caucasian Elm. It was received at Kew in 1886 and remains rare. It grows slowly into a low bushy tree. It rarely flowers but when it does the fruit are 5mm globes deeply grooved into two halves. 2–5–10m. III.

KEAKI 15m

KEAKI *Zelkova serrata* (many-toothed; leaf) is a Japanese tree of great merit formerly seen only in some big gardens but now planted more in city squares and parks, where in the USA, it has shown much promise. The well-stalked leaves hang in elegant lines from the shoot and turn shades of yellow, pink and red in autumn. Old shoots have short stalked leaves like Caucasian Elm but with a finely tapered tip. Raised from seed only. 5–10–20m. I.

CHINESE ZELKOVA *Zelkova sinica* (from China) is an attractive little tree in some collections, known from other Zelkovas by the untoothed lower third of the leaf, which is also hard and often tinged crimson beneath and on the veins. Fruit only 2mm across, deep green, are often borne at the base of each leaf. 3–5–15m. I.

fruit

bark at 30cm

NETTLE TREES *Celtis* (classical Latin name transferred from a lotus). About 70 species from the tropics and northwards, related to elms. They have leaves 3-nerved at the base and the fruit are fleshy berries.

HACKBERRY *Celtis occidentalis* (western) ranges from SE Canada to NW Texas and was introduced to Britain in 1636 but has never been much planted perhaps because it has few attractions. The most unusual feature is the bark with its knobs and winged flanges. The crown is domed with long shoots arching out from near the top. The leaf is hard, rough and variably toothed but always entire at the base and sometimes all down one side. 6–11–15m. III.

unripe fruit

bark at 30cm

SOUTHERN NETTLE-TREE *Celtis australis* (southern) grows from SW Asia to S France where its big smooth silver-grey boles are a feature of city streets and squares. In Britain, however, it is usually little more than a tall bush. The slender, slightly twisted leaf-tip distinguishes this from the Hackberry, together with the smooth bark. It has a thin and open crown and a leaf much roughened by bases of stiff hairs which remain when the tips are shed. 3–5–12m. II.

unripe fruit

bark at 30cm

young fruit

● MULBERRY FAMILY Moraceae (named from the Mulberry, *Morus* in classical Latin) is a mainly tropical group of 1000 species. There are 12 **Mulberries** *Morus* of which only two are normally grown in Britain. They have separate male and female catkins on the same tree and broad alternate leaves sometimes very irregularly lobed.

COMMON MULBERRY, BLACK MULBERRY *Morus nigra* (black; fully ripe fruit) is probably a native of the Black Sea region but has been cultivated so long and so widely this cannot be known for certain. In Britain it is as much a tree of village gardens, church-yards and town parks as of the big gardens, and mainly found in the south. Seedlings are slow so many trees are raised from 'truncheons', 1m lengths of branch 10–20cm through, set halfway into the ground in winter. These sprout masses of shoots and soon look much older than they are. One of the biggest Mulberries is only 80 years old and they grow far too fast for quite small trees to be of the great ages often claimed for them. Autumn colour is late and pale yellow. 2–4–13m. I.

WHITE MULBERRY *Morus alba* (white; pale pink fruit) came from China to Europe in early times and to Britain about 400 years ago. It is uncommon but reaches S Scotland. It does not thrive for long and branches decay and break easily. It is the traditional food-plant for silkworms although they will feed on Common Mulberry and some other trees. It is distinguished by the glossy smooth upper surface of the leaf and sometimes by odd leaves elaborately lobed. Propagation as for Common Mulberry. 3–6–16m. III.

OSAGE ORANGE *Maclura pomifera* (apple-bearing; large rounded fruit). Native to the southern central USA from Arkansas to Texas, this needs warmth and apart from two fine trees in Kew Gardens it is rarely seen. Seedlings are easily raised and very spiny but are also easily killed by frost. Cuttings and layers will grow but both sexes need to be grown together to yield the heavy inedible stringy fruit. In winter it is identified by the zigzag green shoot with a single 1cm green spine at each angle and by the bark. The flowers are little clusters of 30 on a 1cm stalk, and open yellow-green. 2–5–16m. III.

FIG *Ficus carica* (possibly from Caria in Asia Minor where extensively cultivated) is native to the Levant and was brought to Britain very early, perhaps by the Romans. It can be grown well northward in England, against a south facing wall, but will not yield useful fruit. In the south the fruit ripen and trees can grow in the open, as in St James's Park, to make sturdy if far from straight, small trees. Only female trees are grown and they need no males to produce good fruit. The flowers are grouped inside a nearly closed receptacle which itself ripens as the fruit. The shoot is stout, ribbed and seg-mented. Raised from seed and by grafting. 2–3–5m. III.

bark at 30cm

fruit

BLACK MULBERRY

10m

fruit

WHITE MULBERRY

bark at 30cm

bark at 30cm

fruit

OSAGE ORANGE

15m

bark at 15cm

fruit

FIG

161

● MAGNOLIA FAMILY Magnoliaceae (Pierre Magnol, French botanist). 220 species of trees and shrubs from the Americas and (principally) SE Asia. Flowers large and primitive. Raised from seed, layers, and by grafting. The genus Magnolia has 35 species.

fl. 7–10

fruit

△

SOUTHERN MAGNOLIA *Magnolia grandiflora*
(large flowered) is the common evergreen Magnolia grown against walls over much of England and Ireland and as a free standing tree in the south. In the wild from N Carolina to Texas it can be 30m tall and varies in the intensity of the orange shown on the leaf underside: in Britain this is thickly covered in rusty brown hairs except in the forms 'Exmouth' and 'Goliath' which are both common. Being grafts or layers these forms flower within a few years of planting while a seedling tree may take 25 years. 'Exmouth' has narrower leaves than the species type, and 'Goliath' has broader, more rounded. The sweetly scented flowers open few at a time from July to late autumn. 3–5–10m. I.

underside

CHINESE EVERGREEN MAGNOLIA *Magnolia delavayi* (discovered by Pierre Delavay, French Jesuit missionary-botanist in China). This fine plant with leaves to 35 ×18cm is grown on sheltered walls in S England and in the open in the southwest and in S Ireland. It makes a broad tree with strong low branches and a thick, corky and scaling yellowish-white bark. New growth is tinged pale coppery-brown. Growth is more rapid than in Southern Magnolia and is good on chalky soils. The dense grey woolly hairs on the leaf-stalk are shed in stripes. 5–8–15m. I.

underside

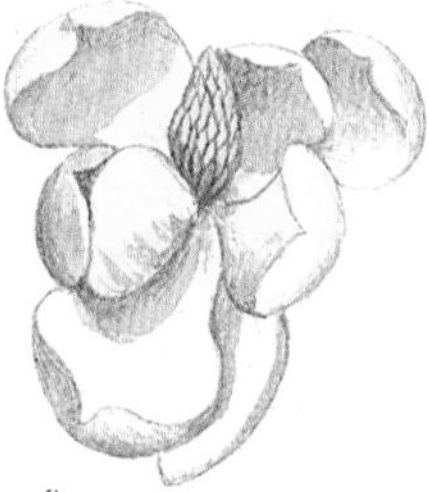

fl.
6–9

bark at 30cm

JAPANESE BIGLEAF MAGNOLIA *Magnolia hypoleuca* (white beneath; leaf) is generally a tree of southern gardens and uncommon, but in favoured areas and well placed it can grow and flower as far north as Morayshire. It grows fast as a young tree but is liable to damage or breakage and is often seen as a group of stems from the ground which are sprouts from the original tree. The bark is smooth pale grey and the branches are in whorls, bare inside their upcurved tips where a whorl of a few leaves is borne. The rich fruity scent of the flowers can be enjoyed 20m or more from the tree around midsummer. 6–12–18m. I.

fl. 8

fruit

fl. 7–8

Japanese Bigleaf

BIGLEAF MAGNOLIA *Magnolia macrophylla* (Greek, large-leafed) is a scarce and local tree in the SE of the USA as it is in S and W Britain. It can bear the largest simple leaf of any tree we grow, 60–70cm long, auricled at the base (an 'ear' each side) and silvered with fine hairs beneath. It is a gaunt tree with few branches and stout shoots which are bloomed blue-grey. The bark is dark grey and scaly. The stout leaf-stalk, 5–12cm long, is covered in fine pale downy hairs. The flowers can be 30cm across but are often only half as big here, and are sweetly scented with thick, fleshy tepals, six in number. 3–5–13m. II.

CUCUMBER TREE *Magnolia acuminata* (tapering to a narrow point; leaf) ranges from Florida just into S Canada and was sent to Britain first in 1736, not flowering until 1762. The English name refers to the fruit when still green but is hopelessly inappropriate as they are then barely 5cm long and become egg-shaped and bright pink as they ripen. It grows to be one of the biggest magnolias and has bark unlike any other, dark brown and purplish narrow ridges and deep fissures. Being an American species its flowers open only when the tree is in full leaf, and as they are greenish they hardly show. The crown maintains a good conic shape even in old trees. 6–11–26m. II.

fl. 7

fruit

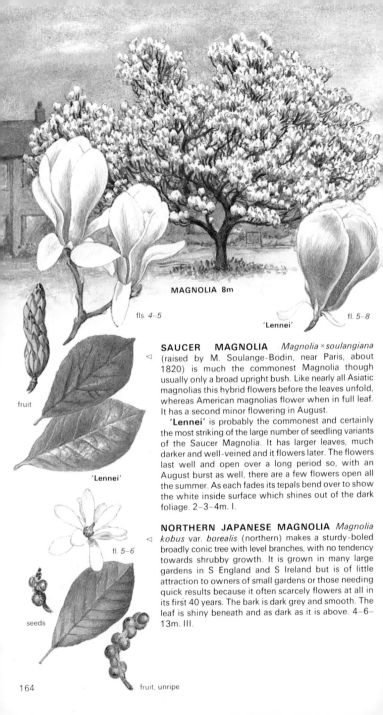

MAGNOLIA 8m

fls. *4–5*

'Lennei'

fl. *5–8*

fruit

'Lennei'

fl. *5–6*

seeds

fruit, unripe

SAUCER MAGNOLIA *Magnolia × soulangiana*
(raised by M. Soulange-Bodin, near Paris, about
1820) is much the commonest Magnolia though
usually only a broad upright bush. Like nearly all Asiatic
magnolias this hybrid flowers before the leaves unfold,
whereas American magnolias flower when in full leaf.
It has a second minor flowering in August.

'Lennei' is probably the commonest and certainly
the most striking of the large number of seedling variants
of the Saucer Magnolia. It has larger leaves, much
darker and well-veined and it flowers later. The flowers
last well and open over a long period so, with an
August burst as well, there are a few flowers open all
the summer. As each fades its tepals bend over to show
the white inside surface which shines out of the dark
foliage. 2–3–4m. I.

NORTHERN JAPANESE MAGNOLIA *Magnolia
kobus* var. *borealis* (northern) makes a sturdy-boled
broadly conic tree with level branches, with no tendency
towards shrubby growth. It is grown in many large
gardens in S England and S Ireland but is of little
attraction to owners of small gardens or those needing
quick results because it often scarcely flowers at all in
its first 40 years. The bark is dark grey and smooth. The
leaf is shiny beneath and as dark as it is above. 4–6–
13m. III.

fls. 4

WILLOW-LEAFED MAGNOLIA *Magnolia salicifolia* (willow-leafed) is a Japanese tree valued in many southern gardens, as in the Savill Gardens, Windsor, for its elegant growth and abundance of early pure white flowers on bare shoots. It soon makes an open dome of shoots and branches which are unusually slender for a magnolia, and it flowers well when young. The leaves vary in size between trees but are narrow, tapering gently to the base and when crushed give a scent of aniseed. 4–7–15m. I.

VEITCH'S HYBRID MAGNOLIA *Magnolia × veitchii* (raised at Veitch's Nurseries in Exeter in 1907) is a cross between Campbell's Magnolia and the Yulan Lily, raised partly to have flowers like Campbell's Magnolia without waiting 25 years for them. Four of the five seedlings bore white flowers; it is the fifth which is seen in many southern and western gardens where it makes a tall tree with grey bark, which flowers profusely. 6–15–27m. II.

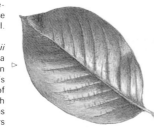

fl. 4–5

Veitch's Hybrid

fl. 2–4

Campbell's

CAMPBELL'S MAGNOLIA *Magnolia campbellii* (Dr A. Campbell travelled with the botanist Hooker, in Sikkim in 1849) grows in the Himalayas from Nepal to Assam and is regarded by many as the king of the magnolias. It grows well at Kew but is mainly a feature of big gardens from Sussex west and north to Argyll. The stout, elephant-grey, smooth trunk bears a wide level-branched crown. The flowers are unharmed by frost when in the closed bud but are vulnerable once the scales open. In 1975 some opened successfully in January but March is the usual time. 8–12–20m. II.

TULIP-TREES *Liriodendron* (Greek, lily and tree). The two species below are the only Tulip-trees in the world and they are a good example among many, of the survival of the long pre-Ice Ages flora in China and eastern N America and nowhere else. Raised from seed.

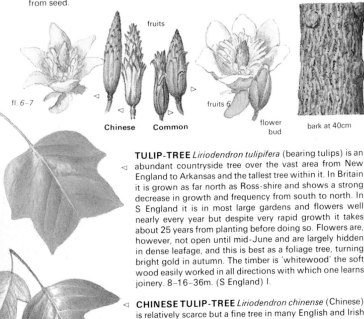

fl. 6-7

fruits

Chinese   Common   fruits 6   flower bud   bark at 40cm

TULIP-TREE *Liriodendron tulipifera* (bearing tulips) is an abundant countryside tree over the vast area from New England to Arkansas and the tallest tree within it. In Britain it is grown as far north as Ross-shire and shows a strong decrease in growth and frequency from south to north. In S England it is in most large gardens and flowers well nearly every year but despite very rapid growth it takes about 25 years from planting before doing so. Flowers are, however, not open until mid-June and are largely hidden in dense leafage, and this is best as a foliage tree, turning bright gold in autumn. The timber is 'whitewood' the soft wood easily worked in all directions with which one learns joinery. 8-16-36m. (S England) I.

CHINESE TULIP-TREE *Liriodendron chinense* (Chinese) is relatively scarce but a fine tree in many English and Irish gardens, growing quite as fast as the common species. New growth emerges orange-red and the leaf-stalk often remains dark red. The whole crown has the more deeply cut leaves that are confined to the sprouts in the common tree, and can be 22×25cm and silvery beneath. 8-16-27m. I.

● **TETRACENTRON FAMILY** Tetracentraceae (4-spurred – the fruit). Allied to magnolias. A single species, and one of the only three broad-leaved trees with the primitive wood-structure of a conifer: it has tracheides instead of vessels and fibres. Raised from seed.

fl. 6

SPUR-LEAF *Tetracentron sinense* (Chinese) is a curiosity grown in some botanic gardens and a few others mostly in the south and west but there are good trees at Cambridge and Edinburgh. One peculiar feature, inspiring the English name used here, is the slender spurs along the shoots each capped by the base of the stalk of a single leaf. The leaf is hard and so are the small, regular and sharp teeth on its margin. Each spur also grows a slender catkin of flowers in spring which remains with green fruit until autumn, then turns brown and persists into winter. There is usually more than one bole, with rather sparse somewhat raised slender branches, and rarely any autumn change of colour, mostly the leaves fall when dark green. 3-5-15m. II.

| TULIP-TREE | 30m | KATSURA 20m |

● **KATSURA FAMILY** Cercidiphyllaceae (leaf like *Cercis*, the Judas-tree). Has but one species, closely related to the magnolias. Like *Tetracentron* (above) it has the primitive wood of a conifer, but unlike it, whole trees are of one sex.

KATSURA TREE *Cercidiphyllum japonicum* (Japanese) also occurs in China. It is easily raised from seed and makes large and shapely plants in the first year, when it should be planted out. With dainty foliage, fine autumn colours and strong growth it has become a popular plant but early plantings were confined to large gardens mainly in the west but also from Sandringham, Norfolk to Novar, Ross-shire in the east. Late frosts can damage the first flush of shrimp-pink leaves but do no lasting harm. There is a tendency to have many stems but good trees have a single axis right to the tip. The tree suffers in droughts and needs a damp soil. 7–13–25m. I.

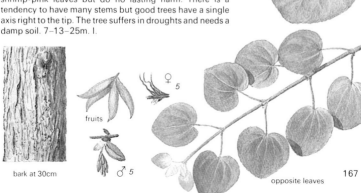

fruits

♀ 5

♂ 5

bark at 30cm

opposite leaves

167

● **WINTER'S BARK FAMILY** Winteraceae (William Winter, a captain under Drake, found Tierra del Fuegan Indians using leaves for medicine and flavouring). A few southern aromatic evergreens related to magnolias.

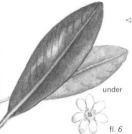

WINTER'S BARK *Drimys winteri* (see above) in its typical form comes from southern Chile and Argentina but it has varieties ranging north to Mexico. In Britain it is biggest and most frequent in Ireland, less so in Cornwall and other west coast areas, and rare and confined to growing against walls further east, seldom far from the south coast. It is a loosely columnar tree, rather pendulous outside. A superior form in some gardens has a regular, conic crown with whorled branches, bright red buds and soft silver-blue underside to the leaf. Raised from seed or cuttings. 4–9–17m. l.

under

fl. 6

● **PROTEA FAMILY** Proteaceae. A large and varied assemblage of trees and shrubs of the southern hemisphere, many with large and brilliantly coloured flowers, scarlet or yellow.

CHILEAN FIREBUSH *Embothrium coccineum* (scarlet; flowers) has a wide range N–S in Chile and varies in the length of leaf. A long-leafed evergreen form *'E. longifolium'* is very vigorous and floriferous in Ireland with leaves to 22cm long. In England the shorter leafed and semi-deciduous form 'Norquinco' is the most planted and carries the densest display of flowers, but the older trees in the west and northwest are the type *coccineum*, of intermediate leaf-length, evergreen. The flowers of all these forms are similar and spectacular. East winds damage them and the tree is scarce in the east and needs planting in shelter. It can be raised from either seed or suckers. 6–9–15m. l.

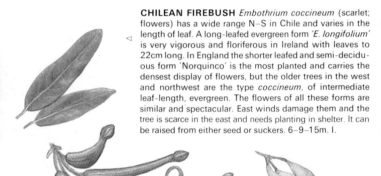

fl 5–6

fruit

● **LAUREL FAMILY** Lauraceae (classical Latin name for Bay) is a large group of about 1000 mainly evergreen, aromatic and tropical trees and shrubs with few hardy species.

BAY *Laurus nobilis* (noble, from the Roman use of the leaves in victors' garlands) is also known as Poets' Laurel or True Laurel to distinguish it from other plants called 'Laurel' like the shrub *Aucuba* and the Portugal and Cherry-laurels. It is often seen as a mop-headed clipped tree in tubs and as a trimmed bush by the kitchen door to provide the leaves which flavour stews, but in most areas not too exposed to eastern winds it grows into a tree of moderate size, often with several stems. Long periods of freezing winds brown the foliage but rarely kill the plant. It can be raised from cuttings. 4–7–17m. ll.

fruit

fl. 4

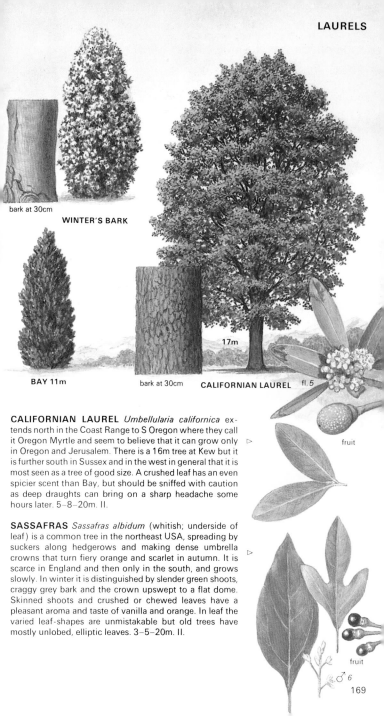

bark at 30cm

WINTER'S BARK

BAY 11m

bark at 30cm

CALIFORNIAN LAUREL fl.5

17m

fruit

fruit

CALIFORNIAN LAUREL *Umbellularia californica* extends north in the Coast Range to S Oregon where they call it Oregon Myrtle and seem to believe that it can grow only in Oregon and Jerusalem. There is a 16m tree at Kew but it is further south in Sussex and in the west in general that it is most seen as a tree of good size. A crushed leaf has an even spicier scent than Bay, but should be sniffed with caution as deep draughts can bring on a sharp headache some hours later. 5–8–20m. II.

SASSAFRAS *Sassafras albidum* (whitish; underside of leaf) is a common tree in the northeast USA, spreading by suckers along hedgerows and making dense umbrella crowns that turn fiery orange and scarlet in autumn. It is scarce in England and then only in the south, and grows slowly. In winter it is distinguished by slender green shoots, craggy grey bark and the crown upswept to a flat dome. Skinned shoots and crushed or chewed leaves have a pleasant aroma and taste of vanilla and orange. In leaf the varied leaf-shapes are unmistakable but old trees have mostly unlobed, elliptic leaves. 3–5–20m. II.

♂ 6

● **WITCH-HAZEL FAMILY** Hamamelidaceae (from the Greek name for Medlar – no relation) is named from the shrubs known as Witch-hazels but contains many trees in both hemispheres.

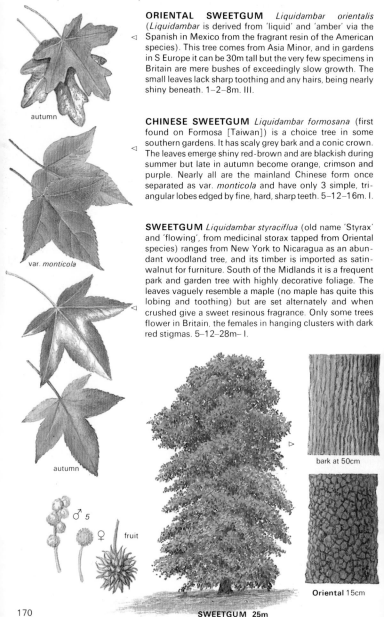

ORIENTAL SWEETGUM *Liquidambar orientalis* (*Liquidambar* is derived from 'liquid' and 'amber' via the Spanish in Mexico from the fragrant resin of the American species). This tree comes from Asia Minor, and in gardens in S Europe it can be 30m tall but the very few specimens in Britain are mere bushes of exceedingly slow growth. The small leaves lack sharp toothing and any hairs, being nearly shiny beneath. 1–2–8m. III.

autumn

CHINESE SWEETGUM *Liquidambar formosana* (first found on Formosa [Taiwan]) is a choice tree in some southern gardens. It has scaly grey bark and a conic crown. The leaves emerge shiny red-brown and are blackish during summer but late in autumn become orange, crimson and purple. Nearly all are the mainland Chinese form once separated as var. *monticola* and have only 3 simple, triangular lobes edged by fine, hard, sharp teeth. 5–12–16m. I.

var. *monticola*

SWEETGUM *Liquidambar styraciflua* (old name 'Styrax' and 'flowing', from medicinal storax tapped from Oriental species) ranges from New York to Nicaragua as an abundant woodland tree, and its timber is imported as satin-walnut for furniture. South of the Midlands it is a frequent park and garden tree with highly decorative foliage. The leaves vaguely resemble a maple (no maple has quite this lobing and toothing) but are set alternately and when crushed give a sweet resinous fragrance. Only some trees flower in Britain, the females in hanging clusters with dark red stigmas. 5–12–28m. I.

autumn

♂ 5   ♀   fruit

bark at 50cm

Oriental 15cm

SWEETGUM 25m

170

PERSIAN IRONWOOD *Parrotia persica* is often only a very widely spreading shrub with long shoots arching out of the top at a low angle. It can, however, be more like the tall trees on the southern shores of the Caspian Sea and grow a good single bole. When cleaned of branches for 2–3m, it shows the mottled bark well. The flowers open in late January. In autumn the foliage on the top shoots tends to turn deep red early and to be shed by the time the rest of the crown is turning yellow then red. 4–7–13m. II.

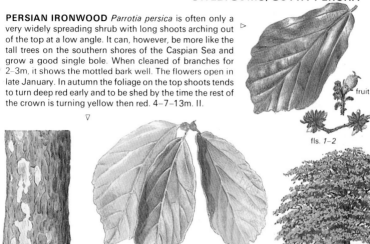

fruit

fls. *1–2*

bark at 30cm

autumn

PERSIAN IRONWOOD

● **GUTTA-PERCHA TREE FAMILY** Eucommiaceae ('good' and 'gum' from the latex prized in China for medicinal use) is a family of this single species, which has affinities with Elms and Witch-hazels. The bark is corky and deeply fissured.

GUTTA-PERCHA TREE *Eucommia ulmoides* (like an Elm; flowers and fruit) is grown in plantsmen's gardens as far north as Edinburgh. It can be a puzzle as it has no marked features beyond a slender-pointed glossy leaf, but if a leaf be slowly torn across the middle, latex from the veins will harden in the air and suspend the lower half from the upper. Only the Dogwoods will also do this. The trees seen are all males and have little bunches of brown flowers. 6–9–15m. II.

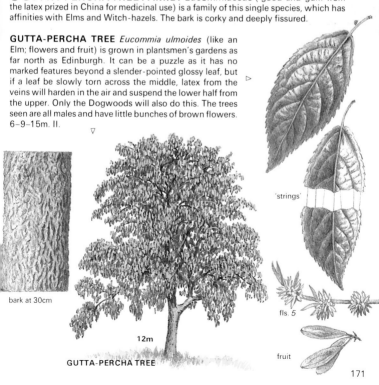

'strings'

bark at 30cm

fls. *5*

12m

fruit

GUTTA-PERCHA TREE

171

● PLANE FAMILY Platanaceae

('Platanus' was the classical name for the Oriental Plane, derived from Greek for 'broad', referring to the leaf). The whole Family composed of the 8 species of Plane, all but the Oriental, native to the USA and Mexico. Their nearest relatives are in the Witch-hazel Family. The base of the leaf-stalk enfolds the lateral bud. Male and female flowers are on the same tree but in different clusters.

♀ 5

♂

25m

◁ **ORIENTAL PLANE** *Platanus orientalis* is native in Crete and the Balkan Mountains but has been planted since ancient times through Iran to Kashmir. The date of introduction to Britain is lost in early records which fail to distinguish this from London Plane and Sycamore. Its spreading, often low crown make it unsuitable for city streets and since it needs warmer summers than the London Plane, the big trees are all in S England. The foliage unfolds covered in pale orange-brown hairs which soon rub off. In autumn it turns pale brown with a distinctive shade of pale bronzy purple. Old trees may have extensive burrs on the trunk and some trees rest the lower branches on the ground. 6–12–32m. II.

bark at 40cm

fruit

'Pyramidalis'

♂

♀

5

LONDON PLANE *Platanus × acerifolia* (maple-leafed) is ▷
a hybrid between the American and the Oriental planes,
arising around 1650 in S Europe. Until 1900 it was much
confused with both parents, and the Americans calling
their plane 'Sycamore' and the Scots calling Sycamore
'Plane' keep this alive. It is the common town and city tree,
but the finest specimens are in southern gardens. It has
hybrid vigour and even the biggest and oldest are still
adding rapidly to their girth. They are hardly known to blow
down and they suffer only one disease, an anthrax fungus
killing new shoots in some years. In London the distinct
form **'Pyramidalis'** is common in streets. It has a burred
stem, rich glossy green 3-lobed leaf and only one or two
very large fruit on each stalk, and is close to the American
Plane. 8–15–44m. III.

30m

fruit

bark at 40cm

173

● **ROSE FAMILY** Rosaceae includes 2000 very varied species of herbs, shrubs and trees, including all the common fruit trees. They have a simple flower structure of 4–5 petals on top of a receptacle with the ovaries. None of the trees is of great size and many are near shrubs. Most are extremely tolerant of different soils. Propagation of the trees is by seed or grafting.

fl. 5

fruit

6m

MEDLAR *Mespilus germanica* is the only species of *Mespilus* and differs from the closely related thorns in having large solitary flowers. It is native to S Europe and Asia Minor and has been cultivated since early times. Its introduction was not recorded, being before such notes were made and it seeds itself in a few woods in S England but is not much seen. Some old gardens grow one or two but young ones are rare. The bark is grey-brown fissured into long, lifting plates. The fruit need to be rotting before they are palatable. 3–5–9m. II.

THORNS *Crataegus* (classical Greek name for Hawthorn) are a complex group across the northern hemisphere. Some can set seed without being pollinated, thus preserving small differences. In the USA, 1100 were distinguished by 1910 but only 35 are now accepted as other than minor local variants. Many are very resilient and are useful and decorative in cities.

HAWTHORN *Crataegus monogyna* (with one style, and hence seed) is the common plant of the quickset hedge and of chalk hills and scrub, but it can grow into a tree 15m tall. It grows rather slowly but is very long-lived so there are some reasonably big trunks in old gardens. It grows from seed but cuttings are easier and quicker. The leaves on the more tree-like plants turn orange, dark red and then purple in a good autumn. The wood is very dense, pale pinkish and has high fuel value and is excellent for turnery. The bark cracks into orange-brown rectangles. 4–6–15m. II.

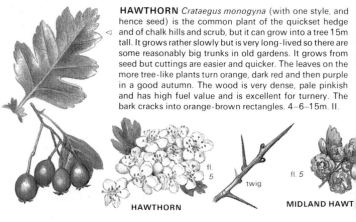

fl. 5

twig

fl. 5

HAWTHORN

MIDLAND HAWT

MIDLAND HAWTHORN *Crataegus oxyacantha* (sharply thorned) is native in the shade of woodlands on the clay soils of C England. The flower has 2–3 styles and the fruit 2–3 seeds. It hybridises with Hawthorn and intermediates in leaf-shape are widespread. In gardens and city parks it is common in the form **'Paul's Scarlet'**, the double red-flowered thorn, which originated near Waltham Cross in about 1858 and is now in every suburban street. Unlike the type it can have a clean stout trunk. The bark is similar to Hawthorn's. 2–4–8m. II.

174

COCKSPUR THORN *Crataegus crus-galli* (cock's spur; long curved thorns) is a rare American tree, since the tree sold here under this name for years is the Broadleafed Hybrid (also in some American parks). There is a genuine tree in the Hillier Arboretum, Hants. It is distinct from all the hybrids by the profusion of slender, curved spines and by completely hairless stalks to the flowers and fruit. 3–5–9m. III.

fl. 5

autumn

BROADLEAF COCKSPUR THORN *Crataegus × prunifolia* (plum-leafed) is of obscure, probably hybrid origin. For some 30 years it has been planted by roads, often at the approach to a village, in road reserves, in parks precincts and gardens. It is tough, spined and almost vandal-proof and is decorative in flower, leaf, fruit, and in autumn when its leaves turn from yellow to orange then a splendid copper then dark red. It is grown either as a squat broad bush or on a cleaned trunk of 1–2m. The shoot and sparse but stout 2cm thorns are rich, shining deep purple-brown. 3–5–8m. I.

fl. 5

fruit, Sept

8m

autumn

BROADLEAF COCKSPUR THORN

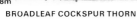

Cockspur   Broadleaf   Hybrid

HYBRID COCKSPUR THORN *Crataegus × lavallei* (Lavallée, of Segrez Arboretum raised the tree, described in 1880 by Carrière – it is often called 'Carrière's Thorn, *C. × carrierei*') is mainly a tree of urban streets, common notably in W London suburbs. It is at once known in winter by the pale grey coarsely scaled bark and level branches with short, dense twig systems on their upper side. The leaves are glossy and narrow. They become dark in late summer, and very late in the year they turn dark red.

fruit, winter

COTONEASTERS *Cotoneaster* ('Cotoneum', a quince; '–aster' resembling a little; the leaves) are about 70 shrubs and this tree. They differ from thorns only in their entire leaves and lack of spines.

HIMALAYAN TREE-COTONEASTER *Cotoneaster frigidus* (cold – from its provenance?) may be a tree to 17m on a single bole or a tall shrub with many stems. It is most often a tree in the western high rainfall areas. The bole tends to lean and then to grow strong vertical sprouts several metres long. It flowers at midsummer and the fruit last well in the autumn, birds eating them late. It is the parent of many hybrids, several of them tall bushes with spectacular fruit like 'Cornubia' and × 'Watereri'. 4–8–17m. II.

under

fl. *5*

COTONEASTER

SNOWY MESPIL

fl.

SNOWY MESPILS *Amelanchier* (French, Amelanche) are 25 white-flowered shrubs or bushy trees.

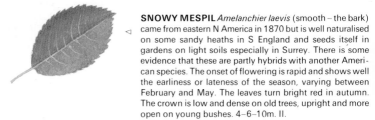

SNOWY MESPIL *Amelanchier laevis* (smooth – the bark) came from eastern N America in 1870 but is well naturalised on some sandy heaths in S England and seeds itself in gardens on light soils especially in Surrey. There is some evidence that these are partly hybrids with another American species. The onset of flowering is rapid and shows well the earliness or lateness of the season, varying between February and May. The leaves turn bright red in autumn. The crown is low and dense on old trees, upright and more open on young bushes. 4–6–10m. II.

autumn

'Beissneri'
20cm

ROWAN
12m

TRUE SERVICE TREE
15m

ROWANS and WHITEBEAMS *Sorbus* (classical Latin for True Service Tree) are more than 80 species and differ in having pinnate (rowans) or simple (whitebeams) leaves, but there are hybrids between them.

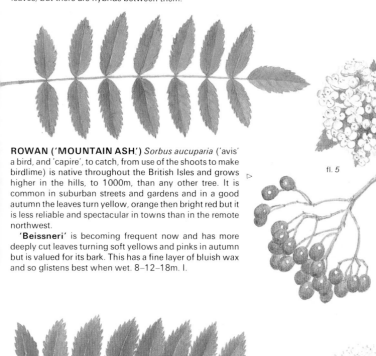

fl. *5*

ROWAN ('MOUNTAIN ASH.') *Sorbus aucuparia* ('avis' a bird, and 'capire', to catch, from use of the shoots to make birdlime) is native throughout the British Isles and grows higher in the hills, to 1000m, than any other tree. It is common in suburban streets and gardens and in a good autumn the leaves turn yellow, orange then bright red but it is less reliable and spectacular in towns than in the remote northwest.

'**Beissneri**' is becoming frequent now and has more deeply cut leaves turning soft yellows and pinks in autumn but is valued for its bark. This has a fine layer of bluish wax and so glistens best when wet. 8–12–18m. I.

fl. *5*

TRUE SERVICE TREE *Sorbus domestica* (used around the house) has been grown since early times but is nowhere now common. It can be known all the year by its bark of close, narrow fissures rich dark brown and grey ridges, and wide, open crown. The obvious difference in foliage from the Rowan is the smooth, rounded green buds (instead of pointed, dark purple with grey hairs) but the leaves also hang down and the branches are level. In one form, shown here, the fruit are apple-shaped, and in another, about equally frequent form they are pear-shaped. They come true from seed, so the desired form can be chosen. The wood is white, hard and strong. 5–9–20m. I.

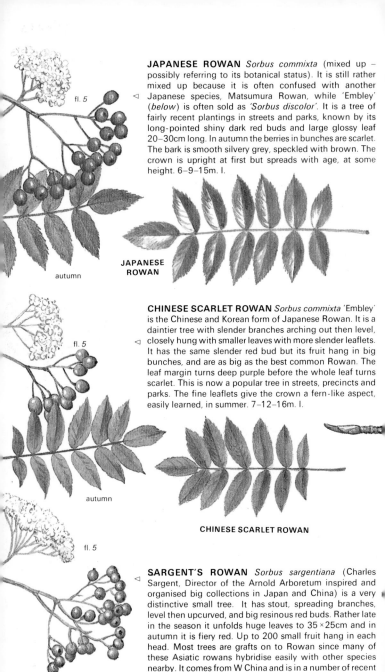

JAPANESE ROWAN *Sorbus commixta* (mixed up – possibly referring to its botanical status). It is still rather mixed up because it is often confused with another Japanese species, Matsumura Rowan, while 'Embley' (*below*) is often sold as *'Sorbus discolor'*. It is a tree of fairly recent plantings in streets and parks, known by its long-pointed shiny dark red buds and large glossy leaf 20–30cm long. In autumn the berries in bunches are scarlet. The bark is smooth silvery grey, speckled with brown. The crown is upright at first but spreads with age, at some height. 6–9–15m. I.

fl. 5

autumn

JAPANESE ROWAN

CHINESE SCARLET ROWAN *Sorbus commixta* 'Embley' is the Chinese and Korean form of Japanese Rowan. It is a daintier tree with slender branches arching out then level, closely hung with smaller leaves with more slender leaflets. It has the same slender red bud but its fruit hang in big bunches, and are as big as the best common Rowan. The leaf margin turns deep purple before the whole leaf turns scarlet. This is now a popular tree in streets, precincts and parks. The fine leaflets give the crown a fern-like aspect, easily learned, in summer. 7–12–16m. I.

fl. 5

autumn

CHINESE SCARLET ROWAN

fl. 5

SARGENT'S ROWAN *Sorbus sargentiana* (Charles Sargent, Director of the Arnold Arboretum inspired and organised big collections in Japan and China) is a very distinctive small tree. It has stout, spreading branches, level then upcurved, and big resinous red buds. Rather late in the season it unfolds huge leaves to 35×25cm and in autumn it is fiery red. Up to 200 small fruit hang in each head. Most trees are grafts on to Rowan since many of these Asiatic rowans hybridise easily with other species nearby. It comes from W China and is in a number of recent plantings in S England. 3–5–9m. I.

bark at 30cm

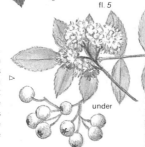

HUPEH ROWAN

fl. 5

under

HUPEH ROWAN *Sorbus hupehensis* (Hupeh Province, C China) raised from seed or grafted on to Rowan makes a sturdy tree which moves well even when 3m tall. It is thus of value where vandalism is likely and it is planted often in public places. The greyish tint to the large leaves pick it out in summer, with the pinkish leaf-stalks turning by the autumn to dark red. The bark is grey and scaly. The crown is nearly erect at first then becomes domed. In one form the fruit turn wholly bright pink and, hanging on after the leaves, look at a distance like flowers. 6–11–15m. I.

'JOSEPH ROCK'

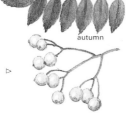

autumn

Sorbus **'JOSEPH ROCK'** (American botanist who brought quantities of plants from China). This is grafted from a tree at Wisley Gardens, Surrey of uncertain origin, probably sent by Rock and from China. It is becoming popular for its many great merits, and will be more so as it becomes more available. Its narrow, erect crown and small leaflets suit it well to street plantings. Its fiery autumn colours and lemon-yellow berries make it stand out among the rowans. 6–12m. I.

Sargent's

autumn

ROWANS

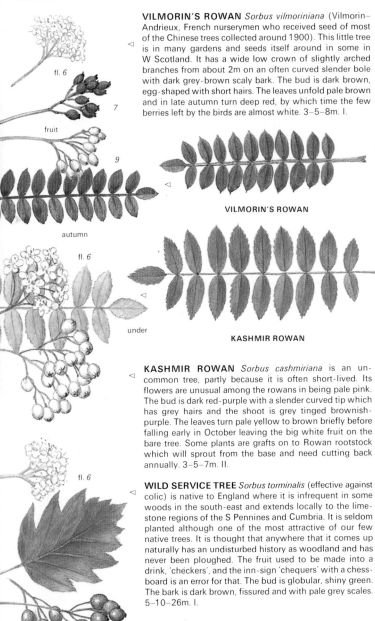

VILMORIN'S ROWAN *Sorbus vilmoriniana* (Vilmorin–Andrieux, French nurserymen who received seed of most of the Chinese trees collected around 1900). This little tree is in many gardens and seeds itself around in some in W Scotland. It has a wide low crown of slightly arched branches from about 2m on an often curved slender bole with dark grey-brown scaly bark. The bud is dark brown, egg-shaped with short hairs. The leaves unfold pale brown and in late autumn turn deep red, by which time the few berries left by the birds are almost white. 3–5–8m. I.

fl. 6

7

fruit

9

autumn

VILMORIN'S ROWAN

fl. 6

under

KASHMIR ROWAN

KASHMIR ROWAN *Sorbus cashmiriana* is an uncommon tree, partly because it is often short-lived. Its flowers are unusual among the rowans in being pale pink. The bud is dark red-purple with a slender curved tip which has grey hairs and the shoot is grey tinged brownish-purple. The leaves turn pale yellow to brown briefly before falling early in October leaving the big white fruit on the bare tree. Some plants are grafts on to Rowan rootstock which will sprout from the base and need cutting back annually. 3–5–7m. II.

WILD SERVICE TREE *Sorbus torminalis* (effective against colic) is native to England where it is infrequent in some woods in the south-east and extends locally to the limestone regions of the S Pennines and Cumbria. It is seldom planted although one of the most attractive of our few native trees. It is thought that anywhere that it comes up naturally has an undisturbed history as woodland and has never been ploughed. The fruit used to be made into a drink, 'checkers', and the inn-sign 'chequers' with a chessboard is an error for that. The bud is globular, shiny green. The bark is dark brown, fissured and with pale grey scales. 5–10–26m. I.

fl. 6

ripe fruit, Sept.

unripe

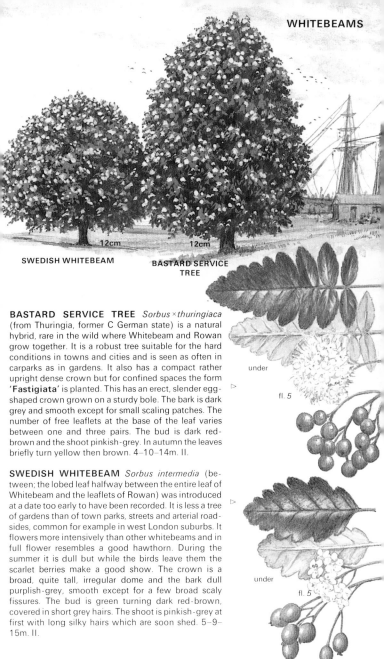

SWEDISH WHITEBEAM

BASTARD SERVICE TREE

BASTARD SERVICE TREE *Sorbus ×thuringiaca* (from Thuringia, former C German state) is a natural hybrid, rare in the wild where Whitebeam and Rowan grow together. It is a robust tree suitable for the hard conditions in towns and cities and is seen as often in carparks as in gardens. It also has a compact rather upright dense crown but for confined spaces the form **'Fastigiata'** is planted. This has an erect, slender egg-shaped crown grown on a sturdy bole. The bark is dark grey and smooth except for small scaling patches. The number of free leaflets at the base of the leaf varies between one and three pairs. The bud is dark red-brown and the shoot pinkish-grey. In autumn the leaves briefly turn yellow then brown. 4–10–14m. II.

SWEDISH WHITEBEAM *Sorbus intermedia* (between; the lobed leaf halfway between the entire leaf of Whitebeam and the leaflets of Rowan) was introduced at a date too early to have been recorded. It is less a tree of gardens than of town parks, streets and arterial road-sides, common for example in west London suburbs. It flowers more intensively than other whitebeams and in full flower resembles a good hawthorn. During the summer it is dull but while the birds leave them the scarlet berries make a good show. The crown is a broad, quite tall, irregular dome and the bark dull purplish-grey, smooth except for a few broad scaly fissures. The bud is green turning dark red-brown, covered in short grey hairs. The shoot is pinkish-grey at first with long silky hairs which are soon shed. 5–9–15m. II.

under

fl. 5

under

fl. 5

WHITEBEAM

under

'Majestica'

'Lutescens'

fl. 5

WHITEBEAM *Sorbus aria* (an old name) is native in the chalk downlands of SE England, where it is very common in hedges and copses on some of the North Downs and Chiltern Hills, and on some limestones further west and in Co. Galway. It is commonly planted in England, more in streets than in gardens – often as one of the varieties. It does not colour so well in the autumn in streets as it does in the hills where the leaves stay on longer when they have turned a pleasant biscuit-brown with the underside still white. Coming into leaf, the whole crown is silver-white until the leaves bend to show the upper sides from which the white hairs are being shed. 5–9–20m. l.

'Majestica' is mostly seen in streets and is more handsome in foliage than the type. The leaf is thicker and to 15×9cm and the tree has sturdy upright branches. 6–10–20m. l.

'Lutescens' is the most popular form in small gardens and is frequent in street plantings because of its neat, upright, egg-shaped crown and small leaves. The shoots are dark purple. 5–8–12m. l.

WHITEBEAM   'WILFRID FOX'   SERVICE TREE
                                        of FONTAINEBLEAU

under

under

Sorbus 'WILFRID FOX' (Dr Fox of Godalming, Surrey, studied the genus Sorbus, founded Winkworth Arboretum and raised this hybrid). This is a hybrid between the common Whitebeam and the Himalayan Whitebeam, raised in about 1920 and multiplied by grafting. It is becoming more frequent in decorative plantings in England but is not yet common. As a young tree it has stout erect branches bearing very small side-shoots. The shoot is stout, smooth, brown speckled white. The leaf is 14–16cm long and varies more in breadth. The bark is purplish-grey, scaling finely in patches. 6–11–15m. l.

SERVICE TREE of FONTAINEBLEAU *Sorbus × latifolia* (broad leafed) is one of a group of hybrids between Whitebeam and Wild Service Tree. It includes several forms native to Britain, each restricted to a small area like the Avon Gorge at Bristol; a part of N Exmoor; the Wye Valley or Brecon Beacons, not really separate full species. Still quite rare but more seen in gardens is the bigger leafed Service Tree of Fontainebleau, from that château in N France. The leaf can be 20×12cm. Many of the older trees have broken trunks and grow out from the base and young trees are seldom seen. The bark is dark grey, flaking coarsely. The fruit ripen yellow-brown. 3–6–15m. ll.

182

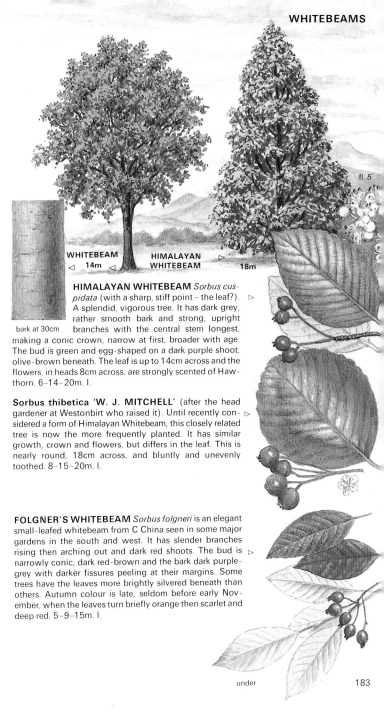

WHITEBEAM ◁ 14m ◁

HIMALAYAN WHITEBEAM ▷ 18m

fl. 5

bark at 30cm

HIMALAYAN WHITEBEAM *Sorbus cuspidata* (with a sharp, stiff point – the leaf?). A splendid, vigorous tree. It has dark grey, rather smooth bark and strong, upright branches with the central stem longest, making a conic crown, narrow at first, broader with age. The bud is green and egg-shaped on a dark purple shoot, olive-brown beneath. The leaf is up to 14cm across and the flowers, in heads 8cm across, are strongly scented of Hawthorn. 6–14–20m. l.

Sorbus thibetica 'W. J. MITCHELL' (after the head gardener at Westonbirt who raised it). Until recently considered a form of Himalayan Whitebeam, this closely related tree is now the more frequently planted. It has similar growth, crown and flowers, but differs in the leaf. This is nearly round, 18cm across, and bluntly and unevenly toothed. 8–15–20m. l.

FOLGNER'S WHITEBEAM *Sorbus folgneri* is an elegant small-leafed whitebeam from C China seen in some major gardens in the south and west. It has slender branches rising then arching out and dark red shoots. The bud is narrowly conic, dark red-brown and the bark dark purple-grey with darker fissures peeling at their margins. Some trees have the leaves more brightly silvered beneath than others. Autumn colour is late, seldom before early November, when the leaves turn briefly orange then scarlet and deep red. 5–9–15m. l.

under

APPLES *Malus* (classical Latin name) are about 25 northern species and innumerable hybrids and selections both for ornament and for fruit. They are exceedingly tough and will grow in almost any soil and transplant well. They are easily raised from seed but named varieties must be grafted to remain true.

fl. 5

7m

6m

JAPANESE
CRAB

PURPLE CRAB

fl. 4–5

fl. 5

JAPANESE CRAB *Malus floribunda* (prolific of flower) is not known as a wild species and is no doubt a garden hybrid arising long ago between two Japanese species. It makes a very twiggy, dense, low and broad crown on a stout trunk with dark brown shallowly fissured bark. It is very common in suburban gardens and parks and is one of the first trees into leaf in spring but the foliage is hidden every April by the profuse flowers. In some years the little fruit are abundant but in others they are very few. The green shoot and the 3cm grooved leaf-stalk are covered in fine dense down. 3–4–8m. I.

PURPLE CRAB *Malus × purpurea* is a hybrid between a form of the Japanese Crab and a Siberian apple that suffuses the hybrid from roots and wood to leaves, in dark purple-red. Briefly spectacular in flower but soon fading and blued, this tree is ungainly and unsightly for the rest of the year. The branches bend at ugly angles and carry a thin cover of muddy purple greenish leaves, greyed as if with blight. **'Lemoinei'** is a common form, stronger growing and with larger deep red flowers. **'Profusion'** has respectable foliage and numerous sprays of deep purple-red flowers wreathed along the shoots among deep red leaves. 3–4–10m. III.

CRAB APPLE *Malus sylvestris* (of the woods) is native to Britain and found in woods and hedges except in C and N Scotland. It has an open, domed crown and the shoots are soon smooth brown, sometimes bearing long thorns. The bark is dark brown, finely and deeply cracked into small rectangular plates. The wood is close-grained, dense and heavy and takes a good polish. It is excellent for turnery and inlay work so only odd pieces will be burned to see its fine burning qualities, high fuel value and sweet aroma. On frequented commons, apple-trees spring up from the pips of dessert apples and are known from wild crabs by their hairy shoot and leaf undersides, and often more pink flowers. **Orchard apples** derive from this and other species.

Crab Apple twig

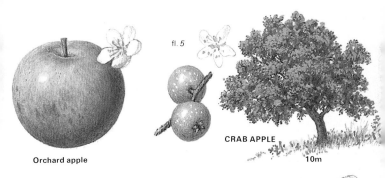

Orchard apple

fl. 5

CRAB APPLE

10m

CHINESE CRAB *Malus spectabilis* (showy) is not known in the wild in China but has long been in gardens there and was growing in Britain by 1780. The tree given this species name was in fact a garden form with semi-double flowers. Each has 6–8 petals. It is uncommon, mainly in the older established gardens and grows bigger than most flowering apples and is one of the few with semi-double flowers. The crown of big twisting branches droops from a stout bole with purple-brown bark in spiralling ridges with thick grey scales. The apples are 2cm across and ripen yellowish. 4–7–12m. II.

fl. 5

MAGDEBURG APPLE *Malus × magdeburgensis* is a hybrid between an orchard apple and an unknown species. It is quite common and can be spotted in flowering time in many a suburban garden although unnoticed at any other time of year. Young trees have upcurved branches but soon become broad and rather pendulous. It is early among apples into flower and the first flowers nestle in close rosy pink bunches among grey-green leaves but more open and the spreading bunches hide much of the foliage. Each flower has twelve petals, a degree of doubleness uncommon in apples. 3–4–5m. I.

fl. 5

SIBERIAN CRAB 10m

fl. 5

SIBERIAN CRAB *Malus baccata* (bearing berries; small fruit which shed their calyx and so are more like berries than apples) is a name which covers a species, a variety and at least one hybrid, none sufficiently distinct to warrant a common name. The species has smooth stalks to its massed starry white flowers and var. *mandschurica* has downy stalks and grows bigger. Both make broadly domed, twiggy, rather pendulous crowns on a stout bole with brown closely fissured bark. The hybrid, *Malus × robusta* has much larger fruit of dark red – abundant and conspicuous in winter. 4–9–15m. II.

fl. 5

HUPEH CRAB *Malus hupehensis* (Hupeh Province, C. China) was considered by its discoverer and collector, Ernest Wilson, to be the finest flowering tree that he collected. In full flower followed by myriads of glossy dark red fruit it certainly has few equals. Being genetically triploid it does not hybridise so that seed taken from garden trees is true to type. It grows fast, with a shoot to 1m long in the 2nd and 3rd years. At first narrowly crowned, it becomes a tall spreading dome on a stout short bole with orange-brown, coarsely plated bark. It is now becoming better known and more obtainable and should soon be less scarce. 7–10–13m. I.

fl. 5

HALL'S CRAB *Malus halliana* (Dr. G. R. Hall introduced it to America from Japan) is not known in the wild but is grown in gardens in China and Japan. It makes a low, spreading tree with an open crown, lovely in flower but of no merit at other times. It is not seen in many gardens here. It has small clusters of rosy-pink flowers, single and semi-double, paler inside. 2–3–4m. II.

HUPEH CRAB 10m

PILLAR CRAB 12m

fl. 5

PILLAR APPLE *Malus tschonoskii* (Tschonoski a Japanese collector, working about 1865) from Japan is now much planted as one of the best trees in towns. It is not only as tough as any and moves well when big, but the branches on newly planted trees, clean-boled for 2m, turn straight up out of reach of casual vandalism and are very strong, as well as making a neat narrow crown for a confined space. The leaves emerge silvery with hairs; the flowers are rather few – which means fewer fruit to fall on to pavements. Autumn colours are superb. The leaf is thick and leathery with a dense cover of white hairs beneath. 7–11–16m. l.

JOHN DOWNIE CRAB *Malus* 'John Downie' (friend of the raiser) not only has the prettiest fruit, but they make the most delicious and splendidly coloured apple-jelly. It was raised near Lichfield in 1875 and is common in suburban and other gardens, slender and upright as a young tree, broad with age. 5–8–10m. l.

fl. 5

Malus **'GOLDEN HORNET'** is a broad, low-crowned weeping tree, pretty when covered in starry white flowers but grown for the long drooping sprays of yellow fruit. It has been available only since about 1949 and is becoming frequent in parks and gardens 2–3–3m.

JOHN
DOWNIE
CRAB

GOLDEN HORNET

187

PEARS

PEARS *Pyrus* (classical name) are about 20 species in the temperate parts of the Old World. Their timber is strong, finely grained and durable but logs being scarce, it is used for turnery and inlay work only. Fruiting forms must be grafted but others are raised from seed.

WILLOW-LEAFED PEAR 8m

COMMON PEAR 13m

under

WILLOW-LEAFED PEAR *Pyrus salicifolia* (leaves like a Willow) from Asia Minor and SW Russia is frequent in decorative plantings to give the silvery colour of its foliage and the low weeping form of its crown. A few trees grow quite tall without weeping. The flowers are densely bunched and before the petals open they have bright red tips which are very attractive amongst the unfolding white leaves. The bark is dark grey or blackish-brown, coarsely scaled. The tree is tolerant of almost any soil but grows slowly. 3–5–10m. I.

COMMON PEAR *Pyrus communis* or Wild Pear – but probably not native to Britain. It was one of the species from which the fruiting pears originate and these seed themselves, the seedlings are varied and many are, or resemble, the old wild type. They sometimes bear a few thorns, and occur in hedges and woodland edges. The big trees in gardens are old fruiting kinds, covered in flowers before the leaves open and with a good bole of dark brown bark cracked into small squares. They often carry mistletoe and colour beautifully in autumn. 5–9–18m. II.

Common

Willow-leafed

fl. 3–4

fl. 4

188

PRUNUS Cherries, Plums, Almonds, Peaches etc. Unlike Apples and Pears, each flower has a single style, thus producing a single seed known as a stone. Many throw root-suckers.

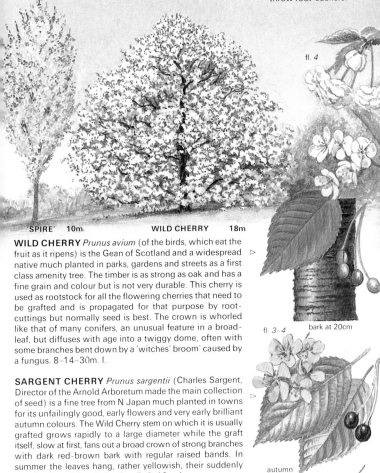

fl. 4

'SPIRE' 10m   WILD CHERRY 18m

bark at 20cm

fl. 3–4

autumn

fl. 3

fl. 1–3

WILD CHERRY *Prunus avium* (of the birds, which eat the fruit as it ripens) is the Gean of Scotland and a widespread native much planted in parks, gardens and streets as a first class amenity tree. The timber is as strong as oak and has a fine grain and colour but is not very durable. This cherry is used as rootstock for all the flowering cherries that need to be grafted and is propagated for that purpose by root-cuttings but normally seed is best. The crown is whorled like that of many conifers, an unusual feature in a broad-leaf, but diffuses with age into a twiggy dome, often with some branches bent down by a 'witches' broom' caused by a fungus. 8–14–30m. I.

SARGENT CHERRY *Prunus sargentii* (Charles Sargent, Director of the Arnold Arboretum made the main collection of seed) is a fine tree from N Japan much planted in towns for its unfailingly good, early flowers and very early brilliant autumn colours. The Wild Cherry stem on which it is usually grafted grows rapidly to a large diameter while the graft itself, slow at first, fans out a broad crown of strong branches with dark red-brown bark with regular raised bands. In summer the leaves hang, rather yellowish, their suddenly tapering broad tips distinctive. 5–9–13m. I.

PRUNUS 'SPIRE' was one of a batch of seedlings from a Sargent Cherry and perhaps a cross with the Yoshino Cherry. It is strictly upright and so is planted where space is restricted and early flowers and good autumn colour are needed. 6–7m. I.

PRUNUS 'ACCOLADE' is a seedling from a Sargent Cherry and makes a low spreading open crown of thin, slender foliage of no merit in summer but superb in flower and more floriferous every year. It flowers several weeks before Sargent Cherry and sometimes in January. 3–4–5m. I

189

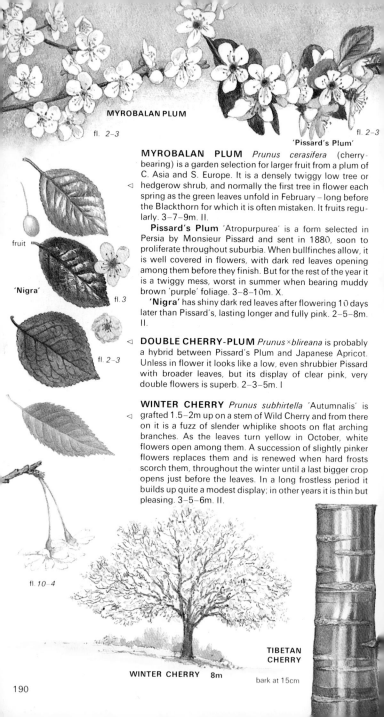

MYROBALAN PLUM

fl. 2–3

'Pissard's Plum'

fl. 2–3

fruit

'Nigra'

fl. 3

fl. 2–3

MYROBALAN PLUM *Prunus cerasifera* (cherry-bearing) is a garden selection for larger fruit from a plum of C. Asia and S. Europe. It is a densely twiggy low tree or hedgerow shrub, and normally the first tree in flower each spring as the green leaves unfold in February – long before the Blackthorn for which it is often mistaken. It fruits regularly. 3–7–9m. II.

Pissard's Plum 'Atropurpurea' is a form selected in Persia by Monsieur Pissard and sent in 1880, soon to proliferate throughout suburbia. When bullfinches allow, it is well covered in flowers, with dark red leaves opening among them before they finish. But for the rest of the year it is a twiggy mess, worst in summer when bearing muddy brown 'purple' foliage. 3–8–10m. X.

'Nigra' has shiny dark red leaves after flowering 10 days later than Pissard's, lasting longer and fully pink. 2–5–8m. II.

DOUBLE CHERRY-PLUM *Prunus ×blireana* is probably a hybrid between Pissard's Plum and Japanese Apricot. Unless in flower it looks like a low, even shrubbier Pissard with broader leaves, but its display of clear pink, very double flowers is superb. 2–3–5m. I

WINTER CHERRY *Prunus subhirtella* 'Autumnalis' is grafted 1.5–2m up on a stem of Wild Cherry and from there on it is a fuzz of slender whiplike shoots on flat arching branches. As the leaves turn yellow in October, white flowers open among them. A succession of slightly pinker flowers replaces them and is renewed when hard frosts scorch them, throughout the winter until a last bigger crop opens just before the leaves. In a long frostless period it builds up quite a modest display; in other years it is thin but pleasing. 3–5–6m. II.

fl. 10–4

WINTER CHERRY 8m

TIBETAN CHERRY

bark at 15cm

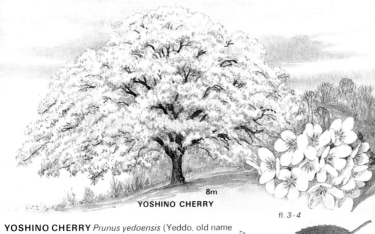

8m
YOSHINO CHERRY

fl. 3–4

YOSHINO CHERRY *Prunus yedoensis* (Yeddo, old name for Tokyo). Seen in March or early April, completely wreathed in dainty flowers and loud with bees, it is irresistible. Seen where bullfinches remove all but the outer tip flowers, or at any other time of year, it has no charms at all. The crown is badly shaped, flat and drooping on thick shoots and the foliage is heavy and lifeless. It is not known as a wild tree and is assumed to be a hybrid arising in Japan. It is frequently seen, and flowers best in towns and busy housing estates which deter bullfinches. 3–5–5m. I (II).

fruit

Prunus 'UMINEKO' (the sea-eagle; branching like half-spread eagle-wings) is a hybrid between two Japanese species, raised by Capt. Collingwood Ingram in Kent in about 1925. It is very erect when young, then the branches arch out. The flowers open among the unfolding bright green leaves on smooth olive-green shoots. The leaf-stalk is grooved and softly hairy. Scarce now, this soon will surely be more available and planted. 4–6m. I.

fl. 4

TIBETAN CHERRY *Prunus serrula* (a small saw; toothing of leaf) comes from W and SW China and is now in many gardens and a few parks, often grafted at base on to Wild Cherry. Wise gardeners plant it beside a well-used path for although the branches will usually shed their outer bark unaided, the bole is apt to go black and thickly scaled without frequent rubbing and removal of the loose outer layers. But do *not* try to strip any firmly fixed inner layers. The thick bands of pores may also grow sprouts unless the buds are rubbed off. The height to which people can reach is often marked on long trunks by a change from shiny bark to rough and scaly. 3–6–13m. I.

fl. 4

fruit

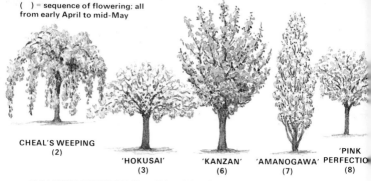

CHEAL'S WEEPING
(2)

'HOKUSAI'
(3)

'KANZAN'
(6)

'AMANOGAWA'
(7)

'PINK PERFECTIO[N]
(8)

JAPANESE CHERRIES 'Sato Zakura' (purely ornamental cherries) were raised in Japan from several Japanese and Chinese species and selections. They flower later than most species and are all grafted on Wild Cherry. Some 70 forms grow in the Hillier Arboretum and at Westonbirt.

CHEAL'S WEEPING CHERRY is among the first of the Sato cherries to flower. The flowers open among greyish-green leaves and are very double. The tree has branches of uneven length and is very common in town gardens. 2–3–3m. I.

'HOKUSAI' was here long before 'Kanzan' and tends to be in the older gardens in villages. It flowers 3 weeks or so before 'Kanzan' and makes the stockier tree with more level branching. In autumn the leaves turn bright orange and scarlet. 5–6–7m. I.

'KANZAN' the universal double pink cherry in suburban and city parks and gardens. With age, the branches arch out and droop. Autumn colours are yellow, pink and some red. 5–9–12m. II.

'AMANOGAWA' common in small gardens and sometimes a street tree. It opens out rather badly after some 20 years. Its flowers are late and fragrant, and autumn colours are mottled yellow, orange and red. 5–7–10m. I.

'PINK PERFECTION' is the only Sato cherry not from Japan. It is a cross between 'Kanzan' and 'Shimidsu'. The flowers open late and deep pink, lasting well, fading gradually to nearly white. 5–6–8m. I.

'SHIROFUGEN'
(10)

'UKON'
(5)

'TAI HAKU'
(4)

'SHIMIDSU'
(9)

'SHIROTAE' (1)

'SHIROTAE'. Many of the flowers are single, the others have only a few extra petals. The bright green leaf is shiny in summer and identifies this when not in flower, helped by the long, level slightly drooped branches. 4–5–6m. l.

'SHIROFUGEN' is one of the best. Beneath dark red leaves, pink buds open pale pink, soon pure white and turn pink again before they fall. The tree spreads widely and droops from a stout bole, growing much more strongly than 'Shimidsu'. 5–8–11m. l.

'TAI HAKU' was lost in Japan over 200 years ago and re-discovered in a Sussex garden in 1923. Every tree known all over the world is derived from that one, moribund plant. The flower is bigger than any other cherry, to 6cm across. The leaf is dark and hard, 20cm long. 6–8–8m. l.

'UKON' is distinct in flower at first, with brown leaves and pale yellow flowers but they soon fade white and show a red eye. It is then like 'Tai Haku' but the flowers are smaller and semi-double and the leaves narrower, oblong. 7–8–8m. l.

'SHIMIDSU' is among the last to flower when buds and leaves hazed in violet hairs turn to green leaves and long pendent flowers of purest white. It grows slowly and sideways. 4–5–5m. l.

193

ALMOND

8m

BLACK
CHERRY

15m

fl. 2–3

fruit

fl. 5–6

◁ **ALMOND** *Prunus dulcis* (sweet) is native to SE Europe and SW Asia but has been planted further afield for so long that its original range cannot be known. The forms grown in S Europe for fruit are mainly white-flowered but there are many pink-flowered garden forms. The flowers open later than the Myrobalan or Pissard plums but before the equally pink Sargent Cherry and are much bigger than all of these. When they fade the red stamens remain after the petals have fallen. The leaves often turn partly red in early summer with a fungus disease, peach leaf curl. The fruit remain on in winter. 5–6–8m. I.

◁ **SOUR CHERRY** *Prunus cerasus* 'Rhexii' is usually the last cherry to flower and is charming in a quiet way. Unnoticed until it flowers, it may be found in many areas of suburban and village gardens. The crown is flattened and untidy, dark in leaf although each leaf is quite bright green. The very double flowers open fully before they fade, to reveal a green eye. 5–6–8m. II.

◁ **MANCHURIAN CHERRY** *Prunus maackii* (Richard Maack, Russian naturalist collected in Manchuria) is grown for its shining honey-brown then orange bark in some of the major gardens. It grows faster than would be preferred, for wide, rough grey fissures split the smooth bark all too soon. The erect rounded heads of white flowers are numerous and fragrant but are among leaves and are not showy. The crown is broad with arched branches although erect at first 6–8–13m. II.

bark at 20cm

BLACK CHERRY *Prunus serotina* (late – ripening fruit) ranges in various forms right from Nova Scotia to Guatemala and is a fine tree to 35m tall in parts of the USA. It is scarce as a garden tree in Britain but used to be planted as cover and feed for pheasants on a number of estates and has run wild on some southern commons. It is often bushy in such places but with very strong shoots which can grow 2m a year if they are cut back. The patches of hairs along the midrib beneath are highly distinctive. 9–12–22m. II.

BIRD CHERRY *Prunus padus* (Greek name used for a wild cherry). This is a native of Scotland, N England and Ireland with outliers in the English Midlands, and is common by streamsides high into the limestone hills. It has a slender, shiny, dark brown shoot and a narrow, beech-like bud. The leaves in early autumn turn yellow, pink and a little red. It is less often planted than the coarse growing 'Watereri' which has longer, spreading flowerheads and bigger but fewer leaves. 5–10–15m. I (type) 6–13–20m. II ('Watereri').

fl. *6*   fl. *4–5*   fl. *3–5*   **Portugal Laurel**   fl. *6*

Black Cherry   **Bird Cherry**   **Cherry Laurel**

CHERRY LAUREL *Prunus laurocerasus* (laurel-like cherry) is commonly called 'laurel' and is very common in shrubberies, as garden hedges and for low cover in woods for game. In mild, wet western areas it spreads rapidly by seeds, rooting branches and suckers and makes acres of woods with pure laurel undergrowth. Cut or crushed leaves emit a pleasant sweet scent but in a closed jar give enough prussic acid gas to kill small insects. 5–8–15m. III.

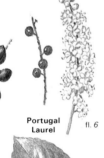

PORTUGAL LAUREL *Prunus lusitanica* (from Portugal; old name Lusitania) is common as a clipped hedge or an unclipped flowering shrub and in the west it makes a modest tree with smooth black bark. The heavily fragrant flowers open in mid June. The shoot is dark red-purple above and green beneath and the bud deep bright red and sharply pointed. 5–7–12m. II.

● **PEA FAMILY** Leguminosae (bearing legumes or pods). A worldwide and varied family of 7000 species. All have root-nodules with nitrogen-fixing bacteria. All except the Judas trees have compound leaves; the trees have hard, durable wood and many are thorny.

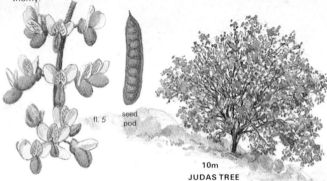

fl. 5
seed pod

10m
JUDAS TREE

◁ **JUDAS TREE** *Cercis siliquastrum* (bearing a siliqua or thin pod) was brought from the Near East before the flowers were appreciated for ornament but when sugar was rare; their sweetness was valued. Petals pulled from the flower were used to sweeten salads. It is a frequent tree in southern village gardens and churchyards. It bears upright branches but droops with age and the whole tree may bend down when senile. Flowers sprout straight from big branches and from the bole as well as on small shoots. 3–5–12m. I.

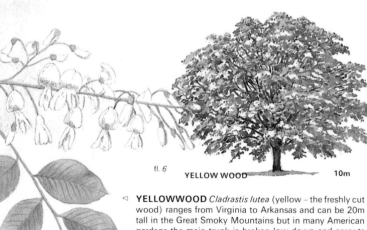

fl. 6
YELLOW WOOD   10m

◁ **YELLOWWOOD** *Cladrastis lutea* (yellow – the freshly cut wood) ranges from Virginia to Arkansas and can be 20m tall in the Great Smoky Mountains but in many American gardens the main trunk is broken low down and sprouts grow up from the base. It is scarce in Britain and seen mainly in the eastern, sunnier parts. It is most easily recognised in leaf because the large leaflets are not opposite but mostly alternate on the central stalk. The bark is smooth and dark grey. The base of the leaf-stalk covers several buds and the leaflets turn bright yellow in autumn. 3–5–10m. II.

MOUNT ETNA BROOM *Genista aetnensis* (from Etna) is wild also in Sardinia and is the only Broom to achieve tree-size in Britain. It is frequent in S England as a rather upright tree with pendulous outer shoots. It has a few tiny narrow leaves to 1cm long and most of the work of the leaves, photosynthesis, is done in the shoots, which are thus bright green for many years. This makes it as green in winter as in summer. It flowers prolifically after midsummer and into August, and is raised from seed. 5–7–10m. I.

seed pod

MOUNT ETNA BROOM   8m

seed pod

fl. 1–4

MIMOSA

MIMOSA or SILVER WATTLE *Acacia dealbata* (whitened with powder; appearance of foliage) comes from SE Australia and Tasmania and is only marginally hardy. It is very common on the Isle of Wight and by the south coasts of Devon, Cornwall and Ireland, and frequent north to the Isle of Man; less so from Hampshire to London. In the worst winters it is cut to the ground but seedlings or shoots spring up and within 3 years the tree is back up to the roof. The bark of young stems is bright blue-green and ribbed, then it becomes rich chocolate-brown and finally black, deeply fluted. 9–15–?m. I.

12m

bark

197

fl. 6

seed pod

'Frisia' **ROBINIA 25m** bark at 40cm

'Frisia'

ROBINIA or LOCUST TREE *Robinia pseudoacacia* (false acacia, a name often used) is native to the Appalachian Mountains but has run wild from S Canada to California. It has done the same in S England on light soils, spreading by root-suckers and grows well in towns and cities but is uncommon north and west of the Midlands. The side-buds have no scales and are hidden in the base of the leaf-stalk. In warm springs flowers cover the tree by early June but late frosts or prolonged cold prevent full flowering. The well-grained brown timber lasts as a fence-post longer than oak. 9–15–30m. III.

'Frisia' from Holland is now a common small-garden tree sometimes greening in summer, usually gold until it turns orange in autumn. 8–12–?m. I.

fl. 7–8 **ROSE-ACACIA** *Robinia hispida* (rough with bristles) is a low shrub from the southern Appalachian region spreading by root-suckers and rarely known to produce seeds. It is grown in some southern gardens, sometimes against a wall, as at Wisley Garden, Surrey. It is often grafted on a stem of Locust-tree and can be worked 1.5–2m up to form a mop-head. The densely set dark red or purple bristles spread from the shoot to the calyx of the flower. Flowers may open in June but some are often still opening in August. I.

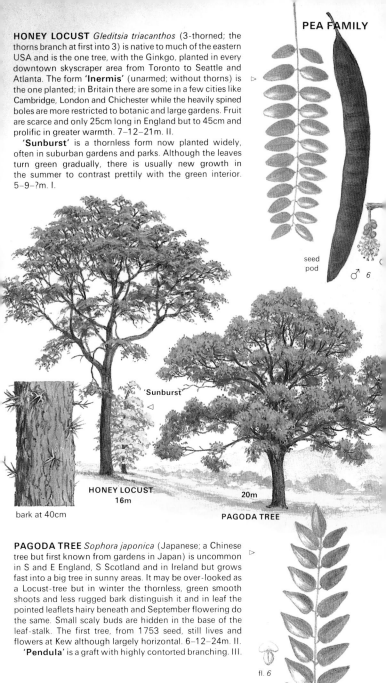

PEA FAMILY

HONEY LOCUST *Gleditsia triacanthos* (3-thorned; the thorns branch at first into 3) is native to much of the eastern USA and is the one tree, with the Ginkgo, planted in every downtown skyscraper area from Toronto to Seattle and Atlanta. The form **'Inermis'** (unarmed; without thorns) is the one planted; in Britain there are some in a few cities like Cambridge, London and Chichester while the heavily spined boles are more restricted to botanic and large gardens. Fruit are scarce and only 25cm long in England but to 45cm and prolific in greater warmth. 7–12–21m. II.

'Sunburst' is a thornless form now planted widely, often in suburban gardens and parks. Although the leaves turn green gradually, there is usually new growth in the summer to contrast prettily with the green interior. 5–9–?m. I.

seed
pod

♂ 6

'Sunburst'

HONEY LOCUST
16m

bark at 40cm

20m

PAGODA TREE

PAGODA TREE *Sophora japonica* (Japanese; a Chinese tree but first known from gardens in Japan) is uncommon in S and E England, S Scotland and in Ireland but grows fast into a big tree in sunny areas. It may be over-looked as a Locust-tree but in winter the thornless, green smooth shoots and less rugged bark distinguish it and in leaf the pointed leaflets hairy beneath and September flowering do the same. Small scaly buds are hidden in the base of the leaf-stalk. The first tree, from 1753 seed, still lives and flowers at Kew although largely horizontal. 6–12–24m. II.

'Pendula' is a graft with highly contorted branching. III.

fl. 6

199

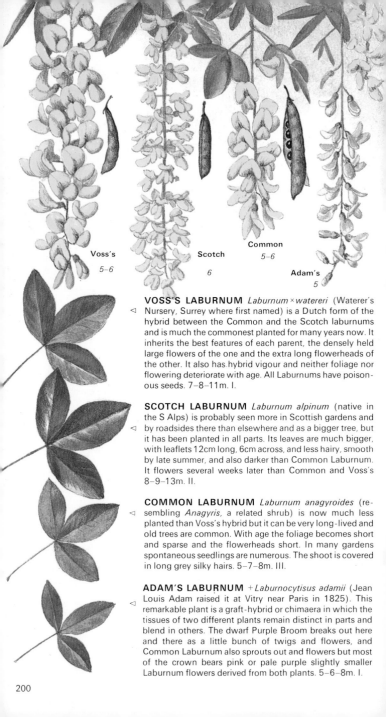

Voss's

5–6

Scotch

6

Common

5–6

Adam's

5

VOSS'S LABURNUM *Laburnum × watereri* (Waterer's ◁ Nursery, Surrey where first named) is a Dutch form of the hybrid between the Common and the Scotch laburnums and is much the commonest planted for many years now. It inherits the best features of each parent, the densely held large flowers of the one and the extra long flowerheads of the other. It also has hybrid vigour and neither foliage nor flowering deteriorate with age. All Laburnums have poisonous seeds. 7–8–11m. I.

SCOTCH LABURNUM *Laburnum alpinum* (native in the S Alps) is probably seen more in Scottish gardens and ◁ by roadsides there than elsewhere and as a bigger tree, but it has been planted in all parts. Its leaves are much bigger, with leaflets 12cm long, 6cm across, and less hairy, smooth by late summer, and also darker than Common Laburnum. It flowers several weeks later than Common and Voss's 8–9–13m. II.

COMMON LABURNUM *Laburnum anagyroides* (resembling *Anagyris*, a related shrub) is now much less ◁ planted than Voss's hybrid but it can be very long-lived and old trees are common. With age the foliage becomes short and sparse and the flowerheads short. In many gardens spontaneous seedlings are numerous. The shoot is covered in long grey silky hairs. 5–7–8m. III.

ADAM'S LABURNUM *+Laburnocytisus adamii* (Jean Louis Adam raised it at Vitry near Paris in 1825). This ◁ remarkable plant is a graft-hybrid or chimaera in which the tissues of two different plants remain distinct in parts and blend in others. The dwarf Purple Broom breaks out here and there as a little bunch of twigs and flowers, and Common Laburnum also sprouts out and flowers but most of the crown bears pink or pale purple slightly smaller Laburnum flowers derived from both plants. 5–6–8m. I.

VOSS'S LABURNUM

9m

15m

KENTUCKY COFFEE TREE

KENTUCKY COFFEE TREE *Gymnocladus dioicus* (trees of separate sex). Quite rare in S England and Ireland but easily identified when found. Its stout shoots are blue-green, bloomed pink and violet. They are knobbly with the raised edges of concave leaf-scars and yellow-brown buds. The bark is grey-brown, with curving, scaly ridges and flanges. The unfolding leaves are pink. In full leaf, each leaflet often appears to be a complete normal leaf. In autumn it turns pale yellow and falls, but the leaf-stalk remains on the tree for many days after. 5–7–17m. I – though in winter it is rather gaunt.

fl. 6

●RUE FAMILY Rutaceae.

A large family of mostly woody plants of warm climates, including oranges, lemons and the other *Citrus* fruiting trees.

12m

under

fruit

fl. 6

Japanese Cork Tree

△

bark at 30cm

bark at 30cm

JAPANESE CORK TREE *Phellodendron japonicum.* This
◁ is one of the little group of 3 species of Cork-trees, all
found in NE Asia. They have opposite compound leaves of
which the stalks enfold the winter buds. Only the Amur
species (below) has a thickly corky bark; in this Japanese
species it is a network of ridges, quite thick but not corky.
The main difference is that the leaf-stalk and the leaf underside are thickly coated with short white hairs. Each tree is of
one sex only and in the absence of seeds they can be raised
from cuttings. 3–5–12m. II.

◁ **AMUR CORK TREE** *Phellodendron amurense* (from the
Amur River region of E Siberia and Manchuria) is the least
rare of the Cork trees and has two very similar varieties also
in cultivation, but is confined to S England. The grey bark is
thickly ridged. The shoot is wrinkled and orange-brown.
The flowers have no petals. 4–7–15m. II.

12m

EUODIA

trunk

fl. *9*

fruit

EUODIA *Euodia hupehensis* (Hupeh Province, C China) may be seen in a few gardens or city parks in all parts. It is most readily seen when in full flower in September, but in winter the unusually smooth grey bark is a feature. The male and female flowers are in separate flower-heads but on the same tree. The bud lacks scales and is a folded leaf covered in dense red-brown hairs. The leaves are opposite, firm and leathery and usually cupped. Trees with shorter leaflet-stalks but otherwise almost the same are *E. daniellii* William Daniell, British surgeon discovered it) from N China and Korea. 8–11–20m. l.

203

● **QUASSIA FAMILY** Simaroubaceae is a large tropical family of 150 species. Only three trees from it are grown in N Europe – two Trees of Heaven and Picrasma. Both these genera have alternate, long-pinnate leaves and come from E Asia.

◁ **DOWNY TREE OF HEAVEN** *Ailanthus vilmoriniana* (Maurice de Vilmorin, French nurseryman received the first seeds.) This tree from W China is very rare and is known by its darker, longer leaves hanging and showing the bright red central stalk which, like the underside of the leaflet, is covered in fine hairs. New shoots on young trees bear soft, green spines. There may be sprouts on the bole. 8–12–22m. II.

◁ **TREE OF HEAVEN** *Ailanthus altissima* (very tall; applies more to a related Moluccan species from which the name 'Tree of Heaven' has been transferred). This tree from N China has been grown in Britain since 1751, most commonly in squares and parks in London but also in other cities and in gardens mainly in the south and east. It spreads widely by suckering from the roots sometimes 20–30m from the tree, but fortunately, in Britain not by seeds for it is an invasive nuisance in the warmer cities of the USA. The leaves unfold red in late May and fall early without autumn colours. Crushed, they have a sour, fetid smell, like old tennis shoes. On sprouts, they can be 90cm long with 40 or more leaflets. The 1–3 broad teeth at the base of the leaflet are found only in *Ailanthus*. 9–15–30m. II.

♂ 7

seeds 9

PICRASMA *Picrasma quassioides* (resembling the Quassia tree) is a small tree ranging from Japan through ◁ Korea and China to the Himalayas. It is rarely to be seen outside botanic gardens, Westonbirt and Wakehurst Place in S England. The bud is naked, just two leaves pressed together, small and scarlet, becoming pale brown as it swells. The leaf has a rich red central stem, and often a long stalk on the end leaflet, and turns orange and scarlet in autumn. The shoot is dark chocolate-purple. The orange-red fruit are freely borne and blacken before falling. 3–5–12m. I.

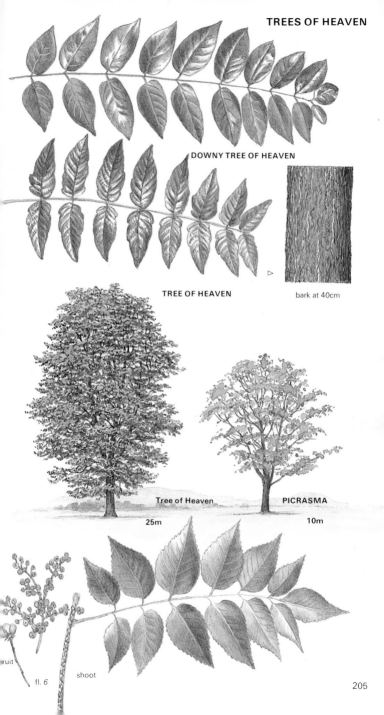

TREES OF HEAVEN

DOWNY TREE OF HEAVEN

TREE OF HEAVEN

bark at 40cm

Tree of Heaven

25m

PICRASMA

10m

fruit

fl. 6

shoot

● MAHOGANY FAMILY Meliaceae (Melia, Greek for Ash, was applied to the China Berry. *Melia azedarach*, common in S Europe and southern USA, but not hardy in Britain, where only one tree of the family is grown.)

CHINESE CEDAR *Cedrela sinensis* is closely related to the Spanish Cedar used for cigar-boxes. They are both called 'cedar' because of their fragrant timber. In Britain, it is grown in botanic gardens in each country but not often elsewhere. The bark, at first smooth coppery-grey plates becomes dark pink-grey and shaggy with age. The very open crown has a few stout branches with upcurved shoots which are warty and pale orange. The white flowers droop on branched heads 50×20cm. Raised from seeds. 6–9–20m. II.

● CASHEW FAMILY Anacardiaceae (Anacardium is the Cashew nut; a name transferred from a heart-shaped (cardium) nut in India). A large tropical and semi-tropical family.

VARNISH TREE *Rhus verniciflua* (flowing with varnish; tapped in Japan). This handsomely foliaged tree grows in a number of good gardens as far north as Edinburgh. In winter it is known by the numerous, stout upright branches and dark grey flaking bark. Also by the stout, upcurved shoots of pale grey, freckled orange, and the broad, brown buds. The flowers are in groups on the end of spoke-like whorls of stalks 50cm long. Fruit glossy, pale brown berries. Autumn colours are orange and scarlet. 4–10–20m. I.

CHINESE VARNISH TREE *Rhus potaninii* (Grigori Potanin, Russian botanist who collected widely in China) is less seen than the Japanese species (above) and less of a tree, being seldom a single bole but more usually 3–4 rather snaky stems, leaning out away from each other. The bark is nearly smooth, grey-pink and the leaves are half as long with fewer and more slender leaflets. They tend to droop but the end leaflet bends out to be level. In autumn they turn yellow then through pink to dark red, usually late and not reliable for good colour. 4–9–18m. II.

autumn

15m
Chinese Varnish Tree

Chinese
Cedar
16m

Box

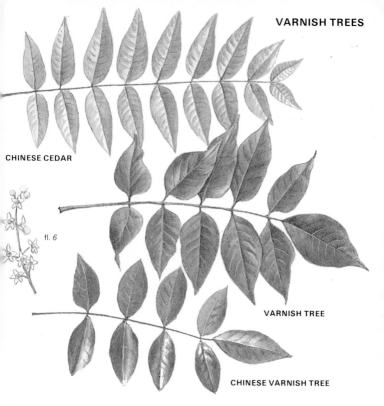

CHINESE CEDAR

fl. 6

VARNISH TREE

CHINESE VARNISH TREE

● **BOX FAMILY** Buxaceae (classical Latin). About 30 small trees with evergreen, opposite leaves and very dense, hard wood. They inhabit the Old World and extend into C America and the W Indies. Raised from seeds or cuttings.

BOX *Buxus sempervirens* (evergreen) was the last native tree to cross into England before the Channel opened. A few wild stands grow on chalk in Kent, Surrey and the Chiltern Hills and on limestone in Glos. and in these many trees have slender conic crowns not seen in gardens. The wood is dark yellow and brown and heavy enough to sink in water. It was the best wood for engraving-blocks and is still used for the heads of mallets and for best quality drawing instruments like rulers. It clips well and lives very long so is a good tree for topiary. Flowers are either male or female but they are in the same cluster. 2–3–10m. II.

fl. 3–4

fruit

fl. 4

BALEARIC BOX *Buxus balearica* is native to the Balearic Islands, S Spain and Sardinia and is grown in S Europe where we would have common Box. It is rare but sufficiently hardy to grow near Edinburgh, although slowly. The leaves lack the shine of Common Box and are larger, at 3–5cm and more widely spaced. It is an upright, rather dull little tree usually with low branches. The flowers are bigger and the stamens of males have broadened white stalks. 2–5–11m. III.

●HOLLY FAMILY Aquifoliaceae. A large family of both evergreen and deciduous trees of medium to small size and shrubs, found almost all over the world. Sexes usually on different plants.

HOLLY *Ilex aquifolium* (the classical name for Holly. *Ilex* is Latin for Holm Oak, which has spined juvenile leaves). Holly is a native and common undershrub in oak and beechwoods everywhere and by rocky streams in the hills. The wood is smooth, hard and white, very strong and heavy. It makes good kitchenware and chessmen. It is easily raised from seeds from berries rotted by storage in damp sand or passing through a bird, but the varieties are grafted since cuttings succeed only with difficulty. Old leaves are shed around midsummer. Birds eat the berries of a few trees in autumn but the rest remain through winter until June. 4–6–20m. II.

COMMON HOLLY

fl. 5

'Ferox'

'Handsworth New Silver'

'Pyramidalis'

'Golden Queen'

young tree

mature tree 15m

bark at 30cm

'Bacciflava'

HIGHCLERE HOLLIES *Ilex × altaclarensis* (Latinised form of 'Highclere' a Berkshire Castle where the cross occurred). The Madeira Holly used to be grown for its berries and had to be taken out of the conservatory for the flower to be pollinated. The bees had usually come from nearby Common Holly so any berries sown might give the hybrid. Thus arose a series of extremely robust hollies with broad, flat leaves. There are scores of cultivars. **'Hodginsii'** a male tree, is commonest, notably good in smoky air and sea-winds. Its leaves have a dull metallic sheen. 5–9–18m. II.

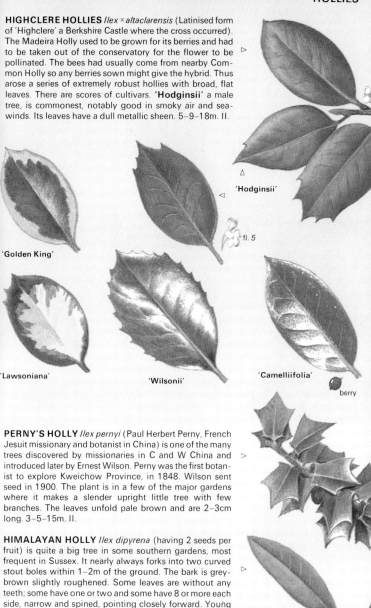

'Hodginsii'

fl. 5

'Golden King'

'Lawsoniana'

'Wilsonii'

'Camelliifolia'

berry

PERNY'S HOLLY *Ilex pernyi* (Paul Herbert Perny, French Jesuit missionary and botanist in China) is one of the many trees discovered by missionaries in C and W China and introduced later by Ernest Wilson. Perny was the first botanist to explore Kweichow Province, in 1848. Wilson sent seed in 1900. The plant is in a few of the major gardens where it makes a slender upright little tree with few branches. The leaves unfold pale brown and are 2–3cm long. 3–5–15m. II.

HIMALAYAN HOLLY *Ilex dipyrena* (having 2 seeds per fruit) is quite a big tree in some southern gardens, most frequent in Sussex. It nearly always forks into two curved stout boles within 1–2m of the ground. The bark is grey-brown slightly roughened. Some leaves are without any teeth; some have one or two and some have 8 or more each side, narrow and spined, pointing closely forward. Young plants bear the more spined leaves. The shoots are angular and dark green. Most trees seen are male, without berries. 3–5–13m. III.

berry

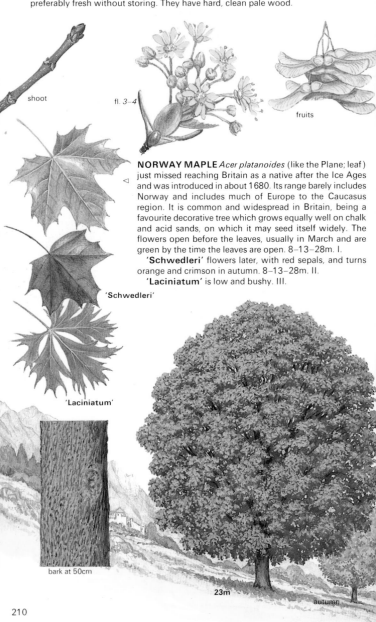

● **MAPLE FAMILY** Aceraceae (classical name, from 'acer' sharp, as the wood can take a sharp point and be used for skewers). 130 species of which all but two are true maples, *Acer*. Opposite leaves. Flowers arranged in every way possible: the sexes are in some on separate trees; in others in separate heads, mixed within the same head, or both in the same (perfect) flower; sometimes all these on one tree. Raised from seed, preferably fresh without storing. They have hard, clean pale wood.

shoot

fl. *3–4*

fruits

NORWAY MAPLE *Acer platanoides* (like the Plane; leaf) just missed reaching Britain as a native after the Ice Ages and was introduced in about 1680. Its range barely includes Norway and includes much of Europe to the Caucasus region. It is common and widespread in Britain, being a favourite decorative tree which grows equally well on chalk and acid sands, on which it may seed itself widely. The flowers open before the leaves, usually in March and are green by the time the leaves are open. 8–13–28m. I.

    'Schwedleri' flowers later, with red sepals, and turns orange and crimson in autumn. 8–13–28m. II.

    'Laciniatum' is low and bushy. III.

'Schwedleri'

'Laciniatum'

bark at 50cm

23m

autumn

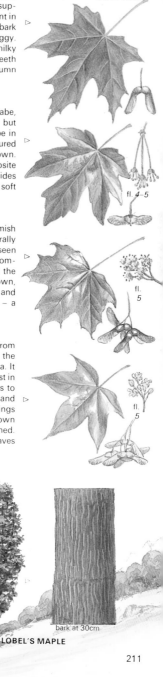

SUGAR MAPLE *Acer saccharum* (sugar; the tree that yields maple syrup in America) is less scarce than is supposed as it is passed as a Norway Maple. It is as frequent in Scotland and Ireland as in England and Wales. The bark has a few broad fissures in dark grey, and becomes shaggy. Other differences from Norway Maple are watery, not milky sap; lobes of the leaf narrowing to their bases, and the teeth at their sides finely rounded, not whiskered. Autumn colours are briefly yellow and red. 7–12–26m. I.

MIYABE'S MAPLE *Acer miyabei* (Kingo Miyabe, Japanese botanist) is a very rare tree in N Japan but Charles Sargent sent enough seed in 1892 for it to be in many collections in Britain. It has a scaly and fissured orange-brown and grey bark and a broadly domed crown. The base of each leaf-stalk is swollen and with its opposite one, enclasps the brownish-purple shoot and nearly hides the bud at the tip. The veins beneath are covered in soft white hairs. 4–6–15m. II.

fl. 4–5

LOBEL'S MAPLE *Acer lobelii* (Mathias de l'Obel, Flemish botanist) is one of the very few trees which grows naturally strictly upright. It is native to S Italy. It is sometimes seen planted in restricted places and in streets, but is not common. In many ways it is between the Norway and the Cappadocian maples but its blue-white shoot is its own, like its habit. The flowers are in erect heads, pale green and not obvious among the open leaves. 9–15–26m. I – a useful and vigorous tree.

fl. 5

CAPPADOCIAN MAPLE *Acer cappadocicum* (from E Asia Minor, once Cappadocia) ranges through the Caucasus, Elburz and Himalayan mountains into China. It is frequent in the larger gardens in all parts, growing best in the wet areas of the west. It is one of the few maples to sucker around the trunk and this it does profusely and widely. It can really only be grown where the surroundings are grazed, mown or under pavings. Suckers have grown up to be 25m tall. The main crown is roundly domed. Sprout leaves unfold red, and the whole crown of leaves turns butter yellow in October. 8–15–26m. II.

fl. 5

bark at 30cm

18m   **LOBEL'S MAPLE**

20m   **SUGAR MAPLE**

211

fl. 4–5

'Brilliant-
issimum'

27m

bark at 80cm

new
growth

SYCAMORE *Acer pseudoplatanus* (false Plane) is native across C Europe to the Caucasus but seems just as at home throughout the British Isles. In the most severely exposed coastal areas it stands up as a tree better than any native species and it thrives on high limestone hills or in smoky city air better than any other broadleafed tree. It invades woods on rich damp soils and shades out the other trees while its heavy leaf-fall destroys the flowers beneath. 10–15–35m. III – a dull tree.

'Brilliantissimum' comes into leaf bright pink then turns successively orange, yellow then white over nearly 2 months. It is a mop-head grafted on a Sycamore stem. 2–3–6m. I.

VAN VOLXEM'S MAPLE *Acer velutinum* var. *vanvolxemii* (Van Volxem discovered and introduced it) is a sort of highly superior Sycamore from the Caucasus region. Although in a different Section of the maples, with flowers in broad, erect heads, it looks like a Sycamore with smooth pale grey bark on a fine trunk marked by ringed scars, with leaves to 15×18cm on a stout stalk to 27cm long, and sharp, dark brown, many-scaled buds. It is seen only in collections. 6–12–24m. I.

212

ITALIAN MAPLE *Acer opalus* (the precious stone) is an uncommon broadly domed tree from S and C Europe. Unless it is in flower, when it is unmistakable, it may be taken for a Sycamore with bluntly lobed broad leaves. The bark, however, is pinkish or orange-grey with square, thick scales when young and is later in big plates and becomes shaggy as their ends lift. In autumn the leaves turn a pleasing yellow. The bud is sharply pointed, pale and dark brown. 5-9-20m. II.

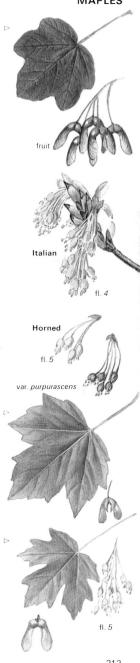

fruit

Italian

fl. *4*

Horned

fl. *5*

var. *purpurascens*

ITALIAN MAPLE   20m

HORNED MAPLE *Acer diabolicum* (devilish; two horn-like styles remain attached between the wings of the fruit) from Japan is scarce and mostly in collections. Its leaf is more like the London Plane than is any other maple but of very different texture with a fringe of soft white hairs standing out from the margin and on the veins beneath. Only the female flowers have petals, and in var. *purpurascens*, which a number of our trees are, these and the young fruit are purple. The dark brown, pointed bud has free spreading scales at the base. 5-8-12m. II.

BALKAN MAPLE *Acer hyrcanum* (from the Caspian Sea area; old name) ranges also into SE Europe and is similar to the Italian Maple, differing most obviously in the long slender leaf-stalk and somewhat longer lobes. It is less frequently seen. The flowers are greenish-yellow in short-stalked bunches of about 20, opening with the leaves. The buds have few red-brown scales with grey margins. The bark is dull grey, pink and orange with thin scales and the crown is rather open and spreading. 4-9-16m. II.

fl. 5

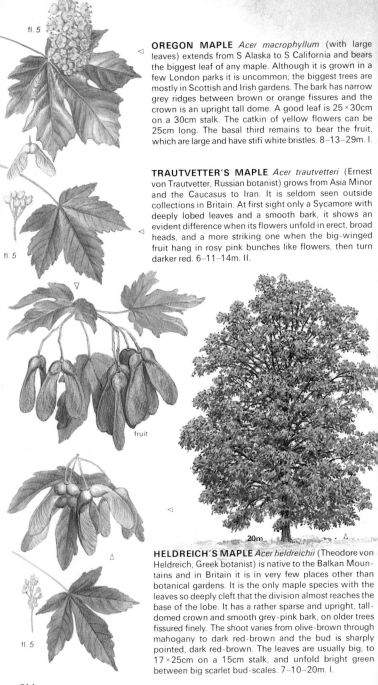

OREGON MAPLE *Acer macrophyllum* (with large leaves) extends from S Alaska to S California and bears the biggest leaf of any maple. Although it is grown in a few London parks it is uncommon; the biggest trees are mostly in Scottish and Irish gardens. The bark has narrow grey ridges between brown or orange fissures and the crown is an upright tall dome. A good leaf is 25×30cm on a 30cm stalk. The catkin of yellow flowers can be 25cm long. The basal third remains to bear the fruit, which are large and have stiff white bristles. 8–13–29m. I.

TRAUTVETTER'S MAPLE *Acer trautvetteri* (Ernest von Trautvetter, Russian botanist) grows from Asia Minor and the Caucasus to Iran. It is seldom seen outside collections in Britain. At first sight only a Sycamore with deeply lobed leaves and a smooth bark, it shows an evident difference when its flowers unfold in erect, broad heads, and a more striking one when the big-winged fruit hang in rosy pink bunches like flowers, then turn darker red. 6–11–14m. II.

fl. 5

fruit

20m

HELDREICH'S MAPLE *Acer heldreichii* (Theodore von Heldreich, Greek botanist) is native to the Balkan Mountains and in Britain it is in very few places other than botanical gardens. It is the only maple species with the leaves so deeply cleft that the division almost reaches the base of the lobe. It has a rather sparse and upright, tall-domed crown and smooth grey-pink bark, on older trees fissured finely. The shoot varies from olive-brown through mahogany to dark red-brown and the bud is sharply pointed, dark red-brown. The leaves are usually big, to 17×25cm on a 15cm stalk, and unfold bright green between big scarlet bud-scales. 7–10–20m. I.

fl. 5

fl. 2–4

autumn

under

new

SILVER MAPLE
20m

SILVER MAPLE *Acer saccharinum* (sweet; the sap, which can be made into syrup although it is the Sugar Maple that provides commercial maple syrup). This is native from SE Canada to Louisiana. In Britain it is quite the fastest maple in growth to a good size and becomes about as big as any. The smooth pale grey bark is much beset with sprouts and sometimes burrs and eventually has loose long plates. At no great age the bole is very big and the branches start to be blown off until it is left as a stump. The flowers are often out by March, long before the leaves emerge orange, but rarely set fruit, shed in May, in Britain. 11–20–30m. II.

fl. 4

autumn

DEEP-VEINED MAPLE *Acer argutum* (sharply toothed) comes from Japan and is grown in collectors' gardens. It usually has several stems and is dark green all over even in winter as the bark is greyish dark green with blisters and raised pores. The fruit are also bright deep green from May, soon after flowering, through the summer, and are numerous, about 12 in each of the many clusters. The leaves are hard and deeply crinkled at each vein and rather late in autumn they turn bright but soft yellow. Male and female flowers are on different trees but the fruit will grow in the absence of males. 3–5–10m. II.

⊲ **SMOOTH JAPANESE MAPLE** *Acer palmatum* (with leaves like an open hand). This is the common 'Japanese Maple' seen as a shrub in many forms, all too often dreary purple, in gardens everywhere. The 'smooth' is to separate it from the other 'Japanese Maple' usually of taller growth and less common, in which the shoot and leaf-stalk are downy. The ordinary *A. palmatum* can be a 17m tree with brown bark striped buff and a domed crown. Autumn colours are yellow, red and crimson. 3–6–17m. I.

'**Artropurpureum**' is bushy but can be 9m tall. 3–5–9m. III – dingy.

'**Ozakazuki**' has fresh green leaves 9 ×12cm in summer with scarlet fruit hanging in bunches beneath and in autumn is an intense fiery scarlet, even in some shade. 2–5–10m. I.

Coral-bark Maple, 'Senkaki' turns soft yellows and pinks in autumn. 3–5–?m. I.

⊲ **DOWNY JAPANESE MAPLE** *Acer japonicum* is an upright, low-branched tree with smooth grey bark. The big-leafed form, 'Vitifolium' is a better tree to 15m tall and a spectacular display of autumn colours, scarlet where the sun strikes, gold, plum-purple and green in the less exposed parts. 3–6–15m. I.

Golden Moon Maple 'Aureum' has butter yellow, 11-lobed leaves and is a low bush for a lifetime, good in rock and heather gardens but apt to scorch in full sun. 2–4–6m. I.

⊲ **KOREAN MAPLE** *Acer pseudosieboldianum* (false, i.e. resembling, Siebold's Maple, a similar plant but with yellow flowers). This tree, which extends into Manchuria, is a rare plant, and scarcely more than a broad bush, in a few collections in the British Isles. Even in summer, the leaves have a very distinctive warm orange-red tinge about them and in autumn they are brilliant orange, scarlet and crimson-purple. The flowers are purple. 2–3–5m. I.

⊲ **ZOESCHEN MAPLE** *Acer × zoeschense* (distributed by the Zoeschen Nurseries, Germany) is a hybrid between the Field Maple and probably the Cappadocian Maple rather than Lobel's because it suckers profusely. It is a broad-crowned sturdy tree seen in collections and a few other gardens in each country. The leaves, 10 ×14cm, are held out level and look almost black from a distance. About 12 yellowish-green, petal-less flowers are borne on each erect head. 6–9–18m. II.

⊲ **FIELD MAPLE** *Acer campestre* (of the fields) is a native common as a hedge and fair sized tree in S England around the chalklands and has been much planted in Scotland and Ireland. When cut, as often for a hedge, it develops thick corky wings on the shoots. New leaves unfold pinkish or, on late sprouts, red, and in the autumn they turn bright yellow, often with some red and dark purple. The small, yellow-green flowers open on erect heads with the leaves. The crown is a dense dome of straight shoots curving up towards their tips. The bud is red-brown with a grey, hairy tip. The bark is pale to dark grey-brown with narrow fissures. 5–8–25m. I.

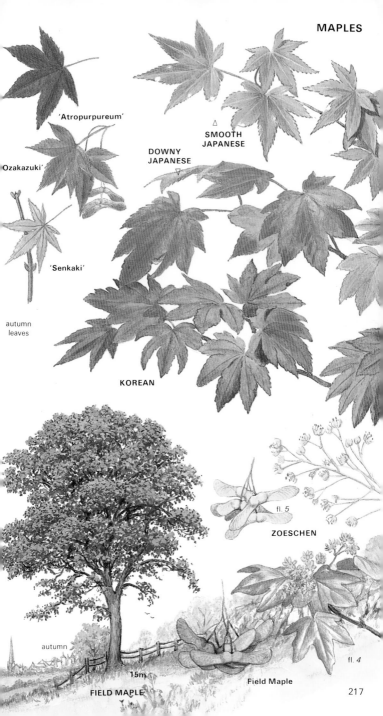

MAPLES

'Atropurpureum'

Ozakazuki'

SMOOTH
JAPANESE

DOWNY
JAPANESE

'Senkaki'

autumn
leaves

KOREAN

fl. 5

ZOESCHEN

autumn

15m

FIELD MAPLE

Field Maple

fl. 4

fl. 5

fl. 5

fl. 5

fl. 5

fl. 5

◁ **PÈRE DAVID'S MAPLE** *Acer davidii* (Abbé Armand David, French missionary who discovered many plants and a species of deer in China) is one of the snakebark maples most frequent in gardens, in 3 of its 4 or more forms. One, 'George Forrest' has broad, shiny blackish leaves with 3 lobes, and a scarlet stalk but no autumn colour. Another has slender, long-pointed leaves without lobes, 15 ×8cm or, in a variant, 13 ×5cm, and these turn yellow-brown to orange in autumn. A third has little 6 ×3cm unlobed elliptic leaves that colour similarly. The fourth, 'Ernest Wilson' is the rarest, with light green partly folded leaves with many small lobes, pale grey beneath and on a short pink stalk. 8–11–16m. I.

HERS'S MAPLE *Acer hersii* (M. Hers, French collector ◁ discovered and introduced it). This Chinese snakebark is now frequently planted but older trees are in collections only. It is distinctively olive-green in almost all its parts, from bark to shoot, leaf-stalk, new leaf, flowers and fruit. Only some strong new shoots are pale pink with leaf-stalks the same colour, and sometimes the mature foliage is very dark green. This grows rapidly at first into a vase-shaped crown of arching branches. Later long shoots droop from the crown 2–4m with only small spurs all the way. Autumn colours are rich orange and dark red. 9–10–14m. I.

◁ **RED SNAKEBARK MAPLE** *Acer capillipes* (slender-footed – perhaps the flower-stalks). This Japanese tree is the best snakebark for scarlet shoots, leaf-stalks and glossy well-veined leaves as well as a bark as brightly striped as any, but it tends to be short-lived. It is less common than the others given here, perhaps for that reason. The foliage is known by the long, gently tapered central lobe with many prominent parallel veins. Autumn colours are orange and scarlet. Flowers and fruit are very prolific. 7–13–16m. I.

◁ **MOOSEWOOD** *Acer pensylvanicum* (in error for 'pennsylvanicum', of Pennsylvania state) is the only snakebark not native in Japan or China and is one of the best. Unmistakable with its upright crown of big bright green leaves, this is easily raised from the abundant seed borne. The leaves vary in size up to 22 ×20cm and the largest have the two lobes nearest the tip while they may be halfway down the smaller leaves. The leaves turn bright yellow early in autumn and are soon shed. 6–9–14m. I.

GREY-BUDDED SNAKEBARK MAPLE *Acer* ◁ *rufinerve* (with red veins; new leaves have rusty red hairs on the veins beneath, later reduced to a little tuft in the angles at the base). This Japanese tree has a greyer bark than other snakebarks, often striped in pink, and buds and young shoots bloomed blue-white. The mid-lobe of the leaf is short and broad with some rusty red remaining beneath. Autumn colours are orange and red with upper branches tending to turn first. 6–9–13m. II

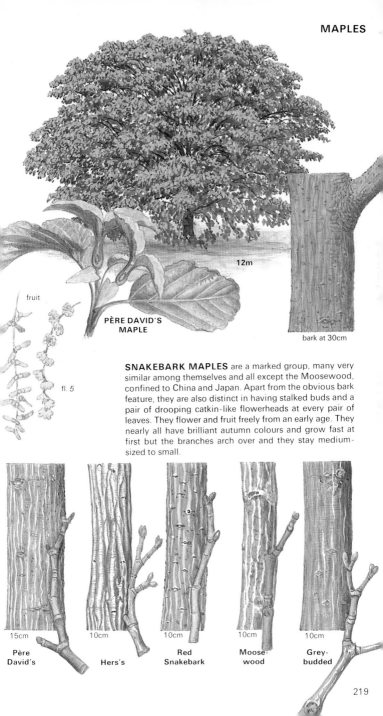

fruit

fl. 5

PÈRE DAVID'S MAPLE

12m

bark at 30cm

SNAKEBARK MAPLES are a marked group, many very similar among themselves and all except the Moosewood, confined to China and Japan. Apart from the obvious bark feature, they are also distinct in having stalked buds and a pair of drooping catkin-like flowerheads at every pair of leaves. They flower and fruit freely from an early age. They nearly all have brilliant autumn colours and grow fast at first but the branches arch over and they stay medium-sized to small.

15cm	10cm	10cm	10cm	10cm
Père David's	Hers's	Red Snakebark	Moose-wood	Grey-budded

219

HAWTHORN-LEAFED MAPLE *Acer crataegifolium* (with leaves like the Hawthorn, *Crataegus*). This rather dainty little snakebark comes from Japan and is uncommon. It has a slender bole and branches, the latter bending out to spread flat with small twisting shoots lined along their upper side, and is irregular in shape. In summer there is much red about it as the shoots are dark red striped white, the leaf-stalk is scarlet, the veins pink, and the fruit are soon red. The leaf is very small, only 6 × 3cm. 3–5–12m. II.

fl. 5

FORREST'S MAPLE *Acer forrestii* (George Forrest, Edinburgh collector in W China, discovered and introduced it). This Chinese snakebark is unfortunately rare even in collections. It is extremely attractive with its well-lobed rather ivy-like leaves on scarlet stalks and a good green and white striped bark. It also has a fountain-like crown of long arched and drooping shoots without side-shoots. The leaves hold on long in autumn but seldom change colour. A form in Silk Wood, Westonbirt has added small lobes, more irregular toothing and an even more flowing crown. 6–9–11m. I.

fl. 5

BIRCH-LEAF MAPLE *Acer tetramerum* (with four parts) is not a snakebark maple although it looks very like one and may have a similar bark, but is in another group in which the trees are either male or female. The bark is usually much blistered and roughened, dark grey-green. This tree is rarely on a single bole; more usually there are 4–5 equal slender stems, tall and lightly branched. It is known in leaf by the long, slender scarlet stalk to a rounded leaf-base on an unlobed leaf, coarsely toothed. It is rare but most seen in the west. 6–9–15m. II.

fl. 5

LIME-LEAF MAPLE *Acer distylum* (with 2 styles and hence 2 seeds in the fruit). This Japanese tree is very distinct in the summer and not much like a maple. Although among maples it most resembles the snakebarks and has a striped green and pale orange bark and a broad unlobed leaf, it is not one of that group. Its flowers are on the upper half of vertical spikes which stand through the summer holding the fruit. The leaves are leathery and large, 13 × 11cm on a stout stalk 4cm long, and turn pale yellow briefly in autumn. 5–8–11m. I.

fl. 5

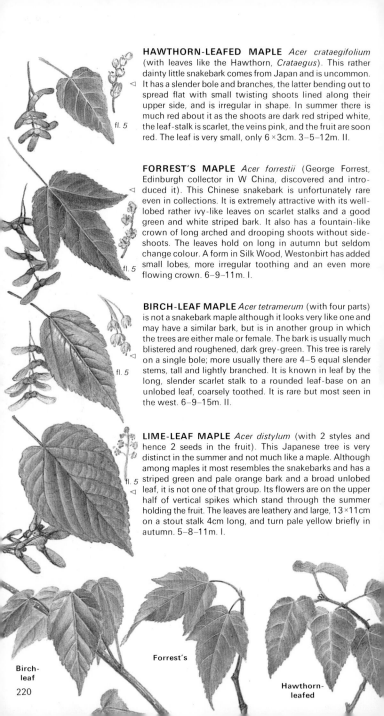

Birch-leaf

Forrest's

Hawthorn-leafed

fl. *2–3*

autumn

RED MAPLE

20m

bark at 50cm

under

△

▷

RED MAPLE *Acer rubrum* (red; the flowers) is abundant in swampy woods from Newfoundland to Texas. In autumn the colours of trees in the same wood range from gold through orange and scarlet to deep royal purple. In Britain where it is reasonably common in the south but scarce in the north, many young trees turn bright yellow and scarlet and old trees mostly dark red and there is much less variety. The crown is an untidy dome of whippy curved shoots which are red to coppery-brown with small dark red-brown buds. Unfolding leaves are reddish and glossy. Flowers may start to open in February or March, at first clustered on short stems which lengthen as more flowers open for several weeks. 8–12–23m. I.

TRIDENT MAPLE *Acer buergeranum* (Buerger) is an attractive little tree from China seen in all too few of our gardens. It makes a densely leafy low domed crown, quite unlike any other, and turning crimson in the autumn. The bark is orange to dark brown in rough edged, lifting square plates, paler when young, and flaky. Most trees bear some unlobed, elliptical leaves among the trident ones. New leaves are covered in pale orange hairs soon shed, and the erect flowerheads opening at the same time are similarly covered. The flowers are yellow and leave a purple disk on the base of the fruit. 5–7–16m. l.

AMUR MAPLE *Acer ginnala* has a wide range in China, Manchuria and Japan. It is very hardy, as is shown by its thriving in Winnipeg and use in tubs in the streets of Montreal. In Britain it is a plant of suburban or semi-rural gardens as much as in large plantings and is usually an open upright bush but may be a small tree on a sinuous stem, with dark grey, smooth bark. The leaves open pale yellow with the whitish flowers, small in erect wide heads, following soon in May. Early in autumn the leaves turn bright red then soon turn dark and fall off. The fruit hang in nodding bunches which may remain pale dull brown well into winter. 3–5–10m. l.

TARTAR MAPLE   6m

TARTAR MAPLE *Acer tataricum* (from C Asia) occurs also in SE Europe and was introduced to Britain in 1759. In flower especially, from a little distance it looks more like a thorn than a maple, a likeness enhanced by the low spreading crown. The bark is smooth brown striped paler. The veins of the leaf are impressed from above and prominent on the underside. The stalk, red or pale pink is grooved above. The fruit take on the red colour soon after midsummer and are then the most prominent feature of the plant. It is scarce but some are seen in town parks as well as in gardens. 3–4–6m. l.

5m

CRETAN MAPLE

10m

MONTPELIER MAPLE

MONTPELIER MAPLE *Acer monspessulanum* (from Montpellier, S France). This tree of the hot dry hills of S Europe and N Africa is uncommon and mostly seen in southern parts and London parks but is grown in Dunkeld, Perthshire and sparingly elsewhere in the north. In summer it looks as if it were an evergreen, the leaves are so dark and hard and remaining so late into the autumn, but they fall by November. New leaves in spring are late and bright green. The pale yellow flowers hang in small clusters in June. The bark is dark grey with black fissures. 3–6–15m. I.

CRETAN MAPLE *Acer sempervirens* (evergreen). The only evergreen maple hardy in SE England although rarely more than semi-evergreen here. This is no more than a twiggy little bush except for one fine specimen in Cornwall. It has no value other than as a curiosity so it is planted only in a few collections. The leaves are mixed, lobed, partly lobed, scarcely lobed and unlobed all together, and are hard, on brown shoots. 1–2–2m. III.

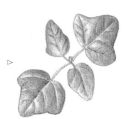

HORNBEAM MAPLE *Acer carpinifolium* (with leaves like a Hornbeam, many parallel veins) is a highly attractive Japanese species that seems to be anything but a maple until the leaves are seen to be opposite or the flowers and fruit show. It is an unusual, wide bushy plant rarely on a single bole, with shiny brown shoots. The leaves are 15–17cm long and have 20 or more pairs of veins. They turn pale bright yellow then brown in autumn. Starry green flowers hang on slender catkin-like heads, 10–12cm long. The bark is smooth and dark grey. 4–6–10m. I.

fl. 5

223

autumn

NIKKO MAPLE

12m

fl. *5*

fruit

fl. *5*

fl. *4–5*

NIKKO MAPLE *Acer nikoense* (from Nikko, in NE Honshu, Japan) is native to C China and Japan and has a compound leaf with 3 leaflets, bigger and broader than the others of this group. The buds are small and blunt, with blackish scales tipped with grey hairs. The flowers hang in threes on long-haired stalks when the leaves are nearly fully expanded. The petals are broad and yellow and point straight down giving the flower a bell-shape. The leaves are bluish-white underneath, densely hairy. Autumn colour is reliable even on chalky soils (on which this tree grows well) turning from scarlet to deep red rather late in the season. 3–5–15m. I – an attractive tree, and useful for its moderate size.

ROUGH-BARKED MAPLE *Acer triflorum* (with flowers in threes) is the Korean and Manchurian equivalent of the Nikko Maple, differing more strikingly in the bark than in any other feature. Also the leaflets, smaller and thinner in texture usually have one broad, blunt tooth. This tree has a reputation for superb autumn colours, but it is unreliable for this. 2–4–8m. II.

VINELEAF MAPLE *Acer cissifolium* (Greek 'kissos', ivy, also used now for a group of vines) is a 3-leaflet maple from Japan of moderate scarcity. From a 1–2m trunk with smooth grey bark ageing in patches to white, it spreads a broad low canopy dense with level shoots. Among these tri-foliate maples it is known by the wire-thin stalks to the leaflets and main leaf-stalks. Spikes of flowers spread stiffly in pairs in large numbers then bear the little fruit. In autumn the leaves turn pale yellow then pinkish-brown. There are tiny white knobs in the vein-angles beneath the leaf. 2–4–9m. II.

224

Nikko 30cm

Rough-barked
30cm

trunk 30cm

under

**PAPERBARK
MAPLE**

autumn

fl. 5

PAPERBARK MAPLE *Acer griseum* (grey; distant view in leaf). One of Ernest Wilson's earliest and best finds in central China this is planted as often as supplies allow ▷ and is now a frequent feature of parks and gardens. It will grow on chalk and in light shade but is always slow after the first few years. The bud is only 1mm long and is black on a dark red-brown shoot which is at first hairy, later smooth. The leaves unfold pale orange-brown and turn pinkish then yellow before becoming green. As they unfold, bunches of 3–5 greenish-yellowish bell-shaped flowers open, each flower on a 3cm hairy stalk. Seed is abundant and fat, but few are fertile so it has to be imported from S Europe, and the tree is often in short supply. 3–5–12m. I – outstanding in bark and autumn colour.

ASHLEAF MAPLE *Acer negundo* (Malayan common name for Chaste-vine, transferred to this tree) is called ▷ 'boxelder' also, but with less apparent reason. It has a remarkable range across America in various forms from Ontario to Guatemala, changing from very smooth and hairless in the north-east to densely soft-downy all over in the far south-west. In Britain it is a very common, if little known and puzzling tree, in suburban areas. Usually planted as a coloured leaf form, it reverts unless the numerous sprouts of stronger plain green foliage are ruthlessly cut out. 8–11–12m. X – sprouty, short-lived and dull.

'**Auratum**' is one of the best golden trees, frequent around London. 8–11–13m. I.

'**Variegatum**', one of the whitest variegated trees, is female. 8–11–15m. I.

'Variegatum'

225

● **HORSE CHESTNUT FAMILY** Hippocastanaceae. **HORSE CHEST-
NUTS** *Aesculus* (classical Latin name for some fruit-bearing tree). A group of 13 trees
of tall or medium size, one a suckering shrub; from N America, S Europe, the Himalayas,
China and Japan. Timber pale, soft and weak, used for carving. Raised by seed or
grafting. Flowers in tall panicles; fruit a prickly or smooth husk round 1–2 big nuts.

autumn

25m

HORSE CHESTNUT

**RED HORSE
CHESTNUT**

fruit

conker

HORSE CHESTNUT *Aesculus hippocastanum* (Greek
for horse and Latin for Sweet Chestnut). So familiar that it
is often supposed to be native, and it seeds itself around as
if it were. But in fact it is native only to a few mountains in
Greece and was not grown in W Europe until after 1600.
The finest trees are on deep, rich valley soils but it will
grow quite well on any soil that is not too acid or dry. The
wood is soft and weak and big branches may break off
during summer rains. 8–11–38m. II.

bark at 60cm

fl. *4–5*

RED HORSE CHESTNUT *Aesculus × carnea* (flesh coloured; deep pink) is a hybrid between the Common Horse Chestnut and a red-flowered American species called there, Red Buckeye. It probably arose in Germany and it has the unusual feature for a hybrid that it breeds true from seed. 4–6–20m. X – dark coarse foliage, and muddy red flowers.

The best trees, however, are all grafts because they are the superior form **'Briotii'**, with shiny leaves and truly red flowers. III.

conker

twig

fl. 5

JAPANESE
HORSE CHESTNUT

Red Horse Chestnut

JAPANESE HORSE CHESTNUT *Aesculus turbinata* (top-shaped). Among foliage of this tree one has the strange feeling of having shrunk to half size for its leaves are twice the size of those of the familiar tree though very similar in shape. The leaflets are stalkless and differ only in their size, gradually tapered tips and whitish underside with small tufts of orange hairs on the midrib. The bark is grey with broad white streaks on young trees, smooth dark grey-pink on old. 8–12–22m. l.

under

conker

SUNRISE HORSE CHESTNUT *Aesculus neglecta* 'Erythroblastos' (red bud) was raised in Germany from an obscure species in the eastern USA. It is propagated by grafting and makes a small tree with a broad, open crown. It is highly decorative for a few weeks in late spring, the leaves unfolding bright pink with scarlet stalks, then turning yellow and, briefly white before becoming green. Some patches of yellow can usually be found on leaves in summer. 2–4–9m. l.

SUNRISE
HORSE CHESTNUT   new leaf

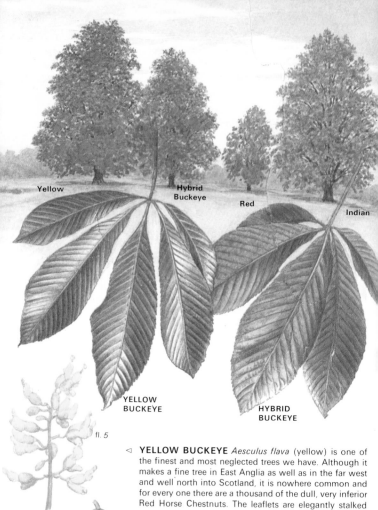

Yellow

Hybrid
Buckeye

Red

Indian

YELLOW
BUCKEYE

HYBRID
BUCKEYE

fl. 5

conker

fl. 6

◁ **YELLOW BUCKEYE** *Aesculus flava* (yellow) is one of the finest and most neglected trees we have. Although it makes a fine tree in East Anglia as well as in the far west and well north into Scotland, it is nowhere common and for every one there are a thousand of the dull, very inferior Red Horse Chestnuts. The leaflets are elegantly stalked and toothed and are bright and glossy and they turn bright orange and scarlet every autumn. The bud is smooth and non-resinous, the scales pale pink-brown edged pink. Many specimens are grafted on common Horse Chestnut. This tree comes from the Appalachian Mountains and is 43m tall in Tennessee. 5–8–20m. I.

HYBRID BUCKEYE *Aesculus × hybrida* is a cross between the Yellow and the Red Buckeyes occurring several times in slightly different forms and once given different
◁ botanical names (*Aesculus × lyonii*; *A. × versicolor*; *A. × discolor*). Grafted trees of these forms are sometimes seen in parks and in botanical gardens, with coarser, flatter leaves than Yellow Buckeye and reddish or partly red flowers. 3–6–10m. II.

INDIAN HORSE CHESTNUT *Aesculus indica* is a Himalayan tree popular with park superintendents in holiday resorts since its flowers open so late that they extend into the early holiday season. It is variable, and the flowers of some are from a distance a good pale pink. The typically hanging red-stalked leaves do not occur on the sturdy form 'Sidney Pearce' raised at Kew, in which stout dark green stalks hold the leaves level. The leaves of the common form unfold pale orange-brown and the conkers can be coal-black. 8–11–20m. l.

conker

fl. 7

RED
BUCK-EYE

fruit

INDIAN
HORSE CHESTNUT

RED BUCKEYE *Aesculus pavia* (after Peter Paaw, Dutch botanist who wrote as 'Petrus Pavius') is native to the southern parts of the Mississippi Valley and the Coastal Plain where it is little more than a 4m shrub. It has been grafted on 2m stems in a few gardens, but some plants bought as Red Buckeye have later been seen to be Hybrid Buckeye. A true one at Kew is quite tall and weeping. The flowers are slender but a genuine bright red, and small though it is this tree (and the Yellow Buckeye), would bring a welcome change to all the Red Horse Chestnuts planted. 2–3–6m. l.

fl. 5

229

● **LIME FAMILY** Tiliaceae (classical Latin, from Greek 'ptilon', a wing; the flower bract) has 300 species but only the 30 limes (lindens) are trees. Most are raised from seed but Common Lime is rarely fertile and is layered. The wood is soft and used for carvings.

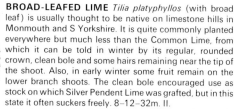

BROAD-LEAFED LIME *Tilia platyphyllos* (with broad leaf) is usually thought to be native on limestone hills in Monmouth and S Yorkshire. It is quite commonly planted everywhere but much less than the Common Lime, from which it can be told in winter by its regular, rounded crown, clean bole and some hairs remaining near the tip of the shoot. Also, in early winter some fruit remain on the lower branch shoots. The clean bole encouraged use as stock on which Silver Pendent Lime was grafted, but in this state it often suckers freely. 8–12–32m. II.

'Rubra' has shoots dark red in winter and green in summer with slightly yellowed leaves. 8–12–30m. II.

COMMON LIME *Tilia × europaea* is a hybrid between the two native limes, Broad-leafed and Small-leafed but is probably not itself a native. It is the common lime for streets and long avenues and is the worst tree known for either purpose. It does achieve a great height and it lives long, but its roots are invasive, it sprouts round the base, it is infested by greenfly, is often badly mis-shapen and has no autumn colours. In places it carries huge bunches of mistletoe among its own sprouty burrs. 8–11–46m. X.

SMALL-LEAFED LIME *Tilia cordata* (heart-shaped; leaf) is native to England and Wales and until Saxon times was the dominant tree in most forests. A few areas remain like that, as in the Forest of Wyre, Worcestershire. It was planted much less frequently than the Common and the Broad-leafed until the recent need to replace elms made it a favourite as a native species of similar stature and needs, and a splendid tree. In leaf it is known by its elegant foliage and in flower the bright starry flowers project at all angles from dark leaves, unlike any other lime. Young trees are shapely and conic but old ones become burred, sprouty and heavily branched. Fewer greenfly than on Common Lime. 6–12–38m. I.

CAUCASIAN LIME *Tilia euchlora* (well green-coloured; shoots and leaves). The glossy foliage, clean of greenfly and good shape of young trees led to quite frequent planting of this tree in parks, streets and squares, and still does. However, old trees grow ever more mushroom-like with thick shoots bending down, and some young trees are suffering a disease which splits the branches. It has a clean bole with leaden-grey bark, smooth and striped darker. The shoot is bright yellow-green, occasionally pink or dark red. In autumn the leaves turn bright yellow, often in parts of the crown only. 7–11–20m. II.

| BROAD-LEAFED | COMMON | SMALL-LEAFED | CAUCASIAN |
| 30m | 40m | 30m | 20m |

close ups of leaf undersides

fl. 6

fl. 6

fl. 7

fl. 7-8

fruits

| Broad-leafed | Common | Small-leafed | Caucasian |

231

under

fl. buds under

under

SILVER LIME *Tilia tomentosa* (densely woolly; shoots and underside of leaf) is a tree of the Black Sea and Caucasus region, and like almost every tree from it, has strong healthy growth and large leaves. The hairy surfaces are unsuited to greenfly making the tree better for sitting under than those limes from which a fine rain of sticky 'honeydew' descends from a hundred million aphids. It is a good tree therefore for city parks and thrives in them. There are many mature and far more young ones in the Royal Parks in London. It flowers late in July. 7–12–28m. l.

SILVER PENDENT LIME *Tilia* 'Petiolaris' (of the leaf-stalk, petiole; the length of which is the foliage distinction from Silver Lime). This tree is known only in gardens and either is a selected variant of Silver Lime or once had a small wild population in the Caucasus region. It is frequent where there is room for a tall tree in gardens and parks. It must be propagated by grafting and is usually on a 2m stem of Broad-leafed Lime and breaks almost at once into 2–3 erect main boles. In autumn parts of the crown turn bright yellow then the whole turns soft yellow-brown. The bark is dark grey with smooth broad pale ridges. Free of greenfly. 8–13–34m. l.

VON MOLTKE'S LIME *Tilia × moltkei* (in honour of Field Marshal von Moltke, of Germany) is a hybrid between the Silver Pendent and American limes seen in a few gardens. Young trees are very vigorous with a shoot to 1.3m long and the leaves can be at least 25 ×15cm, with the silvery haired underside inherited from the Silver Pendent Lime, together with a somewhat weeping habit. 8–14–25m. l.

AMERICAN LIME *Tilia americana* is native from SE Canada to Arkansas and planted in city streets westward to BC and Washington. It is scarce and often not thriving in Britain but there are a few fine trees and at least one suburban street planting. In American streets the leaves are about the size of Common Lime but very different in their bright shiny green and strongly marked parallel veins. Specimen trees in Britain tend to have leaves to 20cm long, or more on sprouts, and the trunks densely ringed with lines of pits made by great spotted woodpeckers sapsucking. The leaf is distinct among limes in being the same colour both sides. 5–7–26m. l.

OLIVER'S LIME *Tilia oliveri* (Daniel Oliver, one-time Keeper of the Kew Herbarium) was discovered in 1888 by Augustine Henry and was one of Ernest Wilson's earliest introductions, in 1900 from Hupeh Province, China. Early trees are in only a few collections but the tree is so handsome that all who know it plant it if they can. The 'chinaman's moustaches' are prominent over branch scars on the otherwise smooth grey bark. Shoots of the lower crown droop and their leaf-stalks point downwards but the blades of the leaves stand out level. The shoot and bud are smooth apple-green sometimes tinged pink. 6–11–24m. l.

under

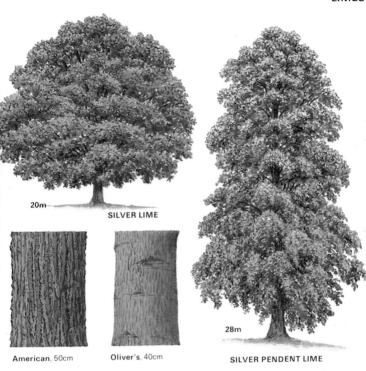

20m SILVER LIME

American, 50cm Oliver's, 40cm

28m SILVER PENDENT LIME

AMUR LIME *Tilia amurensis* (from the Amur River region ▷ of Manchuria and Siberia) is at present a rare tree, but a fine specimen at Westonbirt, by the Morley Ride, attracts attention when it is in flower. It must be the strongest scented of all the limes: the heavy sweet fragrance is evident quite 50m away. The shoot, leaf-stalk and veins beneath the hard, leathery leaves are all densely covered in long yellowish hairs. The bark is smooth grey, striped pale brown. 6–11–18m. l.

MONGOLIAN LIME *Tilia mongolica* was introduced to Kew in 1904 and until some recent plantings, very few other gardens were growing it. Now that it is becoming better known it will be in more demand as a tolerant and shapely tree, with a daintiness not found in other limes. The ▷ slender, rather pendulous shoots are red and smooth, and the leaves emerge tinged red before turning dark shiny green, smooth and hard. It flowers freely after midsummer with thirty or more pale and fragrant flowers in each bunch. The bark of young trees is very smooth, brownish-grey finely striped dark grey, and later becomes purplish-grey with orange and buff fissures. 6–11–20m. l.

fl. 7–8

233

● EUCRYPHIA FAMILY Eucryphiaceae.

A family of only 4 species in one genus, from Chile and Australasia. One is deciduous, the others evergreen. They have given several hybrids and all are useful for their fine late summer display of flower. Raised from seed and cuttings.

fl. *8–9*

NYMANS HYBRID EUCRYPHIA *Eucryphia × nymans-ensis* 'Nymansay' (several hybrid seedlings were raised in Nymans garden, Sussex and named A, B, C etc. The one propagated was 'A' – hence 'Nymansay'). This selection among the hybrids between the rather tender, tall shapely tree *E. cordifolia*, an evergreen, and the deciduous bush *E. glutinosa* is frequent in gardens as a tall dark evergreen background plant which is covered in large white flowers in late summer and often well into autumn. The stems, often more than one from the base, are the favourite sites for the sapsucking activities of the great spotted wood-pecker and are ringed with lines of little pits in the dark grey, otherwise smooth bark. This tree often takes several years to begin to flower but with age it becomes more spectacular every year. 5–9–17m. I.

EUCRYPHIA *Eucryphia glutinosa* (gummy; new foliage) is a Chilean bush occasionally a small tree, common in gardens on acid soils. (The Nymans hybrid, above, will grow on chalk). It is usually deciduous and before falling, the leaves give a fine display of orange and red. 2–3–3m. I.

Eucryphia

fl. *8*

Nymans
Eucryphia   12m

Prickly
Caster-Oil Tree

13m

234

● **TEA FAMILY** Theaceae. A mainly tropical large family with a few species in temperate areas, mainly in China, but two Stewartias are in the eastern USA. Generally raised from seed.

DECIDUOUS CAMELLIA *Stuartia pseudocamellia* (false, i.e. resembling in some ways, the Camellia) is a slender upright-branched tree with shoots fanning out level hardy only in southern and western areas. It is uncommon and is prized for its bark, summer flowers and brilliant dark red autumn colours. A very unusual feature of the leaf is that it is brighter and more shining beneath than above where it is dull and matt. An oval green bract stands erect on either side of the flower bud and is prominent in winter. 5–9–15m. l.

fruit

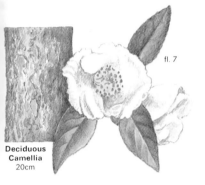
fl. 7

Deciduous Camellia
20cm

fl. 7

Chinese Stuartia
20cm

fruit

CHINESE STUARTIA *Stuartia sinensis* is scarce and confined to the south and when seen, stands out because of its smooth, coloured bark. This may be bright pink, or pale grey suffused pink or grey and yellowish, and is often wrinkled in horizontal bands but is always clear of scales once no longer young. By that time it is a wide-branching low tree. It has crimson-purple new shoots and leaves the same bright green both sides, turning red and dark red in autumn. The flower petals are thick and fleshy. 3–5–10m. l.

● **IVY FAMILY** Araliaceae includes 500 species of evergreen climbers and deciduous thorny shrubs. All have white flowers in umbels – broad heads branched simply from a common stalk.

PRICKLY CASTOR-OIL TREE *Kalopanax pictus* (painted – a confusion with a variegated maple). A strange tree from E Asia, very gaunt and rugged in winter but luxuriantly leafed in summer. The leaves vary in depth of lobing from shallow in the type to deep in var. *maximowiczii*. This has dark red-brown, rough and hairy stalks up to 20cm long. The bark is dull grey and thickly ridged, with short broad-based prickles remaining from the more numerous prickles on the shoots. White flowers open in autumn in small heads at the tips of 30 slender white, spoke-like stalks radiating from each branch-tip, and ripen into black berries. 5–7–18m. l.

twig

var. *maximowiczii*

235

● **SOAPBERRY FAMILY** Sapindaceae has only one tree hardy in Britain, the *Koelreuteria* (Joseph Koelreuter, German professor and pioneer hybridist) one of a few trees of E Asia and Fiji. Raised from seed.

autumn

12m

August

PRIDE OF
INDIA

fl. *8*

PITTOSPORUM

10m

fruit

new
leaves

PRIDE OF INDIA *Koelreuteria paniculata* (with flowers in panicles; many-branched heads with a central stem) is, despite the name, a Chinese tree. It is frequent only in sunny parts, notably in the town parks of Chichester and the college gardens of Cambridge, but local in SE England. The rough bark is purplish-brown with small orange fissures. The shoot is pale copper-brown with squat buds tipped by a curved beak. The leaves unfold red in late May and turn pale yellow before becoming green. In autumn they are yellow and brown. The flowers open in mid August on panicles 30–40cm long. The fruit are papery bladders each containing 3 black seeds. 5–9–15m. l.

● PITTOSPORUM FAMILY Pittosporaceae (with pitch-covered seeds) are
small evergreen trees ranging from Madeira and the Canary Isles to Japan and New Zealand. Raised from seed or cuttings.

PITTOSPORUM *Pittosporum tenuifolium* (with a thin leaf). This tree from New Zealand is normally hardy from Ireland and Cornwall to London but in 1978 most of the biggest, which are in Cornwall where the cold was most intense were badly scorched or killed, while those in Surrey were completely unaffected. Some northward by the west coast to Wigtown were damaged but survive. In SE England it makes a fresh green erect bush and in milder parts it is a tree with a smooth, dull grey bark and flowers heavily in May. 3–6–18m. l.

fl. 4

fruit & seeds

● FLACOURTIA FAMILY Flacourtiaceae (Etienne de Flacourt, director of the French East India Company in 1870). Only one tree in the family grown here.

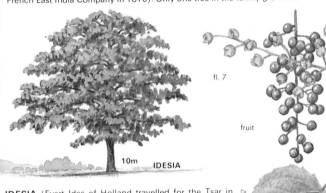

fl. 7

fruit

10m   IDESIA

IDESIA (Evert Ides of Holland travelled for the Tsar in Siberia and China). *Idesia polycarpa* (many fruited), a Catalpa-like tree when not in flower, grown in a few gardens in S England and Ireland. In fact it differs from Catalpa in every detail. The bark is smooth, grey-green and pink; the branches spread less widely; the leaf has a scarlet stalk and hook-tipped teeth; and trees are either male or female. The leaf is 20×20cm on a stalk up to 30cm long and hanging flowerheads are 10–25cm long. 3–6–16m. l.

● MYRTLE FAMILY Myrtaceae. A widespread family – evergreen, aromatic and with bunches of stamens in the flower. Raised from seed.

ORANGE-BARK MYRTLE *Myrtus luma* (probably a native name) from the cool and wet forests of southern S America runs wild and makes thickets in some gardens in W Ireland and thrives in Cornwall and close to the west coast north into SW Scotland but barely survives and is rare east of Devon. It makes an upright, loosely conic black-crowned tree but turns largely white when the masses of flowers open in late summer. The shoot is dark pink above, densely covered in fine hairs. The leaves are in opposite pairs and are sweet and spicy when crushed. 4–6–15m. l.

under

fl. 9
bark, 40cm

GUMS or EUCALYPTS *Eucalyptus* (well-covered – the flowers are enclosed in lidded capsules with holes for stamens and styles). At least 500 species of evergreen aromatic trees dominating the woods of all Australasia except New Zealand. Gums have no resting period; they just stop growing briefly if it is cold. Raised from seed.

fruit

juv.

35m

BLUE GUM

CIDER GUM

20m

238

⊲ **BLUE GUM** *Eucalyptus globulus* (little globe – the flower buds). From Tasmania but now the fastest and biggest growing tree in almost every hot country in the world. Continuously in flower and fruit. In W Ireland it seeds itself widely and seedlings grow 2.5m a year. By the east coast north to beyond Belfast and the Isle of Man it is commonly 35m tall, but on mainland Britain it does not survive the severest winters. The blue seedlings are used everywhere: if planted out in the far south and west they may be 15m tall before a hard winter comes. As with most other gums, the opposite, broad juvenile leaves change with age to slender and alternate. 17–25–45m. I.

CIDER GUM *Eucalyptus gunnii*. This is the common gum planted all over Britain and but rarely damaged in the hardest winters. It is native to C Tasmania where it is not an impressive tree but in Britain it can grow as fast as most other gums and makes shoots 2m long. It sprouts readily if cut down and the first year shoots then bear the round juvenile leaves and are cut for the floristry market. 13–20–30m. I.

SNOW-GUM *Eucalyptus niphophila* (snow-loving) grows at 2000m on the highest mountain in Australia, Mt Kosciusko, and the nearby ranges and is even more hardy than the Cider Gum. It scarcely has any juvenile stage and before it is 1m high, 2 months from seed it has alternate elliptical leaves, which often unfold dark orange. The shoot starts yellow and turns dark red before the blue-white bloom appears on it. The leaf-stalk is thick and wrinkled. The flowers, 9–11 closely bunched can be spectacularly clear white. 9–15m. I.

BROAD-LEAFED KINDLING BARK *Eucalyptus dalrympleana* from Tasmania and SE Australia has been planted recently quite widely and has proved in recent damaging winters to be variably hardy with one tree unharmed near one which was killed. The leaves on older trees may be very long – up to 30 × 4cm. It differs from the Blue Gum in the tiny flower-buds in heads of 2–3 at the base of each leaf. 12–20–?m. I.

juvenile

fl. 8

fl. 8

juvenile

| Blue Gum 50cm | Cider Gum 40cm | Snow 20cm | Broad-Leaf 40cm | Urn Gum 40cm |

URN GUM *Eucalyptus urnigera* (bearing urns; the fruit capsules) comes from Tasmania and is frequent in Ireland and along the British west coast north to W Ross. It usually stands out from other eucalypts by reason of its relatively broad leaves being dark apple-green, but there are some with the more usual blue foliage. The urn-shaped fruit are in 3s dark glossy green at first and broadly rimmed. Juvenile leaves are opposite, nearly round and blue-white. The bark is strips of orange and green leaving pale cream or brown. 12–22–32m. I.

fruit

20m

TUPELO   autumn   **DOVE TREE**   15m

●**TUPELO FAMILY** Nyssaceae (Nyssa, a water-nymph; the first Nyssa described, Water Tupelo, grows in water). A small family of trees with flowers of different sexes on the same tree. Raised from seed.

fruit

TUPELO *Nyssa sylvatica* (of woods, not of water, see above). This species grows on the Coastal Plain and in the lower Mississippi Basin. In Britain it will grow well only in those areas with the warmest summers. Few are seen north of the English Midlands and it is far from common in the south and then grows slowly unless on deep, rich slightly acid soils in some shelter. The bark, like many other trees from the eastern USA, is soon deeply ridged and fissured, dark grey or brownish. In winter the shoots are spiky with short, forward-pointing side-shoots, with small red-brown buds. 2.5–4–24m. I.

240   fruits

DOVE TREE *Davidia involucrata* (with an involucre, bracts around the flower). The form described first by Abbé David in C China and sent by Ernest Wilson in 1903 has soft white hairs on the underside of the leaf and is fairly scarce. The tree quite frequent in all areas is var. *vilmoriniana* which had been sent in 1897 by Paul Farges to Vilmorin's Nurseries in France, unknown to Wilson at the time. Underside of the leaf smooth and shiny green. It is somewhat more vigorous and the leaf tends to be longer, up to 20 × 17cm. The bud is dark shining red and the bark purple, smooth beneath flaking brown scales. The flower head emerges purple between yellow bracts and opens yellow as the bracts turn white. 6–10–21m. I.

10m

TABLE DOGWOOD   fl. 5

10m PACIFIC DOGWOOD

DOGWOOD FAMILY Cornaceae.

PACIFIC DOGWOOD *Cornus nuttallii* (Thomas Nuttall, a British botanist collected it in British Columbia). In SW Britain it is liable to die quite young for no apparent reason. The flowers for next spring are prominent on the tips of winter shoots. After a hot summer it may flower a second time when in full autumn colour. 3–6–12m. II.

fruit

▷

BENTHAM'S CORNEL *Cornus capitata* (growing in a dense head – the flowers). This nearly evergreen broad little tree grows from the Himalayas to China. It is grown in SW Britain, but is barely hardy near London. The shoot and leathery leaves have a soft grey down. The fruits are like erect crimson strawberries. 2–4–15m. I.

fl. 5

▷

TABLE DOGWOOD *Cornus controversa* (doubtful; alternate leaves found only in one other dogwood) is an eastern Asiatic tree of good size mostly in the south but grown north to Edinburgh. The alternate shiny leaves hang from level branches. 5–7–16m. I.

▷

  'Variegata' is a much prized small leafed, white variegated form. Very slow and small I.

fl. 5

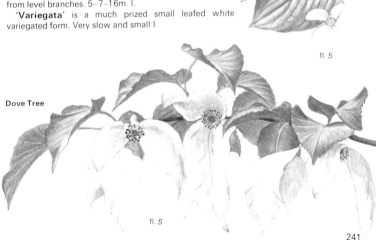

Dove Tree

fl. 5

fl. 5

● **HEATHER FAMILY** Ericaceae (Latin name for Heath) has 1500 species and includes Rhododendrons, Azaleas and heathers. *Arbutus* (classical name for Strawberry Tree) is a group of 15 evergreen trees with alternate leaves and pitcher-shaped flowers. The wood is pink, fine grained and very hard. Raised from seed.

fruit
underside *10*

◁ **STRAWBERRY TREE** *Arbutus unedo* ('I eat one', implying 'only one' as the delicious looking fruit has an unpleasant flavour). This is native to counties Kerry and Cork where it is shrubby over large areas, and in Co. Sligo. In England it is a tree of village gardens, churchyards and town parks, peculiarly ornamental in late autumn when the fruit turn from green to scarlet as the flowers open, but few trees bear as many fruit as those in Ireland. The dark pink shoot bears sparse, long fine hairs and small, blunt purple-red buds. The tree is raised from seed and the plants are slow and tender for a few years. 3–5–10m. I.

underside

◁ **HYBRID STRAWBERRY TREE** *Arbutus ×andrachnoides* (resembling *andrachne*, the Cyprus Strawberry Tree, one of its parents) occurs in the wild where Strawberry Tree and the Cyprus species grow together in Greece. It grows faster and bigger than either parent and is much hardier and grows further north, into S Scotland, but is uncommon. The leaf-stalk can be fleshy and winged, but trees vary in many details and even in whether to flower in the late autumn as in one parent, or in the spring as in the other. 5–8–13m. I.

underside

◁ **CYPRUS STRAWBERRY TREE** *Arbutus andrachne* (classical Greek) grows in SE Europe and around the eastern Mediterranean and needs the hottest and sunniest summers it can find in Britain. This practically confines its growth to East Anglia and the eastern half of the south coast. The shoots are yellow-green as is the bark of the upper crown but the bark of the trunk goes through a cycle from pale yellow to pink, red and rich chestnut orange which then starts to flake away to reveal pale yellow very smooth new bark. During this shedding period it is supremely attractive. 2–5–12m. I.

fruits
9

underside

◁ **PACIFIC MADRONE** *Arbutus menziesii* (Archibald Menzies, collected specimens in 1792) is very common in low hills from the coast of BC to mid-California. In Britain it is hardy as far north, in a sheltered place, as Elgin, Morayshire, but is not often seen. It has an upright, conic crown with curving branches rich red with peeling bark. Young shoots are smooth and green with relatively large green or pale brown conic buds. The thick leathery leaves are often blotched black before they fall. Propagation is from American seed. Seedlings have toothed leaves at first and can be tender. Once established they grow fast and this is among the best evergreen trees for town parks. 4–8–21m. I.

STRAWBERRY TREES

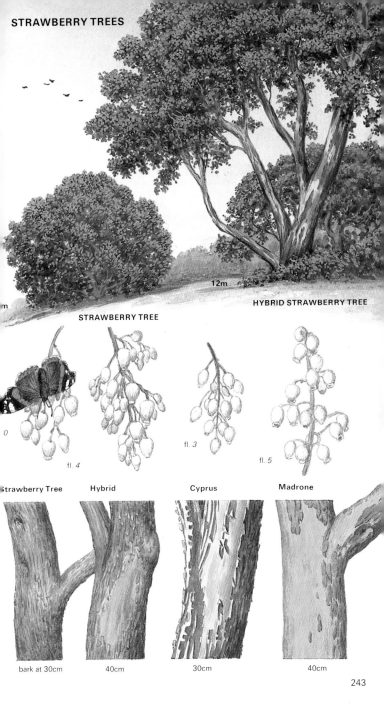

12m

HYBRID STRAWBERRY TREE

STRAWBERRY TREE

0

fl. 4

fl. 3

fl. 5

Strawberry Tree   Hybrid   Cyprus   Madrone

bark at 30cm   40cm   30cm   40cm

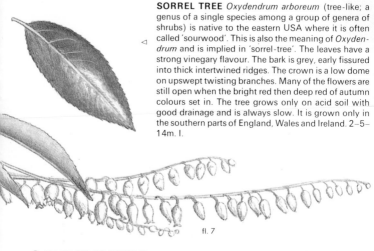

SORREL TREE *Oxydendrum arboreum* (tree-like; a genus of a single species among a group of genera of shrubs) is native to the eastern USA where it is often called 'sourwood'. This is also the meaning of *Oxydendrum* and is implied in 'sorrel-tree'. The leaves have a strong vinegary flavour. The bark is grey, early fissured into thick intertwined ridges. The crown is a low dome on upswept twisting branches. Many of the flowers are still open when the bright red then deep red of autumn colours set in. The tree grows only on acid soil with good drainage and is always slow. It is grown only in the southern parts of England, Wales and Ireland. 2–5–14m. I.

fl. 7

● **STORAX FAMILY** Styracaceae (classical name) extends from E Asia to S America and includes a few hardy deciduous small trees with white flowers. Raised from seed.

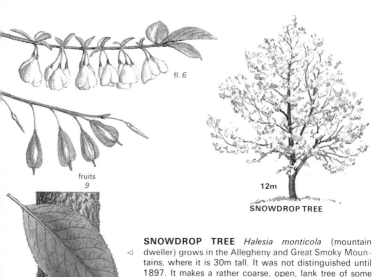

fl. 6

fruits
9

12m
SNOWDROP TREE

bark at 30cm

SNOWDROP TREE *Halesia monticola* (mountain dweller) grows in the Allegheny and Great Smoky Mountains, where it is 30m tall. It was not distinguished until 1897. It makes a rather coarse, open, lank tree of some vigour, splendid only when in flower. Hardy in the north, it is grown in all parts of Britain but not commonly. The bole with fissured grey or brown bark is usually curved and bears rather few spreading branches making a broad, irregular conic crown. The shoot is grey-brown with minute dark purple buds. Some leaves are 25 ×10cm; the stalk and underside are softly hairy. 5–8–15m. II.

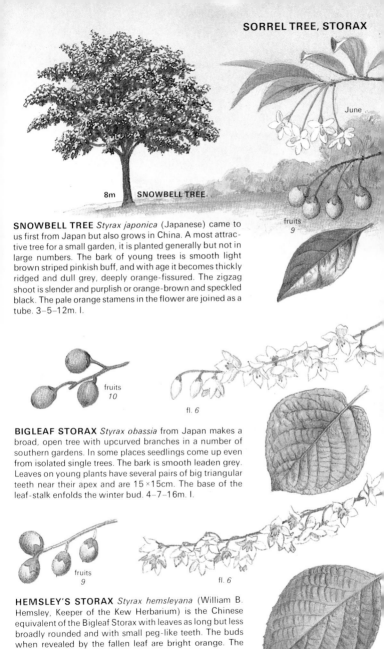

8m SNOWBELL TREE

June

fruits
9

SNOWBELL TREE *Styrax japonica* (Japanese) came to us first from Japan but also grows in China. A most attractive tree for a small garden, it is planted generally but not in large numbers. The bark of young trees is smooth light brown striped pinkish buff, and with age it becomes thickly ridged and dull grey, deeply orange-fissured. The zigzag shoot is slender and purplish or orange-brown and speckled black. The pale orange stamens in the flower are joined as a tube. 3–5–12m. l.

fruits
10

fl. 6

BIGLEAF STORAX *Styrax obassia* from Japan makes a broad, open tree with upcurved branches in a number of southern gardens. In some places seedlings come up even from isolated single trees. The bark is smooth leaden grey. Leaves on young plants have several pairs of big triangular teeth near their apex and are 15 ×15cm. The base of the leaf-stalk enfolds the winter bud. 4–7–16m. l.

fruits
9

fl. 6

HEMSLEY'S STORAX *Styrax hemsleyana* (William B. Hemsley, Keeper of the Kew Herbarium) is the Chinese equivalent of the Bigleaf Storax with leaves as long but less broadly rounded and with small peg-like teeth. The buds when revealed by the fallen leaf are bright orange. The flowers are smaller but more numerous as more spikes are on each shoot. It is a tree with less stout branches and is about as frequent. 5–8–12m. l.

245

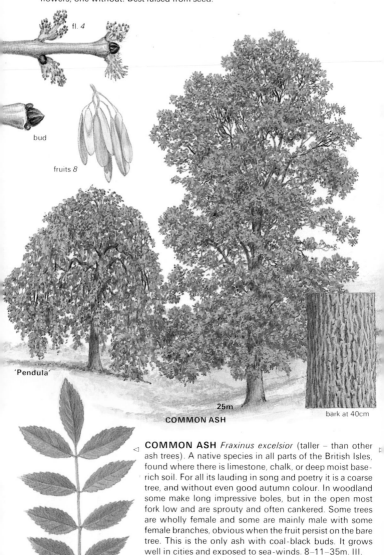

● **OLIVE FAMILY** Oleaceae (Olea – Latin for Olive) contains many fragrant flowering shrubs like Lilac and Jasmine, but also ash trees. All have opposite leaves.

ASHES *Fraxinus* (the Classical name). Two groups, one with petalled scented flowers, one without. Best raised from seed.

fl. *4*

bud

fruits *8*

'Pendula'

25m
COMMON ASH

bark at 40cm

COMMON ASH *Fraxinus excelsior* (taller – than other ash trees). A native species in all parts of the British Isles, found where there is limestone, chalk, or deep moist base-rich soil. For all its lauding in song and poetry it is a coarse tree, and without even good autumn colour. In woodland some make long impressive boles, but in the open most fork low and are sprouty and often cankered. Some trees are wholly female and some are mainly male with some female branches, obvious when the fruit persist on the bare tree. This is the only ash with coal-black buds. It grows well in cities and exposed to sea-winds. 8–11–35m. III.

Weeping Ash 'Pendula' is usually grafted at 2m and its shoots soon scrape the ground. A few, grafted at 10m or more, are tolerable trees. III.

246

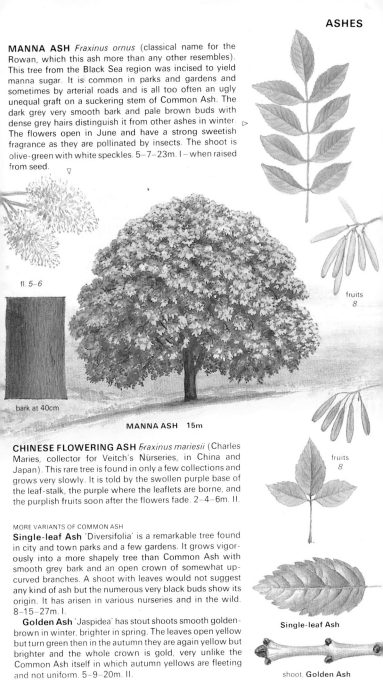

MANNA ASH *Fraxinus ornus* (classical name for the Rowan, which this ash more than any other resembles). This tree from the Black Sea region was incised to yield manna sugar. It is common in parks and gardens and sometimes by arterial roads and is all too often an ugly unequal graft on a suckering stem of Common Ash. The dark grey very smooth bark and pale brown buds with dense grey hairs distinguish it from other ashes in winter. The flowers open in June and have a strong sweetish fragrance as they are pollinated by insects. The shoot is olive-green with white speckles. 5–7–23m. I – when raised from seed.

fl. 5–6

bark at 40cm

fruits 8

MANNA ASH 15m

CHINESE FLOWERING ASH *Fraxinus mariesii* (Charles Maries, collector for Veitch's Nurseries, in China and Japan). This rare tree is found in only a few collections and grows very slowly. It is told by the swollen purple base of the leaf-stalk, the purple where the leaflets are borne, and the purplish fruits soon after the flowers fade. 2–4–6m. II.

fruits 8

MORE VARIANTS OF COMMON ASH

Single-leaf Ash 'Diversifolia' is a remarkable tree found in city and town parks and a few gardens. It grows vigorously into a more shapely tree than Common Ash with smooth grey bark and an open crown of somewhat upcurved branches. A shoot with leaves would not suggest any kind of ash but the numerous very black buds show its origin. It has arisen in various nurseries and in the wild. 8–15–27m. I.

Golden Ash 'Jaspidea' has stout shoots smooth goldenbrown in winter, brighter in spring. The leaves open yellow but turn green then in the autumn they are again yellow but brighter and the whole crown is gold, very unlike the Common Ash itself in which autumn yellows are fleeting and not uniform. 5–9–20m. II.

Single-leaf Ash

shoot. Golden Ash

247

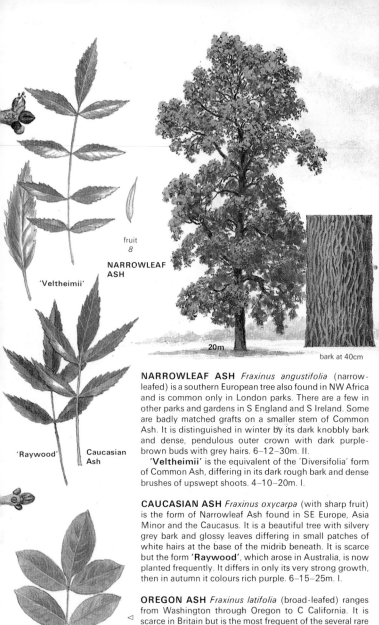

fruit
8

NARROWLEAF
ASH

'Veltheimii'

'Raywood'   Caucasian
              Ash

20m

bark at 40cm

NARROWLEAF ASH *Fraxinus angustifolia* (narrow-leafed) is a southern European tree also found in NW Africa and is common only in London parks. There are a few in other parks and gardens in S England and S Ireland. Some are badly matched grafts on a smaller stem of Common Ash. It is distinguished in winter by its dark knobbly bark and dense, pendulous outer crown with dark purple-brown buds with grey hairs. 6–12–30m. II.

'**Veltheimii**' is the equivalent of the 'Diversifolia' form of Common Ash, differing in its dark rough bark and dense brushes of upswept shoots. 4–10–20m. I.

CAUCASIAN ASH *Fraxinus oxycarpa* (with sharp fruit) is the form of Narrowleaf Ash found in SE Europe, Asia Minor and the Caucasus. It is a beautiful tree with silvery grey bark and glossy leaves differing in small patches of white hairs at the base of the midrib beneath. It is scarce but the form '**Raywood**', which arose in Australia, is now planted frequently. It differs in only its very strong growth, then in autumn it colours rich purple. 6–15–25m. I.

OREGON ASH *Fraxinus latifolia* (broad-leafed) ranges from Washington through Oregon to C California. It is scarce in Britain but is the most frequent of the several rare ashes with hairy shoots and leaf-stalks. The underside of the leaflet is white with soft woolly hairs. The bark is criss-crossed with shallow buff-grey ridges. 6–15–25m. II.

248

bark at 40cm

WHITE ASH 20m

WHITE ASH *Fraxinus americana* has an extensive range
in N America from Nova Scotia to Texas and Florida. It ▷
has long been known to outgrow the Common Ash in
Britain, but it needs good soil to grow well and has not
been widely planted. The leaves are variable in size,
whiteness beneath and toothing, and may even be entire.
The small, conic buds are pale brown. Male and female
flowers are on separate trees. Autumn colour is unreliable
and variable in Britain and is yellow to brown, not showing the purple bronzing so distinct a feature in America.
8–17–26m. II.

RED ASH; GREEN ASH *Fraxinus pennsylvanica* is in
two distinct forms formerly separated under these names,
but there is every gradation between them so they are
now regarded as one species. Both are scarce in Britain. ▷
The Red Ash is like the White Ash but has more slender
leaflets and they are green and finely hairy beneath, as is
the shoot. The Green Ash form has stout shiny green
hairless shoots and leaflets without hairs. In autumn its
leaves start early to turn pale yellow then become a good
bright gold lasting up to a week. In America these trees
have an even wider range than the White Ash, reaching
west to Alberta, Montana and Colorado. 7–15–24m. I.

fl. 4

PRIVETS *Ligustrum* (the Latin name) are 50 Old World species, mainly evergreen.

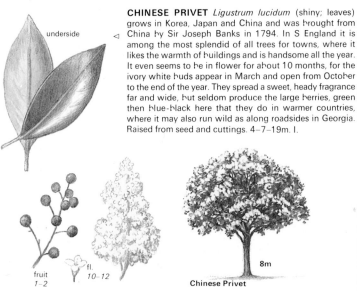

underside ◁

CHINESE PRIVET *Ligustrum lucidum* (shiny; leaves) grows in Korea, Japan and China and was brought from China by Sir Joseph Banks in 1794. In S England it is among the most splendid of all trees for towns, where it likes the warmth of buildings and is handsome all the year. It even seems to be in flower for about 10 months, for the ivory white buds appear in March and open from October to the end of the year. They spread a sweet, heady fragrance far and wide, but seldom produce the large berries, green then blue-black here that they do in warmer countries, where it may also run wild as along roadsides in Georgia. Raised from seed and cuttings. 4–7–19m. I.

fruit
1–2

fl.
10–12

8m

Chinese Privet

PHILLYREA (Greek name) is a small group of Mediterranean evergreen shrubs and small trees.

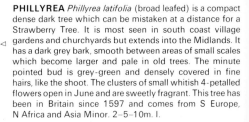

fl. 5

9m

bark at 30cm

◁

PHILLYREA *Phillyrea latifolia* (broad leafed) is a compact dense dark tree which can be mistaken at a distance for a Strawberry Tree. It is most seen in south coast village gardens and churchyards but extends into the Midlands. It has a dark grey bark, smooth between areas of small scales which become larger and pale in old trees. The minute pointed bud is grey-green and densely covered in fine hairs, like the shoot. The clusters of small whitish 4-petalled flowers open in June and are sweetly fragrant. This tree has been in Britain since 1597 and comes from S Europe, N Africa and Asia Minor. 2–5–10m. I.

● **EBONY FAMILY** Ebenaceae is a mainly tropical family which includes the tree giving ebony wood, but only the Date-plums *Diospyros* (the Godsberry, from the edible fruit of some species) are hardy in Britain. Raised from seed.

bark at 30cm

DATE PLUM   12m

DATE-PLUM *Diospyros lotus* (classical Greek name given to many different plants) has, like all species of *Diospyros*, male and female flowers on separate trees, and shoots which do not form a winter-bud at their tip. It is native to a wide area from Japan and China westwards perhaps as far as Asia Minor. It is scarce in Britain but not confined to the south. In autumn it appears to be evergreen as the leaves are green and shiny well into the season but they fall still green. On warm, still days, a scent of black currants is detectable around the trees. The fruit are inedible. 3–6–15m. II.

fl. 8

fruit 9

PERSIMMON *Diospyros virginiana* grows wild from New York State to Texas where the hanging bunches of pinkish yellow fruit amongst leaves turned black are a familiar roadside sight in autumn and the blackish boles of bark ridged in blocks stand out in hillside woods. In Britain it is grown only in a few southern gardens and particularly at Kew. It generally does not ripen the fruit here which in America are highly esteemed. The length of leaf on a single shoot can vary between 1cm and 20cm and when crushed they give a sweet scent. The shoot is red-brown with a slight silver covering. 3–6–11m. III.

The related species grown in S Europe for its decorative and edible fruits is *Diospyros kaki*.

fl. 7

fruit 9

● **BIGNONIA FAMILY** Bignoniaceae (Abbé Jean Bignon, librarian to Louis XIV) is a family mostly of climbers and one genus of trees – *Catalpa* (American Indian name) of which there are 11 species, from N America, W Indies and China. Raised from seed.

NORTHERN CATALPA *Catalpa speciosa* (beautiful; showy) is native to the middle Mississippi Valley. The cold winters there make this tree much more suitable to the British climate than the Indian Bean Tree, but it was introduced 154 years later, in 1880 and has never caught up. It is much less common but there are a few in most southern areas. Some are grafts at 1m or more on Indian Bean stock and the change in the bark from the brown and scaly stock to the grey and deeply ridged upper part is prominent. The flowers open in June–July nearly a month before those of the Indian Bean. 4–8–18m. I.

fl. 7

◁

INDIAN BEAN TREE *Catalpa bignonioides* (related to the Bignonia Vine) comes from the coastal plain of the Gulf of Mexico east of Louisiana. It is the common Catalpa of London and other southern cities, and in gardens it can be found far into NE Scotland but seldom flowers in the north. It fails to ripen its top buds in autumn, so they die in winter. New shoots arise from lower down, and to grow a good bole all but the strongest shoots should be cut out. Easily raised from imported seed. It is the last tree into leaf and one of the first to shed them. 6–9–19m. II.

fl. 8–9

◁

HYBRID CATALPA *Catalpa × erubescens* (growing red; new foliage is purple). This tree arose in Indiana as a cross between Indian Bean and the Yellow Catalpa in a nursery. By grafting it at base on to Indian Bean strong young plants are made which flower within a year of planting and may bear leaves to 38 × 33cm. Old trees are local in S England but young ones are being planted widely. The flowers are small, on a big, open head 30 × 20cm in August–September with a sweet fragrance of lilies. 8–13–20m. I.

fl. 9

◁

YELLOW CATALPA *Catalpa ovata* (with ovate leaves; egg-shaped tapering to the tip). This Chinese tree is unusual in gardens north to Edinburgh but sometimes in small front gardens and one is the central tree in the town of Leatherhead, Surrey. It has a darker crown than other Catalpas and the flowers open in early August. The leaves unfold dark purple and have hard hairs and veins beneath and on the stalks. They are about 20–25cm. 5–7–12m. I.

◁

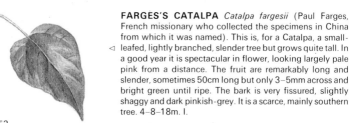

FARGES'S CATALPA *Catalpa fargesii* (Paul Farges, French missionary who collected the specimens in China from which it was named). This is, for a Catalpa, a small-leafed, lightly branched, slender tree but grows quite tall. In a good year it is spectacular in flower, looking largely pale pink from a distance. The fruit are remarkably long and slender, sometimes 50cm long but only 3–5mm across and bright green until ripe. The bark is very fissured, slightly shaggy and dark pinkish-grey. It is a scarce, mainly southern tree. 4–8–18m. I.

◁

10m   **INDIAN BEAN TREE**

bark at 40cm

● **FIGWORT FAMILY** Scrophulariaceae (some herbs in the family were remedies for scrofula) includes a genus of about 10 Chinese trees. *Paulownia*.

ripe fruits, 9

fl. 5

16m   in flower, 5

PAULOWNIA *Paulownia tomentosa* (densely hairy – the foliage. Princess Anna Paulovna was the daughter of Czar Paul I of Russia). First introduced from China *via* Japan. It is fairly frequent in gardens and towns in S England and SE Ireland. Growing very fast from seed, it makes a shoot up to 2.5m long in its second year, 4cm across, but nearly hollow and easily bent. On these young growths leaves can be 40 × 30cm and have slender pointed teeth each side near the base. The brown hairy flower-buds stand through the autumn and winter on branched heads 20–30cm long. The bark is smooth, brown then grey. 9–15–25m. l.

253

● **AGAVE FAMILY** Agavaceae (from the Greek for 'admirable' – many species have imposing candelabras of flowers) contains one genus of one true tree hardy over most of the British Isles – Cordyline (Greek for 'club-shaped' from the shape of the stem in some species). It also includes the Yuccas, which grow from a short woody stem but which do not make trees here. Like the Palms (opposite), plants in this family produce a single, central bud which pushes new leaves up and out at the top. In the Cabbage Tree there is no external cambium; instead, the leaves stay connected to the roots by bundles of tissues.

12m

Cabbage Tree

CABBAGE TREE *Cordyline australis* (southern), from New Zealand, is very common on the Isle of Wight, Isle of Man, and along the coast from S Devon to Tongue on the extreme north coast of Scotland and around the coasts of Ireland. It remains a single stem until it flowers, when it divides. Given a mild winter it is indifferent as to soil. Its hard, tough foliage withstand salt winds, so it is much planted near the sea. It is raised from seed, and in Ireland sows itself freely. Sprouts from the base can also be rooted as cuttings. 3–5–15m. II.

Canary
Palm

12m

Chusan Palm

12m

● **PALM FAMILY** Palmae. A large family widespread in the Tropics. The habit of growth does not allow branching, and unlike all other trees they do not thicken with age. The stem of a palm does not increase appreciably in diameter however old it is. Raised from seed.

CANARY PALM *Phoenix canariensis* is the most handsome palm common in hot dry regions and is hardy in Britain only in the Scilly Isles and in a few gardens by the south Devon and Cornish coast. The stout trunk sheds the leaf-bases, and becomes comparatively smooth with age. The leaves, bright green, can be up to 10m long, each leaf composed of a hundred or more slender parallel leaflets. ▷

CHUSAN PALM *Trachycarpus fortunei* (named after Robert Fortune, who brought tea out of China). This, from S China, is the only palm hardy almost throughout the British Isles. The trunk is encased in spine-edged leaf-bases and a thick layer of hard fibre. Mature trees bear several flower-heads at a time, each a panicle 60cm long with stout central stem, pale orange at base, shading to ivory white in the middle and branches, bearing small pale yellow flowers. The whole panicle is either male or female. The fruits hang in blue-black bunches from June onwards. ▷

Key to Broadleafed trees in winter

This is a key for the recognition of species and some important cultivars in winter. It uses only winter shoots and buds. The first page reference after each tree name is to the main section of the book. Further references, preceded by w, are to pages 259–63 with illustrations of forty types of distinctive winter silhouettes.

SHOOTS WITH THORNS

1 at base of each leaf or bud — **Osage Orange**, 160
2 at base of each leaf or bud — **Robinia**, 198, w 262
3 at base of each leaf or bud — **Honey Locust**, 199
spread along shoot
  well spaced out, 2–5cm long — **Thorns**, 175. **Pears**, 188
  close together, short — **Prickly Castor-Oil Tree**, 235

SHOOTS WITHOUT THORNS

BUDS NAKED – no bud scales
  alternate, stalked — **Wingnuts**, 116
  opposite, not stalked
    shoot fairly slender, pale brown — **Euodia**, 203
    shoot stout, orange-brown — **Amur Cork Tree**, 202

BUDS WITH SCALES
Opposite pairs
terminal bud lacking; laterals minute
  bud dark brown — **Paulownia**, 253
  bud orange-brown — **Catalpa**, 252
terminal bud present
  bud black, broad, low — **Common Ash**, 246, w 263
  bud dark brown, broad, hairy green — **Manna Ash**, 247
  bud medium-small, slender
    shoot smooth and slender
      shoot pale red-brown; bud shiny red — **Katsura Tree**, 167
      shoot red-brown; bud sharply pointed, dark red-brown — **Red Maple**, 221
      shoot dark red; bud stalked — **Snakebark Maple**, 219
      shoot pale orange-brown — **Field Maple**, 216, w 263
      shoot dark green; bud hairy grey — **Ashleaf Maple**, 215
      shoot bloomed grey on purple-brown — **Silver Maple**, 215
    shoot not slender, stout
      bud rounded, green; shoot olive-grey — **Sycamore**, 212, w 263
      bud (terminal) dark red-brown — **Norway Maple**, 210, w 263
  bud big, oval
    bud shiny, resinous, red-brown — **Horse Chestnut**, 226, w 263
    bud dull green, scale-margins dark red — **Red Horse Chestnut**, 227

Alternate (spiralled) buds
shoots harsh with warts
  shoot slender; warts white
    shoot dark brown — **Paper Birch**, 122
    shoot dark grey — **Silver Birch**, 122, w 260
  shoot medium stout; warts green — **Rauli**, 133

a cluster of buds, brown or red-brown, at tip of shoot — **Oaks**, 140–53
  bud with whiskers adhering — **Turkey Oak**, 141, w 261

shoot densely hairy
    shoot stout, pale brown, ribbed — **Hungarian Oak**, 144
    shoot medium-slender, brown, not ribbed — **Downy Oak**, 141
shoot red-brown, slightly ribbed, bud
    red-brown — **Red Oak**, 148
shoot orange-brown, smooth, bud tipped
    by grey hairs — **Scarlet Oak**, 148
shoot pale grey-green, grey or brown
    bud dark red-brown, few-scaled — **Common Oak**, 140, w 261
    bud pale brown, many-scaled — **Sessile Oak**, 140, w 261

buds flattened, like two hands pressed together — **Tulip-tree**, 166

lateral bud stalked — **Alders**, 128
    shoot downy, pale brown, soon grey — **Grey Alder**, 128
    shoot smooth
        purple — **Common Alder**, 128, w 260
        dark purple-brown, speckled — **Italian Alder**, 128
        dark red, bud dark red — **Red Alder**, 128

bud shiny and sticky with resin
    bud slender, laterals pressed closely to the
        shoot, dark brown — **Poplars**, 108–11
        shoot shining pale yellow — **Black Poplars**, 109, w 259
        shoot dark red-brown, purplish — **Western Balsam Poplar**, 111
    bud broad-conic, dark brown — **Aspen**, 110, w 259
    bud bright red
        bud slender, shoot dark grey-green — **'Embley' Rowan**, 178
        bud broad, blunt, shoot dark brown,
        very stout — **Sargent Rowan**, 178
    bud bright green, rounded — **Service Trees**, 177, 180–2
        shoot smooth, brown — **Wild Service Tree**, 180
        shoot downy or smooth, olive — **True Service Tree**, 177

bud with fine, bright yellow scales on each
    bud-scale; slender, curved tip — **Bitternut**, 120

bud broad, flattish, shoot very stout
    shoot orange
        shoot pale, bud hairy grey — **Black Walnut**, 118
        shoot dark, bud very small, smooth — **Tree of Heaven**, 204
    shoot dark purple with grey — **Common Walnut**, 118, w 259
    shoot pale grey
        bud yellow-brown, downy, beaked — **Varnish Tree**, 206
        bud flat, shoot bloomed violet and pink — **Kentucky Coffee Tree**, 201
    shoot less stout, pale copper-brown — **Pride of India**, 236

bud and shoot hairy
    bud hairy at base only, smooth tip — **Grey Poplar**, 110
    shoot with white wool, wearing away to
        leave green
        bud orange-brown, shoots long and
        slender, narrowly angled — **White Poplar**, 110
        bud green and brown, shoots short and
        stout, widely angled — **Silver Lime**, 232
    shoot stout
        shoot green to purple, bud with pale green
        inner scales and brown outer scales — **Shagbark Hickory**, 120
        shoot dark red-brown, bud dull red-brown — **Wych Elm**, 154

shoot slender
  shoot dark grey and pink-brown — **White Willow**, 114, w 249
  shoot red-brown, bud dark brown — **Elms**, 155, w 261
  shoot grey-brown with white hairs — **Zelkovas**, 158–9
shoot medium-slender, grey-brown; bud
  purple-black — **Persian Ironwood**, 171

bud hairy, shoot smooth
  shoot stout
    shoot dark orange-grey, bud purple and grey — **Rowan**, 177, w 262
    shoot green, bud big, hairy grey — **Magnolias**, 162–5
  shoot medium, dark grey, bud dark brown — **Whitebeams**, 182, w 262
  shoot slender, dark green, bud whitish green — **Laburnum**, 200, w 262

bud smooth, shiny, shoot densely hairy
  shoot green, slender — **Japanese Crab Apple**, 184
  shoot green and red, zigzag, medium stout — **Broad-leafed Lime**, 230
  shoot pale brown
    slender — **Roblé Beech**, 133
    stout to medium — **Hazel**, 132, w 260
  shoot red-brown, warted — **Rauli**, 133
  shoot dark brown, slender — **White Birch**, 122

bud smooth, shoot finely downy
  shoot pale grey-brown, stout — **Common Mulberry**, 160
  shoot dull grey-brown to red-brown, ribbed — **Sweet Chestnut**, 138, w 260
  shoot dark red-brown — **Rauli**, 133
  shoot dark green — **Pagoda Tree**, 199
  shoot green and red — **Broad-leafed Lime**, 230

bud smooth, shoot smooth
  shoot zigzag
    shoot slender, bud slender and pointed
      shoot pale red-brown, bud dark
      red-brown — **Hornbeam**, 130, w 260
      shoot dark brown, bud chestnut-brown — **Beech**, 133, w 260
    shoot medium stout
      shoot dark purple — **'John Downie' Crab**, 187
      shoot olive-green to purple-brown — **London Plane**, 173, w 262
  bud deep shiny red
    bud rounded
      shoot red-brown — **Small-leafed Lime**, 230, w 263
      shoot dark brown — **Sallow**, 112, w 259
    bud pointed, shoot dark brown, speckled
    pale — **Dove Tree**, 240
  bud yellow-brown
    shoot shiny bright green — **Sassafras**, 169
    shoot olive-brown — **Crack Willow**, 112, w 259
    shoot yellow — **Weeping Willow**, 114, w 259
  bud shiny green, shoot pale yellow-brown — **Sweetgum**, 170
  bud green and red, shoot green and red — **Common Lime**, 230, w 263
  bud pale brown, shoot glossy olive-green — **Bay Willow**, 112
  bud dark brown, shoot shiny dark brown — **Bird Cherry**, 195, w 262
  bud red-brown
    shoot pale grey, speckled — **Snowy Mespil**, 176
    shoot yellow-brown — **Wild Cherry**, 196, w 262
  bud dark purple-brown, shoot dark purple,
  grey and brown — **Judas Tree**, 196

Winter silhouettes. On these pages are shown the typical silhouettes of forty common broadleafed trees in winter – specimens growing well in the open.

...arch. Central stem continues ...o nearly to the tip, *p.70*

Black Poplar. Shoots bunched; branches ends droop with age, *p.108*

Lombardy Poplar. Far the commonest tree of this shape, *p.108*

...hite Poplar. Rarely makes ...straight tree, *p.110*

Grey Poplar. Sturdy; big branches carry domes of twigs, *p.110*

Aspen. Usually leans, *p.110*

...rack Willow. Heavy, low ...anches make a broad crown, ...112

...allow. Shoots stout ...d short, *p.112*

White Willow. Erect branches carry slender, upright shoots, *p.114*

Weeping Willow. Shoots *yellow*, brightest after mid-winter, *p.114*

259

Walnut. The branches, both large and small, are twisted, *p.118*

Silver Birch. Most weeping when in the open, *p.122*

Common Alder. Usually by water, *p.128*

Hornbeam. Fine straight shoots make a big dome, *p.130*

Hazel. Most often a man stemmed bush, *p.132*

Beech. When in woods, the boles are long and clean, *p.133*

Sweet Chestnut. A tall, irregular dome of stout shoots, *p.138*

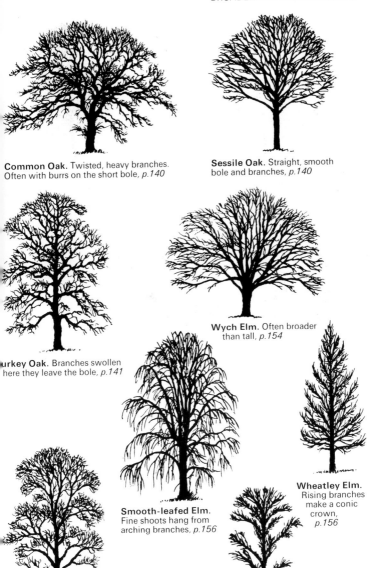

Common Oak. Twisted, heavy branches. Often with burrs on the short bole, *p.140*

Sessile Oak. Straight, smooth bole and branches, *p.140*

Turkey Oak. Branches swollen where they leave the bole, *p.141*

Wych Elm. Often broader than tall, *p.154*

Smooth-leafed Elm. Fine shoots hang from arching branches, *p.156*

Wheatley Elm. Rising branches make a conic crown, *p.156*

English Elm. Only fine shoots and big branches leave the bole, *p.155*

Cornish Elm. Arched branches with shoots held close, *p.156*

BROADLEAFED TREES IN WINTER

Rowan. Stout and upright shoots, *p.177*

London Plane. Twisting branches. Many hanging fruits persist through the winter, *p.173*

Swedish Whitebeam. A low crown but with a stout bole, *p.*

Whitebeam. Upright when young, less so with age, *p.182*

Wild Cherry. A straight stem, continuing well into the crown, *p.189*

Bird Cherry. Slender shoo a small upright tree, *p.195*

Robinia. Becomes irregular, with twisting branches and straight shoots, *p.198*

Laburnum. Branches arching out, *p.200*

Norway Maple. A short bole with long straight shoots, *p.210*

Sycamore. Short-jointed, narrow shoot systems; in woods the bole can be long, *p.212*

Field Maple. A good dome of fine, straight twigs, *p.216*

Common Lime. Vertical branches to the top of the crown, *p.230*

Horse Chestnut. The side branches arch down with age, *p.226*

Small-leafed Lime. Systems of short-jointed, fine shoots, *p.230*

Common Ash. Some branches can carry fruit in winter, *p.246*

263

Notable trees in the British Isles

This section is a guide to the principal specimens of British trees, with their locations and measurements. The specimens have been chosen both to give a range of the finest trees in the land (including some young ones of great promise) and also to give a wide geographical coverage: thus a tree growing well beyond its British range may be included although only a moderate specimen.

Status and **frequency**. After each tree's English name is given the date, where known, of its first introduction to Britain; or the letter N for native species or forms. General frequency in Britain today is given as:

C = common   F = frequent   O = Occasional   R = rare

- sometimes qualified by a further abbreviation in parentheses.
Thus 'O (SW)' indicates a tree to be found occasionally in SW Britain only.

Dimensions. The first figure given after each location is the *height* in metres (for measuring heights, see the inside back cover). The second is the *diameter* of the trunk, in centimetres, measured at 1.5m above ground level except where otherwise indicated. Occasionally a measurement is omitted as uncertain or misleading. Where either height or diameter or both are given in *bold* type, this is the largest specimen of that dimension known in Britain and Ireland.

Any such records are inevitably dated even when published, for two reasons. First, the biggest trees are generally the oldest, and so most liable to death and decay. Second, trees are always growing: with many of the exotic species the biggest specimens in Britain are still growing rapidly.

The gale of 16 October 1987, with winds of up to 100 m.p.h. over a line from the Isle of Wight to East Anglia, struck shortly before this edition went to press. There had been heavy rainfall and the soil gave minimum root-hold. A late wet summer had left foliage still green and well-fixed. The scene was set for maximum destruction.

In fact, it had little effect on the trees listed here *except* for those in Kent and Sussex. In Surrey, there were a few important but isolated losses. In London, it was mainly native trees like oaks and common exotics like lime, horse-chestnut and plane that caused the most spectacular damage. At Kew, nearly all the most important old trees survived, and in London parks only 2 or 3 trees blown down in each was of particular interest.

In Kent and Sussex, however, destruction in places was wholesale. As far as possible, we have revised this list with regard to major collections such as Sheffield Park and Wakehurst Place. But the full extent of the losses will take years to collate. Any tree recorded in this region may now no longer be standing − except for Maidenhair Trees, Giant Sequoias and Dawn Redwoods, not one of which is known to have been blown down.

Access. The gardens and collections cited here are those known to be open to the public. But a few belong to schools or hotels and may not always be open, and some are private gardens only open at certain times under charity schemes. Changes of ownership or policy also affect this and it is always best to enquire before a visit whether a garden is in fact open. In a few cases a tree which is *not* accessible, and whose owner does not welcome publicity, is of such superior size that it has to be mentioned. Its location is given only as a county, eg (Devon).

Addresses. For clarity and ease of reference, and to avoid much repetition of county names, the locations are given in their briefest form. Fuller addresses are given in alphabetical order on pp. 278-81.

Maidenhair Tree 1754 F (s). Cobham Hall Sch 20-118. Blaise Cas 24-125. Whitfield Ho 20-134. Terrace Gdn, Richmond 27-80. Abbotsbury (Lr Pool Walk) 27-44. Bath BG 26-58. Cathays Pk 22-68. Kew 25-135 at 1m. Battersea Pk (Rose Gdn) 20-38. Stowe Pk 25-110. Holker Pk 21-86. Longleat 25-100. *p.24.*

Common Yew N.C. Wardour Old Cas 25-100 at 1m. Close Walks. Midhurst **28**-64. Selborne -255. Brockenhurst 21-196. Tisbury -301. Ulcombe Ch, Kent - **333.** Belvoir Cas **29**-90.
  'Fastigiata' c.1800 C. Lanhydrock 15m. Pencarrow **16m**, 15m. Armadale Cas 12m. Mylor Ch some 20 trees 10-11m. *p.24.*

California Nutmeg 1851 O. Exeter Univ 20-101. Castlewellan 20-104. Batsford Pk 21-82. Stourhead 20-55. Stonefield 13-99. Benmore 14-84. Birr Cas 16-67. Fota 15-**110**. *p.20.*

Japanese Nutmeg 1764 R. Victoria Pk, Bath 13-24. Bedgebury 9-16. *p.26.*

Japanese Cowtail Pine 1829 O. At Bedgebury and Kew. *p.26.*

Chinese Cowtail Pine 1848 O. Leigh Pk 9-18. Borde Hill 9-14. Pencarrow 8-51 at 0.5m. Bodnant 4-13. Nymans 5-14. *p.27.*

Plum-fruited Yew 1860 O. Kew 13-44. Exbury Ho 12-37 at 0.5m. Powerscourt 13-29. Birr Cas 16-33. Bodnant 12-40. Ashbourne Ho 19-62. *p.28.*

Totara 1847 R (S & W). Kilmacurragh 10-33. Morrab Gadns, Penzance 7-34. Trebah 20-97. Lydhurst 10-14. Heligan **19**-99. Inverewe 16-51. Bosahan 14-61. Tregrehan 18-65. *p.28.*

Chilean Totara 1847 O.(SW & Ireland). Kilmacurragh 12-78. Scorrier Ho **19**-87 at 1m. *p.28*

Willow Podocarp 1853 O. (F in SW & Ireland). Bicton 18-57. Trengwainton 19-58. Penjerrick 17-48. Powerscourt 18-**76**. Tregrehan 22-56. *p.28.*

Large-leaf Podocarp 1861 R. (SW) Tregrehan 5-11. Bicton 6.5-10. Nymans 3-5. Singleton Abbey 9-30. *p.28.*

Prince Albert's Yew 1847 O. (S & W). Kilmacurragh **18**-48. Woodhouse 18-55. Castlewellan 14-60 at 1m. Leonardslee 13-24. Fota 14-38. *p.29.*

Monkey-puzzle 1795 O. Lochnaw **29**-99. Bicton Ho 28-126, 29-116. Castle Kennedy 25-96. Armadale Cas 23-98. Cairnsmore 24-115. Hafodunas 25-105. Holker 27-110. Craigievar 22-112. *p.30.*

Incense Cedar 1853 F. Doune Ho **37**-**172**. Killerton 32-102. Orchardleigh 34-126. Eastnor Cas 32-174 at 1m. Westonbirt 33-111. Roche's Arb 34-77. Kinfauns 32-157. Nuneham 31-125. Endsleigh **39**-133. *p.31.*

Chilean Incense Cedar 1847 R. Wakehurst Pl 14-30. Mt Usher 13-**41**. Howick 12-40 at 1m. Tatton Pk 13-22. Wisley 17-35. Westonbirt 13-22. *p.31.*

Lawson Cypress 1854 C. Powerscourt (Dargle Glen) 27-**150**. Killerton 34-101. Balmacaan 40-136. Rhinefield Drive, New Forest 37-136. 34-92. Achnacarry 36-144. Reelig Glen 31-108. *p.32.*

Hinoki Cypress 1861 F. Powerscourt 23-61. Killerton 24-63. Petworth Ho 25-54. Strone 22-78. Culdees 19-78. Cowdray Pk 16-79. *p.34.*

Sawara Cypress 1861 F. Killerton 25-85,23-80. Longleat 24-67. Cowdray Pk 28-88. Strone 24-68. Tottenham Ho 23-78. Glamis Castle 15-68. *p.35.*

Nootka Cypress 1851 C. Eridge Cas 25-101. Moss's Wood, Leith Hill 27-86. Dawyck 27-91. Stourhead 28-86. Cawdor Cas 28-89. Blair Drummond **31**-99. Penrhyn Cas 25-95. *p.36.*

White Cedar 1736 R. Bedgebury **15**-**43**. Woburn Abbey (Playland) 14-37. Borde Hill 15-34. Kew 13-27. *p.36.*

Formosan Cypress 1910 R. Sheffield Pk **22**-48. Headfort 13-58. Nymans 17-45. Borde Hill 16-71 at 1m. Hergest Croft 15-45. Bicton 16-34. Westonbt 15-34. Fota 16-72. *p.36.*

Leyland Cypress 1888 C. Bicton 36-97, 32-80. Leighton Pk 30-108. Haggerston Pk 29-85. Bedgebury 30-74. Wakehurst Pl 33-85. Wisley 28-101. Inveraray Cas 32-**110**. *p.36.*

Italian Cypress c.1500 O. Nymans **22**-35. Hardwicke Pk **22**-74. Killerton 21-61. Blenheim (Rose Gdn) 21-77. Singleton Abbey 20-61. Canon's Park 16-51 at 1m. Hergest Croft 19-41. *p.38.*

Monterey Cypress 1838 C. Montacute Ho 37-243. Abbotsbury 32-156. Melbury Pk 37-190. Powerscourt 31-375 at 0m. Johnstown Cas 33-253. Windsor Gt Pk (Obelisk) 32-146/ Moreton Ho **40**-**302**. Bicton 38-142. Ballywalter 32-210. *p.38.*

Gowen Cypress 1846 R. Wakehurst Pl 26-94, 20-58. Bicton 22-64. Thorp Perrow 18-37. *p. 39.*

Arizona Cypress 1882 R. Avondale **25**-**77** Mt Usher 19-66. Exbury Ho 20-52. *p.40.*

Smooth Arizona Cypress 1907 F. Powerscourt **24**-**76**. Coolhurst 23-48. Wisley 23-58. Birr Cas 23-70. Victoria Pk, Bath 24-55. *p.40.*

Mexican Cypress pre-1680 O. Bicton 24-67. Fota 20-119. Kilmacurragh 26-90. Abbotsbury 18-51. Wakehurst Pl 21-74. Borde Hill (Stonepit) 27-70. Leonardslee 22-59. *p.40.*

Bhutan Cypress 1824 R. Nettlecombe Ct **31**-**144**. Powerscourt 27-70. Abbotsbury 25-63. Hewell Gra 24-56. Batsford Pk 17-41. Keir Ho 22-77. Rossie Priory 22-70. Heanton 26-66. Abbeyleix 21-64. Fota 26-93. *p.40.*

Patagonian Cypress 1849 O. Strone 21-69. Kilmacurragh 17-**74**. Benmore 15-50. Killerton 15-44. Castlewellan 10-54. Belsay Cas 15-51. Bicton 17-49. Tregrehan 20-67. *p.40.*

Temple Juniper 1861 R. St Ronan's Sch **16**-**54**. Exton Pk 12-30. Leonardslee 13-28. Borde Hill 12-27. Bedgebury 11-30. *p.42.*

Syrian Juniper 1854 R. Batsford Pk **21**-68 at 1m. Brickendon Golf Crse 19-40. Leonardslee 20-22. Kew 15-24. *p.42.*

Chinese Juniper 1804 F. Westonbirt **21**-51. Highnam 19-**77**. Bowood 20-58. Possingworth Pk 20-36. Highnam Pinetum 21-67. Caledon Cas 18-73. Castlehill 18-57. *p.44.*

Pencil Cedar pre-1664 O. Holkham Ho 20-84. Ham Ho 15-82. Pittville Pk 14-75. Harkwicke Pk 18-69. Thorp Perrow 15-40. Killerton 14-95. Pains Hill 18-**149** at 1m. Moncrieffe Ho 17-79. Abbeyleix 20-93 at 1m. Wakehurst Pl 21-38. *p.44.*

Meyer's Blue Juniper 1914 C. Westonbirt (Mitch Dr) 9-16. Innes Ho 4-19. *p.45.*

Drooping Juniper 1830 R. Kilmacurragh 19-52. Birr Cas 15-61 + 50. Castlewellan 15-66 at 1m.? Rowallane 13-53. Pencarrow 12-41. Hafodunas 15-66. **Cox's** - Bodnant 10-41. Sheffield Pk 11-31. Exbury **19**-**50**. *p.45.*

Western Red Cedar 1853 C. Bicton 42-145, 39-181. Killerton 38-145. Stourhead 35-160. Armadale Cas 29-156. Powerscourt 35-173. Strone 46-168. Castlehill 37-173. Balmacaan 41-**193**. Belladrum 41-186. *p.46.*

Japanese Thuja 1860 R. Tregrehan **24**-70. Beneden Sch 22-90. Coed Coch 20-86. Patterdale Hall 18-96 at 1m. Avondale 16-64. Linton Pk 22-78. Castelwellan 18-60. Ochtertyre 17-84. *p.47.*

Chinese Thuja 1752 O. Battersea Pk 15-23. Melksham Sports Cl 14-31. Dyffryn Gdn 14m. E Malling Ch 15-54. Ewhurst Ch 12-49. *p.48.*

Korean Thuja 1918 R. Hergest Croft **13-22** Westonbirt 10-11. *p.48.*

Hiba 1853 O. Tregrehan 21-**86**. Penjerrick 23-37. Stonefield 18-59. Portmeirion **24**-40, 21-47. *p.48.*

Coast Redwood 1843 F. Roche's Arb **43**-137. Caledon Cas 37-229. Bowood 35-202. Melbury 41-209. Stourhead 39-206. Taymouth Cas Gdns 39-223, 38-221. Windsor Gt Pk 36-185. Bodnant **47**-159. Stuckgowan 45-196. The Gliffaes 43-205. Longleat 32-208. Fota 30-**230**. *p.50.*

Giant Sequoia 1853 F. Castle Loed **52**-280. Glenlee Pk 51-233. Cawdor Cas 50-238. Balmacaan 30-301, 48-219. Taymouth Cas 50-244. Scone place 40-280. Benmore 50-183. Ashford Old Mnr 49-163. Crowthorne Ave, Berks 42-265, 46-162. Wrest Pk 37-245. Powis Cas 38-306 Cluny Cas 36-**332**. Princeland 32-330. Myarth 50-224. Hutton-in-the-Forest 39-296. Rhinefield Terr 48-250. *p.50.*

Japanese Red Cedar 1842 C. Kilmory Cas 27-186. Monk Coniston 33-173. Windsor Gt Pk 31-129. Fota 35-148. The Gliffaes 22-171. Tregothnan 30-140. Endsleigh **41**-95 ('Lobbii'). *p.50.*

Swamp Cypress 1640 F. Broadlands 36-159. Burwood Pk **38-192**. Dean Court, Wimborne 33-188. Pusey Ho 29-146. R Gade, Watford 28-127. Elvaston Pk 25-123. Melbourne Ho 23-199. Gothic Lodge, Wimbledon 28-158. Arnos Pk, Midd 29-114. Kew (Palm House Pond) 28-116. Knaphill Nsy 31-110. Syon Ho 32-125. Dulwich Art Gall 26-99. Roezel Mnr, Jersey 34-144. The Rectory, Much Hadham 31-165. *p.52.*

Pond Cypress 1789 R. Beauport Pk 20-51. Knaphill Nsy 21-**75**, 20-68. Woburn Abbey 19-52. Nymans 18-37. Kew 18-43. *p.53.*

Dawn Redwood 1948 F. Wisley 26-56. Cambridge BG 21-80. Leonardslee 30-55, 22-78. Stourhead 21-67. Kew 24-74. Savill Gdn, Windsor 27-57. Clapton Ct 19-50. Killerton 19-48. Oxford BG 20-70. Cawdor Cas 10-29. Birr Cas 13-52. Central Pk, Bournemouth 24-**90**. Ladham Ho 21-70. River Dr, Esher 19-80. Penrhyn Cas 18-73. Sheffield Park 18-76. *p.53.*

King William Pine 1857 R. Kilmacurragh 16-**59**. Mt Usher 17-53. *p.54.*

Smooth Tasmanian Cedar 1857 R. Kilmacurragh **16**-47, 11-**50**. *p.54.*

Summit Cedar 1857 R. Scorrier Ho **18**-80. Kilmacurragh 18-61. Tullymore Pk12-33. Tregrehan 17-32. Benmore 13-42. *p.54.*

Japanese Umbrella Pine 1861 F. Beneden Sch 23-50. Chilworth Mnr 9-**57**. Armadale Cas 10-56. Kilmory Cas 12-57. Langholm Chase Hotel, Cumbria 15-44. Tilgate Pk 15-50. Bodnant 23-47. Sheffield Pk 17-48. Killerton 15-50. *p.54.*

Chinese Fir 1804 O. Bicton **31**-79. Pencarrow 25-**86**. Mt Usher 20-82. Oakley Pk 23-66. Claremont 21-72. Trebah 26-75. Killerton (Chapel) 26-77. Bedgebury 19-60. Crarae 13-34. Glendurgan 20-80. *p.55.*

Caucasian Fir 1847 F. Benmore 46-107. Powerscourt 28-**149**. Taymouth Cas 41-141. Stourhead 33-116. Cragside 47-109. Meikleour Ho 46-113. Dunans 43-109. *p.56.*

Beautiful Fir 1830 O. Benmore 35-97. Castlewellan 34-107. Taymouth Cas Gdns **132cm** diam. Hergest Croft 24-76. Leckmelm **40**-77. *p.57.*

Veitch's Silver Fir 1879 O. Gosford Cas 25-77. Hergest Croft 25-71. Glentanar 21-73. Dawyck 27-71, 26-72. Alnwick Cas 22-62. Crarae 19-66. Dunkeld Ho (nr Cathedral) 23-75. Stourhead 22-51. Dochfour 24-**95**. Benmore 27-55. *p.57.*

Maries's Fir 1879 R. Dawyck **23-58**. Leonardslee 22-34, 21-36. Bedgebury 18-40. *p.57.*

Bornmuller's Fir 1880 R. Bicton 30-82. Drum Mnr 20-95. Red Rice Coll 30-**118**. Cairnsmore 25-108. *p.57.*

Low's White Fir 1851 F. Durris Est 42-154. Blair Cas (Diana's Gr) 48-117. Powerscourt 42-112. Kilravock Cas 37-**189**. Bodnant 47-117. Cragside 49-117. Cawdor Cas 46-125. *p.58.*

Subalpine Fir 1863 R. Crarae For Gdn 16-27. Kilmun For Gdn 14-36. Coull Ho 19-**56**. Altyre **21**-35. *p.58.*

Cork Fir 1901 R. Ardross Cas 15-48. Bayfordbury 10-33. Hillier Arb 11-28. Highclere Cas 23-48. Pitcarmick 17-**53**. *p.58.*

Cilician Fir 1855 O. Speech Ho 25-**94**. Glenapp **33**-67. Rhinefield Terr 31-77. Culcreuch Cas 29-85. *p.58.*

Grand Fir 1831 C. Strone Ho 61-180. Moniac Glen 55-140. Lochanhead Hotel, Kirkcudb 43-217. Balmacaan 52-**232**. Blair Cas 56-155, 55-155. Bodnant 56-166. Abercairny 40-190. Glamis Cas 48-169. Dunkeld Ho (nr Cathedral) 51-141. Murthly Cas 55-149, 48-211. Brahan Ho 47-186. Leighton Woods **58**-136. Skelgill Wd 50-119. *p. 59.*

Noble Fir 1830 C. Taymouth Cas Gdns 47-171, 46-164. Durris 47-157, 45-163. Blair Cas (St Bride's chyd) 37-176, (Diana's Gr) 49-117, (drive) 30-160. Kirkerran 39-143. Ardross Cas 32-156. Cawdor Cas 44-158. Huntington Ho 35-177. Armadale Cas 38-141. Gosford Cas 32-165. Opp Benmore **50**-165. Bolderwood 45-135. Glenferness 39-**187**. Ardkinglas Ho 50-102. *p.60.*

Red Fir 1851 O. Cragside 40-94. Blair Cas (St Bride's chyd) **42-159**, (Diana's Gr) 38-100. Dunkeld Ho 41-115. Balmoral Cas 31-112. Walcot Pk 33-88. Taymouth Cas 39-116. *p.61.*

Forrest's Fir 1910 O. (Angus) **26-91**. Headfort 20-77, 21-70. Durris 22-54. Wakehurst Pl (Sands Pine) 21-39. Hergest Croft 14-53. RBG, Edinburgh 21-51. Tigh-na-Bruach 19-70. Crarae 20-56. *p.61.*

Himalayan Fir 1822 R. Powerscourt (Giant's Gr) **34**-86. Gosford Cas 25-**124**. Kilmacurragh 24-118. Aira Force 27-90. Fasque Ho 22-108. Castle Kennedy 26-103, 29-96. Howick 27-98. Portmeirion 29-93. Inveraray Cas (Limekilns) 28-88. *p.61.*

Pindrow Fir 1837 R. Aldourie Cas **34**-90. Kilmacurragh 30-**108**. Monk Coniston 34-102. Whittingehame Sch 28-96. Eastnor Cas 32-57. Mt Stewart 29-86. Eilean Shona 29-82. Kiftsgate 22-70. *p.61.*

East Siberian Fir 1908 R. Wakehurst Pl (Woodland V) **25**-48. Balmoral Cas 13-34. Dawyck Ho13-37. *p.62.*

King Boris's Fir 1883 R. Penrhyn Cas 38-106. Wakehurst Pl (Oaks) 28-113. Mt Stewart 30-106. Stonefield Cas **40-153**. Abbeyleix 31-126. *p.62.*

Sakhalin Fir 1878 R. Glasnevin BG 19-28. Hergest Croft 16-40. *p.62.*

Common Silver Fir 1603 F. Benmore **48**-159. Strone 45-**292**. Kilkerran 46-156. Powerscourt 44-160. Inchmarlo 43-177. Lingholm 44-140. Raehills 50-201. *p.63.*

Grecian Fir 1824 O. Bodnant 41-110. Tullymore Pk 28-**162**. Highclere Pk 35-142. Whittingehame Sch 26-142. Melbury 36-149. Hardwicke Pk 28-114. Oakley Pk 33-121. Hergest Croft 28-160. *p.64.*

Nikko Fir 1870 F. Taymouth Cas **34-115**. Abbeyleix 27-86. Castlewellan 22-97. Monteviot 30-86. Aigas Ho 23-77. Ardross Cas 24-87. Glamis Cas 26-108. Trentham 25-75. Brahan 28-96. *p.65.*

Spanish Fir 1837 O. Rhinefield Drive, New For 34-70. Lydhurst 24-**116**. Longleat 25-103. Windsor Gt Pk 22-83. Thorp Perrow 22-78. Burford Ho 29-92. Rosehaugh 23-115. *p.65.*

Algerian Fir 1862 R. Warnham Ct **33**-82. Castlewellan 26-**111**. Glasnevin BG 24-94. Hardwicke Pk 31-89. Wakehurst Pl 30-80. Borde Hill 30-88. Longleat (Pl Gdns) 25-105. *p.65.*

Korean Fir Hergest Croft 11-34. Dawyck 9-35. Wakehurst Pl 9-20. Tanadyce 10-37. Crarae 12-32. Durris 13-**53**. *p.66.*

Momi Fir 1861 O. Tregrehan 32-103. Balfour Mnr 31-**113**. Lr Combe Royal 31-105. Stourhead 29-99. Nymans **35**-83. *p.67.*

Min Fir 1910 R. Powerscourt 20-**57**. Wakehurst Pl 19-40. Abbotswood 22-50. Durris 17-48. *p.67.*

Santa Lucia Fir 1854 C. Exeter Univ (Streatham Hall) **38**-114, 26-116. Upper Hartfield (gdn) 27-81. Leonardslee 30-45. Althorp 35-**137**(forking). Smeaton Ho 27-64. Wakehurst Pl 31-61. *p.67.*

Manchurian Fir 1904 R. Borde Hill (Tolls) **24**-40. Headfort 21-**62**. Westonbirt (Sand Earth) 20-43. Terling Pl 20-40. Bedgebury 18-44. Birr Cas 18-47. *p.67.*

Deodar 1831 C. Whitfield Ho 37-148. Bolderwood Arb 37-101. Haffield Ho 32-160. Dunrobin Cas 29-112. Walcot Pk 32-132. Cricket Ho 29-141. Orchardleigh 30-136. Bristol Zoo 24-128. Eastnor Cas **38**-169, 38-160. Longford cas 31-136. Conon Ho 27-**180**. Stratford Pk 33-153. Ballindean 30-161. *p.68.*

Blue Atlas Cedar 1854 C. Brockhampton Pk **39**-136. Garston Ho 25-164. Horsley Towers 20-160. Ware Pk 23-146. Sandling Pk 27-134. Eastnor Cas (orig) 34-143, 32-**181**. Scone Pine 31-148. Patshull Ho 32-142. Lynhales 26-150. Merlewood Gra 31-149. Bowood 37-167. *p.68.*

Cedar of Lebanon 1638 C. Bowood 40-208, 40-181. Goodwood Pk 40-**286**. Blenheim Pal (Cascade) 29-269. Chilworth Manr 30-243. Sherborne Cas 37-197. Melbury 38-177. Claremont 32-221. Forty Hall 21-233. Garnons 37-225. Eastnor Cas 38-212. Peper Harow pl 1735 32-254. *p.68.*

Cyprus Cedar 1881 R. Borde Hill (Warren W) 23-50. Wakehurst Pl 21-56, **27**-50. Bedgebury 20-34, 17-43. Windsor Gt Pk (Botany Bay) 22-42, 21-48. Bicton 17-**57**. *p.68.*

European Larch 1620 C. Glenlee Pk 46-95. Monzie Cas 31-187. Dunkeld Ho (Cathedral) 32-173,'6' 40-106. Blair Cas (Old Blair Br) 43-134. Gordon Cas (Drive) 30-170. Downton Ho 20-148. Innes Ho 20-164. Parkhatch 45-98. Kilruddery Ho 19-149. Foulis Cas 20-175. Tottenham Ho 26-154. Nonsuch Ho 24-168. *p.70.*

Japanese Larch 1861 C. Blair Cas (Diana's Gr) 39-92. Dunkeld Ho '2' 31-90, (Drive) '12' 33-**101**, (Bishops Walk) 39-87. Ardross Cas (Ptm) 28-73. Monteviot Pinery 30-76. Glenapp 26-72. Brocklesby Pk 28-65. Avondale 26-77. Abbeyleix 27-85. Glen Ho 31-96. Abercairny 27-96. *p.70.*

Hybrid Larch 1897 F. Stourhead 30-82. Blair Cas (Gunroom Br) 24-**100**. Dunkeld Ho (Bishops' Walk fence) **40**-67. Dawyck 26-83. Glasnevin BG 20-61. Munches 28-99. Strone **40**-80. *p.70.*

Tamarack 1737 R. Wakehurst Pl 20-43. Cambridge BG 20-46. Blairquhan 18-33. *p.72.*

Western Larch 1881 R. Bayfordbury **28**-49. Kew 23-50. Dawyck 24-37. Bedgebury 24-34. Darnaway (old Pine) 19-40. *p72.*

Dahurian Larch 1872 R. Kyloe Wd **25**-39. Hergest Croft (Park Wd) 21-35. Wakehurst Pl 18-48. Brocklesby Pk 16-28. Achamore 17-**67**. *p.73.*

Sikkim Larch 1854 R. Strete Ralegh Pine 19-31, 18-74. Borde Hill (Gores Wd) 12-20. Rowallane 9-12. *p.73.*

Golden Larch 1854 R. Carclew Ho 20-83. Kew 18-60. Leonardslee 18-62. Biddulph Gra 15-35, 15-40. Wakehurst Pl (Drive) 10-50, (Gdn) 12-53. *p.73.*

Tiger-Tail Spruce 1861 O. Stourhead 27-77. Pencarrow 24-99. Petworth Ho 22-58. Trewidden 22-69. Walcot Pk 21-39. Batsford Pk 19-60. Powerscourt 20-49. Endsleigh 24-96. *p.74.*

Schrenk's Spruce1877 R. Nymans **22-34**. Kew 14-28. Wisley 17-29. Glasnevin BG 14-20. *p.74.*

Morinda Spruce 1818 O. Melbury **37**-112. Taymouth Cas Gdns 37-137. Castlewellan 23-133. Penryhn Cas 33-106. Fairburn 26-139. Eastnor Cas 34-112. *p.74.*

Brewer Spruce 1897 F. Wakehurst Pl (Valley) **20**-40. Kilmacurragh 15-**64**. Hergest Croft (Park Wd) 18-47. Dawyck 19-58. Dyffryn Gdn 15-54. Glentanar (Gdn) 18-63. Darnaway (Old Pine) 12-52. Kyloe Wood 14-43. St Ronan's Sch 19-54. Exbury 17-56. Leonardslee 20-49. Pitcarmick 20-51. Hergest Croft 18-61. *p.74.*

Sikkim Spruce 1878 R. Wakehurst Pl (Woodland Valley) **34**-73. Kilmacurragh 24-**77**. Drum Mnr 23-54. Bodnant 25-68. Borde Hill (Warren Wd) **34**-82. Sidbury Mnr 22-70. *p.75.*

Sargent Spruce 1901 R. Stourhead **32**-66. Westonbirt (Morley Dr) 28-62. Wakehurst Pl 26-82. Bicton 24-67. Stanage Pk 24-72. Birr Cas 23-57. Hergest Croft 25-68. Tregrehan 23-**84**. *p.76.*

Serbian Spruce 1889 F. Endsleigh 25-71. Castlewellan 21-68. Wakehurst Pl (Horsebr Wd)28-46. Savill Gdn, Berks 25-49. Colesbourne 25-39. Leonardslee 25-40. Murthly Cas **33**-65. Crarae 24-48. Glasnevin BG 27-29. *p.76.*

Oriental Spruce 1837 F. W Dean (Roche's Arb) 35-84. Blair Cas (Diana's Gr) 35-71. Broxwood Ct 28-118. Bowood 37-101. Bicton 31-85. Monk Coniston 27-90. Petworth Ho 33-85. Castle Milk 31-108. Monteviot Pinery 23-115. Aigas Ho 32-108. Mosses Wd 36-103. Culcreuch 34-107. *p.77.*

Sitka Spruce 1831 C. Kilravock Cas 41-228. Balmacaan 48-216. Castle Leod 51-187. Aigas (roadside) 50-140, Drumtochty Glen (roadside) 46-210. Ardanaiseig 40-200. Monteviot Pinery 38-196. Aira Force 36-200. Benmore (Glen Massen) 46-181, Scone Palace Pine 48-209 (three others similar). Abbeyleix 40-167. Powerscourt (Giant's Gr) 40-207. Randolph's Leap **58**-170. Woodhill 43-**252**. Fairburn 45-246. Castlehill 46-245. Ballogie 48-186. *p.77.*

Hondo Spruce 1861 F. Leonardslee 32-63. Benmore 28-**108**. Gnaton Hall 31-78. Ardross Cas (Pine) 24-86. Glengarry Cas Hotel 19-82. Bodnant 26-81. Glenapp 29-52. Monteviot Pinery 19-85. Eridge Cas **33**-91, 28-99. Tal-y-Garn 31-95. *p.77.*

Norway Spruce c.1500 C. Kincardine Cas (railway bank) 46-125. Lingholm 43-**147**. Cawdor Cas 36-128. Hackwood Pk 37-102. Moss's Wd. Leith Hill 32-100. Glenlee Pk 42-126. Bicton 29-114. Powerscourt 42-109. Moniac Glen **52**-80. Culdees 44-101. Ballindalloch 44-112. *p.78.*

Siberian Spruce 1908 O. Dawyck **19**-40. Glentanar 11-**43**. Westonbirt 15-26. Bedgebury 13-20. *p.78.*

Likiang Spruce 1910 O. Powerscourt 25-69. Bedgebury 19-69. Lamellan 22-62. Stanage Pk 24-61. Hergest Croft 25-58. Walcot Pk 19-51. Glasnevin BG 16-61. Beaufront Cas 21-**70**. *p.78.*

Colorado Blue Spruce 1877 C. Victoria Pk, Bath 25-42. Wimpole Ho 20-**69**. Batsford Pk (2) 27-63. Tring 22-62. Ramster 26-51. Knaphill Nsy 21-61 (Orig). Sandringham 22-55. Radley Coll 25-54. *p.79.*

Engelmann Spruce 1864 R. Dawyck 29-76. Powerscourt 24-38. Abbeyleix 29-42, 22-59. Darnaway (Old Pine) 18-43. Kailzie 21-50. Fairburn 30-48. *p.79.*

Black Spruce c.1700 O. Nymans 21-56, 22-53. Abbeyleix 1956, 19-51. Windsor Gt Pk 17-29. Rhinefield 24-46. Dawyck 20-42. *p.80.*

Red Spruce pre-1750 R. Rhinefield Drive 26-50. Glentanar (Pine) 17-57. Bedgebury 20-48. Dawyck 18-40. Windsor Gt Pk 19-41. Crarae 15-54. *p.80.*

White Spruce pre-1700 O. Merlewood Gra 20-59. Crarae 20-50. Wisley 17-45. Eridge Cas 26-**80**. Castle Milk 23-51. Ardverikie 23-51. *p.80.*

Dragon Spruce 1910 O. Powerscourt 23-45. Eastnor Cas (below drive) **26**-51. Hergest Croft 13-45. Westonbirt (Willesley Dr) 19-43, Dyffryn 16-41. Borde Hill (v. *notabilis*) 23-41. *p.80.*

Alcock's Spruce 1861 R. Bicton 21-**65**. Avondale 16-58. Ardross Cas (Pine) 20-54. Dunkeld Cath. Gr **26**-53. *p.80.*

Western Hemlock 1851 C. Benmore **51**-133. Doune Ho 41-**186**. Scone Pal Pine 43-183. Drum Mnr 33-183. Oakley Pk 32-157. Strone Ho 42-149. Cawdor Cas 44-140. Patterdale Hall 32-142. Ardanaiseig 36-140. Castle Milk 38-144. Bodnant 44-132. Murthly Cas **51**-118. Leny Ho 46-141. *p.82.*

Eastern Hemlock 1736 F. Oakley Pk 33-116, 23-**153**. Walcot Pk 22-117. Alton Towers 21-78. Lowther Cas 26-125. *p.83.*

Carolina Hemlock 1886 R. Wakehurst Pl (Sands Pine) **15**-40. Hollycombe Steam Fair 13-40. Leonardslee (Valley Gdn) 11-36. Wisley 10-22. Fota 11-47. *p.83.*

Chinese Hemlock 1901 R. Windsor Gt Pk 16-46(main stem). Bodnant **18**-57. Headfort 12-46. Glasnevin BG 12-41. *p.83.*

Southern Japanese Hemlock 1861 O. Antony Ho **19**-71. Wakehurst Pl (Bethlehem Gdn) 19-50. Leonardslee (Coronation Gdn) 18-30. *p.84.*

Northern Japanese Hemlock 1861 R. Leonardslee (Top Gdn) **21**-34. Hergest Croft 15-40. Abercairny 18-**80**. Glamis Cas 19-40. *p.84.*

Himalayan Hemlock 1838 R. Tregrehan 23-83. Kilmacurragh 22-83+82. Mt Usher 16-61. Rowallane 15-66. Powerscourt 15-54. Stonefield 23-65+57. *p.84.*

Mountain Hemlock 1854 O. Fairburn **36**-77, 21-**106**. Murthly Cas 26-114. Durris (nr drive) 26-87. Monk Coniston 19-88. Walcot Pk 20-58. Monteviot Pinery 20-102. Blair Cas 31-71. *p.84.*

Jeffrey's Hemlock 1851 R. Bodnant **18**-39. Drum Cas 9-27. *p.84.*

Douglas Fir 1827 C. Moniac Glen 61-96, 60-98, 60-81. Dunkeld Ho (Cathedral) 31-215. Ardanaiseig 37-183. Walcot Pk 35-183. Castle Milk 37-175. Hermitage, Inver 61-131. Broadwood, Dunster 53-144. Balmacaan 40-168, 40-184. Wray Cas 27-166. Glenlee Pk 45-177. Sutherland's Grove 53-144. Blair Cas (Diana's Gr) 56-101. Benmore (Glen Massen) 52-150. Vivod Ho 52-105. Findhorn Gorge 56-135. Bolderwood 47-116. Murthly Cas 54-167. Dunans 61-171. Strone 55-142. Dupplin, Belle Wd 48-195. Randolph's Leap 58-141. Endsleigh 50-187. Belladrum 52-188. *p.86.*

Blue Douglas Fir 1884 O. Balmoral Cas **29**-57. Tilgate Pk 25-48. New Court 20-45. Capenoch 25-42. *p.86.*

Bigcone Douglas Fir 1910 R. Bedgebury **21**-60, 20-55. Hillier Arb 10-22. *p.87.*

Scots Pine N.C. Oakley Pk **36**-89. Colebrooke 24-142. Cawdor Cas 19-140. Powerscourt 31-133. Brockenhurst Pk 31-144. Speymouth For 31-140. Bargany 36-138. Ballogie 37-141. *p.88.*

Red Pine 1756 R. Leonardslee (Coronation Gdn) **21**-42. Borde Hill (Warren Wd) **21**-47. Wakehurst Pl 12-31. Bedgebury 20-44. Wisley 16-26. Ochtertyre 18-40. *p.88.*

Japanese Red Pine 1861 R. Borde Hill (Warren Wd) **22**-35. Wisley 14-36. Birr Cas 17-61. *p.88.*

Bishop Pine 1846 O. Muckross Abbey **30**-85. Eberno Ho 29-**134**. Wakehurst Pl 28-104 at 1m, 24-95. Eastnor Cas (Bridge) 26-105. Bodnant 25-108. Castle Kennedy 25-111. Borde Hill (Warren Wd) **30**-90. *p.88.*

Austrian Pine 1835 C. Bolderwood '40' 36-117. Brocklesby Pk 32-**133**. Sidbury Mnr 33-125. St Fagan's, Cardiff 34-94. Glasnevin BG 25-101. Dawyck **40**-104. Bowood 28-138. *p.90.*

Crimean Pine 1790 F. Bolderwood 40-127. Bowood 28-135. Hanford Ho 30-140. Nuneham Pine 38-127. Ickworth 35-135. Beauport Pk 37-**167**. Beaufort Cas **41**-137. Rossie Pr 38-141. *p.90.*

Corsican Pine 1759 C. Stanage Pk 42-110. Bicton 34-122. Holkam Hall 32-136. Sandringham 34-110. Alton Towers 29-117. Adhurst St Mary **46**-127. Albury Pk 32-129, Offnells 39-99, Dropmore 37-144. *p.90.*

Shore Pine 1855 O. Bodnant **34**-96. Warnham Ct 25-91. Bowood 24-80. Westonbirt (Broad Drive) 19-90. Wakehurst Pl (above lake) 24-81. Castle Milk 24-74. Walcot Pk 22-75+69. Errol Ho 26-**114**. *p.91.*

Lodgepole Pine 1854 R. Westonbirt (Pool Ave) 30-**78**. Borde Hill (Warren Wd) 25-48. Bodnant 21-63. Wisley 17-47. Exeter Univ (Reed Hall) 16-51. Culcreuch Cas 30-70. *p.91.*

Jack Pine pre-1783 R. Wakehurst Pl 17-41. Blairquhan 18-58. Blackmoor **27**-45. *p.92.*

Mountain Pine R. Glasnevin BG 17-41. St James's Ch, Patterdale 17-**94**, 17-79. Kilmacurragh (Drive) 16-27. Bedgebury (Hills Ave) 11-41. Cambridge BG 16-48. Albury Pk **18**-58. *p.92.*

Bosnian Pine 1890 O. Killerton 22-59. Borde Hill (Warren Wd) 24-44. Wakehurst Pl (Sands Pine) 18-75, (Pine) 23-71. Tynninghame 20-**80**. Hergest Croft 20-57. Benmore 21-51. Kew 18-38 (Orig.). Stratfield Saye **26**-68, 21-75. *p.93.*

Japanese Black Pine 1861 R. Borde Hill (Azalea Ring) 25-70. Glasnevin BG 20-52. Westonbirt (Willes Dr) 20-54. Suamarez Pk 25-73+60. *p.93.*

Aleppo Pine 1683 R. Glasnevin BG **14**-56. Kew 12-108 at 0.3m, 11-59, 15-40. Wisley 15-45. *p.94.*

Calabrian Pine 1836 R. Kew 13-**60**. Glasnevin BG **18**-46, 14-58. *p.94.*

Stone Pine pre-1500 O. Crickhowell 20-109. Margam Pk 13-87. Tredegar Pk 16-76+57. St Fagan's 19-86 at 0.3m. Warwick Cas 16-76. Hatfield Forest, Essex 16-80+71. Glasnevin BG 11-76. Hever Cas 18-71. *p.95.*

Maritime Pine pre-1600 O. Garnons Ho **35**-101. W Lavington Rect 23-117. Bolderwood 30-86. Brocklesby Pk 26-86. Holme Lacey 29-107. Carey 25-**133**. *p.95.*

Monterey Pine 1833 C. Castle Kennedy 41-157. Knowle Pk, Devon 27-230. Penrhyn Cas 39-139. Somerleyton Hall 28-148. Castle Horneck 30-204. Bicton 30-211. Sandling Pk 31-221 at 1m. Mt Stewart 31-209. Ballamoar 25-171. Bolderwood 35-157. Powerscourt 32-161. Ballywalter 40-200. Heckfield Pl 36-197. Bowood 26-191. *p.96.*

Knobcone Pine 1847 R. Borde Hill (Warren Wd) 22-56. Bedgebury 16-51. Cawdor Cas 13-36. Wisley 14-44 at 0.5m. *p.96.*

Northern Pitch Pine 1743 R. Blackmoor (Moat) 23-69. Wakehurst Pl 19-74. Batsford Pk 18-64. Wisley 16-76. Inveraray Cas 17-**86**. *p.96.*

Mexican Pine pre-1837 R. Tregrehan 21-65. Powerscourt (Lake) 13-58, (Ent) 11-51. Hillier Arb 11-41. Cockington Court 14-46. *p.96.*

Jeffrey Pine 1852 O. Scone Palace Pine **41-128**. Powerscourt (Field) 35-118. Wrest Pk 23-93. Eastnor Cas 23-93. Holdfast La, Grayswood 22-90. Clumber Pk 16-46. Hampton Pk 30-107. Peper Harow 30-115. Ochtertyre 32-88. *p.98.*

Ponderosa Pine 1827 O. Bowood 41-140. Powis Cas 41-134, 34-**145**. Eastnor Cas 37-105. Lexden, Colchester 22-111. Dunorlan Pk 28-105. Dawyck 30-99. Bayfordbury 25-124. *p.98.*

Bigcone Pine 1832 R. Powerscourt (Pepperpot) **25**-74. Bedgebury (Plot) 19-51. Westonbirt (Sand Earth) 21-65. Wakehurst Pl (Sands Pine) 20-67. Edinburgh RBG 25-57. *p.99*

Lacebark Pine 1846 R. Kew (Pine) **15-38**. Wisley 15-25. Antony Ho 14-27. Bayfordbury 10-31. *p.99.*

Bristlecone Pine 1863 R. Prested Hall 11-24. Talbot Mnr 7-22. Kew 8-18. Edinburgh RBG 9-16. Leicester UBG 12-25. *p.100.*

Foxtail Pine 1852 R. Prested Hall 12-29. Glasnevin BG 11-27. Edinburgh RBG 15-27. Beaufront Cas 12-23. *p.100.*

Montezuma Pine 1839 R. Mt Usher 18-101. Sidbury Mnr 17-117. Powerscourt (Pepperpot) 24-73. Kilmacurragh 23-88. Cairnsmore 17-84. Sheffield Pk 21-80. Culzean Cas 18-70. Grayswood Hill 19-100. Endsleigh 27-**152**. *p.101.*

Bhutan Pine 1827 F. W Dean (Roche's Arb) 35-83. Windsor Gt Pk (nr Botany Bay) 24-**134**. Hewell Gra 26-107. Abbeyleix 37-113. Kilmacurragh 23-120. Hardwicke Pk 23-106. Powerscourt (River Dr) 25-126. Fallbarrow Pk 24-102. Sidbury Mnr 23-97. *p.102.*

Holford Pine 1906 R. Westonbirt (Holford Dr) 30-67, (Willes Dr) 25-75. Wisley 22-100. Wakehurst Pl (Sands) 23-81. Tilgate Pk 22-70. *p.102.*

Mexican White Pine 1840 R. Bicton 29-81, 21-88. Bodnant 25-108. Stratford Pk 22-65. *p.102.*

Weymouth Pine 1705 O. Puck Pits 40-83. Gosford Cas 25-**134**. Leigh Ct 37-118. Rhinefield Drive 33-107. Chatsworth Ho **44**-86, 31-105. Hackwood Pk 33-107. Westonbirt (Circular Dr) 24-101. *p.102.*

Sugar Pine 1827 R. (Shropshire **29-96**). Crarae (For Gdn) 10-21. Batsford Pk 11-21. Hillier Ar 6-18. *p.104.*

Macedonian Pine 1863 F. Stourhead **35-132**. Monteviot Pinery 29-109. Wotton Ho, Surrey 28-105. Woburn (Evergreens) 25-93. Avondale 25-79. Trentham Pk 21-69. Hergest Croft 20-81. Westonbirt (Willes Dr) 26-79. Beaufront Cas 24-92. Bicton 30-86. Ochtertyre 32-126. *p.104.*

Western White Pine 1831 R. Patterdale Hall **38-95**. Wythenshaw Pk, Manchester 22-51. Brickendon Golf Co 24-73. Lude Ho 34-87. Avondale 33-52. *p.105.*

Chinese White Pine 1895 R. Kew 16-43 (orig). Westonbirt (Leyshon Glade) 18-32, (Willes Dr) 14-43. Saltram Ho 22-50. Tatton Pk 20-46. Fota 26-**99**. *p.104.*

Arolla Pine 1746 F. Taymouth Cas Gdns 24-87. Castle Milk **35**-85. Drum Mnr 24-60. Powis Castle (Poaches Gate) 18-87. Dawyck 18-82, 22-71. Capenoch 24-52. Chatsworth 22-76. Monteviot Pinery 26-86. Waddesdon 18-78. *p.106.*

Japanese White Pine 1861 F. Stourhead 26-68. Leonardslee 17-53. Tullymore Pk 11-82. *p.107.*

Limber Pine 1851 O. Brocklesby Pk (Monument) 20-37, (Kennelside) 18-49. Leighton Pk (Arb) 13-52. Kew 19-40. Windsor Gt Pk **27-71**. *p.107.*

Korean Pine 1861 R. Castle Milk 19-35. Sidbury Mnr 18-45. Crarae 22-50. Birr Cas 18-39. Darnaway (Old Pine) 10-34. Wisley 14-19. Fota 20-**54**. *p.107.*

Black Poplar N F. Newtown (Car Park) 31-167. Bury St Edmunds Abbey 20-145. Longnor Hall, Shrops **38**-201, 30-**235**. Cannington, Somerset 27-190. Christ's Sch, Brecon 34-210. *p.108.*

Lombardy Poplar 1758 C. B3001 nr Milford 36-101. Sandford Pk, Cheltenham 36-67. Oxford Univ pks 34-121. The Fen, Cambridge 36-108. Town Meadow, Godalming, Surrey 32-**131**. Henrietta Pk, Bath 37-125. Leigh Village, Kent 32-128. Hall Place, Kent 36-104. *p.108.*

Black Italian Poplar 1750 (Kent **46**-205). Chelsworth 38-**217**. Osterley Pk (below dam) 41-149. Green Pk 31-104. Battersea Pk 34-146. Bowood (Lake) 46-146. Abbeyleix 46-169. *p.108.*

Golden Poplar 1876 F. Osterley Pk (Lake) 33-86. Manor Pk, Aldershot 28-**110**, 30-90. Oxford Univ pks 27-87. Kew 23-60. Sidney Gdns, Bath 31-96. *p.108.*

'Eugenei' 1832 O. Colesbourne **43-135**. Edinburgh 37-128, 36-114. Kew 40-117. Glasnevin BG 37-108. *p.109.*

'Regenerata' 1814 F. Hyde Pk (S of Serpentine) 32-112, (nr Bridge) 28-113. Boultham Pk, Lincoln **40**-140. Harnham Rd, Salisbury 38-**145**. *p.109.*

'Robusta'1895 C. Dyffryn Gdn 33-124. Shinners Br, Totnes 37-112. Colesbourne 33-109. Wakehurst Pl (Serps) 35-106. Glasnevin BG 32-68. Westonbirt 37-70. *p.109.*

Berlin Poplar pre 1810 O. Prested Hall **33-103**. Cannizaro Pk, Wimbledon 26-44. Talbot Mnr 26-47. Kew 24-77. *p.109.*

White Poplar (early) F. Bayfordbury **24-166**. *p.110.*

Grey Poplar (early) C. Birr Cas **38-180**. Broadlands 31-134. Batsford Pk 33-113. Oxford Univ pks 31-138. Dunrobin Cas (shore) 28-130. Leigh Pk 29-122. Castlehill, Devon 38-126. *p.110.*

Aspen N O. Howick 19-24. Batsford Pk 22-34. Munches, Kirkcudb 25-38. *p.110.*

Western Balsam Poplar 1892 C. Bowood **41**-100. Colesbourne 34-97. Cambridge BG 34-**105**. Oxford Univ pks 28-81. Victoria Pk, Leicester 29-72. *p.111.*

Chinese Necklace Poplar 1900 R. Bath BG **26**-75. Drum Cas 17-33. Westonbirt (Mitchell Dr) 15-32. Abbotsbury 13-29. Birr Cas 16-35. Combe Ho, Devon 24-**85**. *p.111.*

Crack Willow N C. Terling Pl (12)-**203**. Ovingdon (rdside) 21-130. Oxford Univ pks 28-108. *p.112.*

Bay Willow N F. Deene Pk 16-**44**. Oxford Univ pks 15-**56**. Wakehurst Pl 23-52+. *p.112.*

Goat Willow N C. Honeyhanger Ho 19-28. Black Rock Gorge 14-**65**. Lael For Gdn, W Ross 16-**75**. Moniac Glen, Inverness 21-51. *p.112.*

Bat Willow (early) R. Marble Hill Pk 32-**128**. Thorp Perrow 25-108. *p.114.*

Violet Willow (early) R. Glasnevin BG **18-50**. *p.112.*

White Willow N C. Woodbrook Coll **33**-79. Hampton Ct (towpath) 21-106. Oxford Univ pks 24-102. Sandringham Pk 26-85. Roath Pk, Cardiff 24-88. Wimbledon Common (SE) 18-101. *p.114.*

Weeping Willow (c.1800) C. Oxford BG 16-116. Regent's Pk 19-105. Radnor Gdns, Twickenham 25-133. W Kingsclere, Berks 18-**172**, 18-146. *p.114.*

Corkscrew Willow c.1925 C. Oxford BG 15-44 (main stem). Cambridge BG 10-32 at 1m. Cannizaro Pk, Wimbledon 16-38. Pershore Coll of Ag 16-57. *p.115.*

Caucasian Wingnut pre-1800 O. Melbury **35-178**. Abbotsbury **38**-127, 32-166. Lacock Abbey 26-193 (triple stem). Rowallane 22-66. Hyde Pk (Rotten Row) 21-129. *p.116.*

Chinese Wingnut 1860 R. Kew (Sundial Lawn) **21-126** at 1m. Dyffryn Gdn 26-90. Hollycombe Steam Fair 20-80. *p.116.*

269

Hybrid Wingnut 1908 O. Westonbirt (Pool Gate) 25-**120**. Kew 23-117. Birr Cas 26-106. Talbot Mnr 17-51. Edinburgh BG 18-76. Glasnevin BG 24-95. Borde Hill (S Park) 20-115. *p.117.*

Common Walnut (introduced by Romans?) F. Gayhurst **24-194** Ribston Hall 16-141. Lydham Hall, Shrops 23-128. Fingask, Perths 28-117. *p.118.*

Black Walnut pre-1656 O. Battersea Pk 33-96. Mote Pk, Maidstone 30-100. Marble Hill Pk 33-177. Brahan Ho 20-100. Oxford BG 30-106. Cambridge BG 24-105. Much Hadham Rect **36-204**. Bisham Abbey (Bucks) 34-132. *p.118.*

Butternut 1656 R. Cliveden **25-60**. Pusey Ho 18-21. Westonbirt (Acer Gl) 20-40. Thorp Perrow 15-27. *p.118.*

Manchurian Walnut 1859 R. Aldenham Pk (Woods) **16-43**. Kew 9-34. Deene Pk 12-40. *p.118.*

Japanese Walnut 1860 R. Edinburgh RBG **16**-60. Batsford Pk 13-**81**. E Bergholt Pl 15-48. *p.118.*

Bitternut 1689 O. Kew (Pagoda V) 32-64. Bicton 26-74. Leeds Cas, Kent (Duckery) **33-89**. Syston Pk, Lincs 24-85. Hollycombe Steam Fair 29-55. *p.120.*

Shagbark Hickory 1629 O. Reading Univ (Whiteknights Pk) 24-79. Fredville Pk 21-90. Orchardleigh 20-40. Cannizaro Pk, Wimbledon 20-22. Westonbirt (Broad Dr) 23-44. Coolhurst 24-56. Osterley Pk 24-64. Hollycombe 28-37. *p.120.*

Pignut c.1750 R. Wakehurst Pl (Serps) **23**-32. Glasnevin BG 17-50. Orchardleigh 18-36. Hergest Croft 12-37. *p.120.*

Shellbark Hickory c.1800 O. Tortworth chyd 17-51. Borde Hill (Lit Bentleys) 23-38. Nymans (Wild Gdn) 24-41. Bicton 22-40. *p.120.*

Mockernut c.1766 O. Oxford Univ pks 20-38. Edinburgh RBG 16-30. Kew (Ash Colln) 24-56. Westonbirt (Vict Gl) 19-38. *p.120.*

Pecan c.1766 R. Cambridge BG **21-38**. Wisley 18-28. Bedgebury 11-18. *p.120.*

Silver Birch N C. Woburn (roadside) **30**-75. Sidbury Mnr 27-**97**. Blair Cas (Hercules Walk) 28-66. Castle Leod 24-95. Rhododendron Wood 266-**133**. *p.122.*

Swedish Birch 1820 F. Taymouth Cas Gdns **33-56**. Sheffield Pk 27-43. Windsor Gt Pk (Botany Bay) 21-37. Hall Place, Kent 26-34. Bulkeley Mill, Gwynedd 25-51. *p.122.*

White Birch N C. Hutton-in-the-Forest, Cumb **27**-96. Oxford Univ pks 24-59. Bohunt Mnr 21-98. *p.122.*

Szechuan Birch 1908 R. Hergest Croft **19**-38. Mt Usher 18-60. Kew (Victoria Gate) 15-30. Windsor Gt Pk (Totem Pole Ride) 17-31. *p.122.*

Paper Birch 1750 O. Westonbirt (Rattrays) 23-35. Belvoir Cas Co Down. 21-**71**. Greenwich Pk 21-56. Cambridge BG 21-65. Sidbury Mnr 20-66. Ascott Pk 16-61. Glasnevin 19-70. Hergest Croft (Azalea Gdn) 24-54. Cockington Ct 16-62. Edinburgh RBG 20-58. Colesbourne 25-**50**. *p.122.*

Erman's Birch 1890 O. Westonbirt (Down Gate) **21-88**. Hergest Croft 19-32. The High Beeches, Sussex 17-38. Cathays Pk, Cardiff 14-44. Windsor Gt Pk 21-44. Edinburch RBG 21-56. Tregothnan 19-57. Thorp Perrow 19-41. *p.124.*

Chinese Red-Bark Birch 1918 R. Bodnant 17-36. Westonbirt (Savill Glade) 22-35. Dyffryn Gdn 17-30. Branklyn Gdn 16-32. Howick 13-22. Tulquhan Cas, Aberdeens 10-38. Castle Milk 18-43. *p.124.*

Himalayan Birch 1849 O. Howick **19**-40. Edinburgh RBG 18-44. Trewithen 17-50. Brook Ho 15-60. Hergest Croft 14-31. *p.124.*

'Jacquemont's Birch' 1880 O. Mt Usher 16-31. Hergest Croft 17-33. Westonbirt (Circular Dr) 12-26. Speech Ho 17-40. *p.124.*

Yellow Birch 1767 O. Tilgate Pk **20-67** at 1m. Furzey Ho, New For 12-34. Whitfield Ho 19-42. Innes Ho 11-51 at 0.5m. Windsor Gt Pk 12-31. Wakehurst Pl (Pheas Walk) 14-36. *p.126.*

Cherry Birch 1759 O. Brocklesby Pk (Kennelside) 17-36. Mt Usher 15-47. Winkworth Arb 14-48 at 1m. Bodnant 17-43 at 1m. Wakehurst Pl (The Oaks) 16-34. Hollycombe 20-66. Wisley 18-51. *p.126.*

River Birch 1736 O. Chiswick Ho 17-47. Petworth Ho 13-50. Windsor Gt Pk (Botany Bay) 19-50. *p.126.*

Transcaucasian Birch 1897 O. Westonbirt (Victory Glade) 10m. Thorp Perrow 9m, 8m, 8m. Aldenham Ho (Woods) 12m. Leonardslee 8m. Talbot Mnr 8-17. *p.126.*

Monarch Birch 1888 O. Killerton 19-56. Windsor Gt Pk 22-29+27. Innes Ho 15-28. Westonbirt (Wigmore 22-48. Wayford Mnr 16-57 at 0.3m. Leonardslee 22-31. Hergest Croft 20-56. *p.126.*

Common Alder N C. Sandling Pk 29-127. Alexandria Pk, Hastings 25-88. Cathays Pk, Cardiff 20-70. Belton Pk 25-73+72cm. Mote Pk, Maidstone 23-70. Dundonnel, W Ross 10-**170**. Ashburnham Pk, Sussex **32**-75. *p.128.*

Grey Alder 1780 O. Castle Milk 28-40. Birr Cas 17-65. Lyndford Arb 20-40. Speech Ho 16-52. Central Pk, Bournemouth 20-57. *p.128.*

Red Alder 1880 O. Kew **19-57**. Bedgebury 19-46. Thorp Perrow 22-47. Crarae 17-29. *p.128.*

Italian Alder 1820 O. Westonbirt (Skillings Gate) 28-87. Canterbury Cathedral 20-93. Bedgebury 22-77. Battersea Pk 19-77, 20-73. Kilmun Arb 20-58. Oxford BG 22-63. Marble Hill Pk 30-71. Smeaton 29-87. Calderstones Pk 19-87. *p.128.*

Hornbeam N C. Wrest Pk **32**-78. Oxford Univ pks 23-97. Bath BG 24-99. Clumber Pk 23-95. Heron Court, Hants 20-146. Trebah, Cornwall 30-86. Hatfield Forest, Essex 16-130. *p.130.*

Fastigiata' 1894 C. Kew **23-68**. College Rd, Dulwich 16-40, Colesbourne 22-48. Welford Pk (roadside) 17-48. *p.130.*

European Hop-Hornbeam pre-1724 O. Killerton (Chapel) 21-50 (main stem). Oxford BG 15-51. Cambridge BG 14-51. Glasnevin BG 14-51. Edinburgh RBG 17-55. Bulstrode, Bucks 13-100. Albury Pk, Surrey 13-61. *p.131.*

Turkish Hazel 1650 O. Brocklesby Pk (Kennelside) **26**-61. Syon Pk 23-**92**. Bury St Edmunds Abbey 19-90+63. Colesbourne 23-68. Oxford Univ pks 21-86. Chiltlee Est, Liphook (roadside) 20-66. Owston 13-69. Hergest Croft 21-59. *p.132.*

Rauli 1913 O. Bergholt Pl 26-89. Muncaster Cas 30-95. Benmore 29-84. Petworth Pk (car park) 24-88. Frensham Hall, Surrey 28-99. *p.133.*

Roble 1902 O. Sunningdale Nsy 23-**105**. Caerhays Cas 28-97. Trewithen 23-84. Cannizaro Pk, Wimbledon 25-61. Killerton (Lawn) 24-71. Borde Hill (Lit Bentleys) 32-69. Benmore 29-60. Glamis Cas 30-62. South Place, Sussex **36**-77. Blairquhan, Ayrs 26-75. Grayswood Hill, Surrey 24-89. Ashbourne Ho 30-100. *p.133.*

Antarctic Beech 1830 O. Abbeyleix (Pleas Grnds) 16-56. Crarae 14-49. Sheffield Pk 16-31+29. Bodnant 14-30+29cm. Wakehurst Pl (Serps) 19-47. St John's IOM 13-31. Arduanie, Argyll **26-70**. *p.134.*

Dombey's Southern Beech 1916 R. Mt Usher 27-104, 27-102. Bodnant 24-125. Rowallane 22-78. Petworth Pk (car park) 27-84. Sandling Pk 26-49. Winkworth Arb 28-73. Muncaster Cas **36**-75, 35-88. *p.134.*

Silver Beech ?1850 R. Trewithen 20-48. Caerhays Cas 27-103 at 1m. Nymans (Magnolia Gdn) 21-71. *p.134.*

Red Beech 1910 R. Castlewellan 22-86. Mt Usher 22-63. Trelissick 24-45. *p.134.*

Black Beech post 1914 R. Wakehurst Pl (below Serps) **26**-60. Rowallane 22-57. Ardanaiseig 20-43. Trewithen 20-37. *p.134.*

Mountain Beech ?1880 R. Lochinch 21-60. Ardanaiseig 16-49. Caerhays Cas 20-61. Muncaster Cas 23-74. Ashbourne Ho, Cork 27-67 at 0.5m. *p.134.*

Common Beech N C. Stourhead (Zigzag) 40-163. Monteviot Pinery 28-229. Ampfield (by A31) 34-118. Bishop's Ct 27-165. Haddo Ho 23-181. Cricket Ho, Som (Lr Walk) 33-183. Howick (nr gate) 34-169. Beaufort Cas 26-**231**. Hallyburton Ho, Perths **46**-151. Beaufront, Hexham 44-171. Blair Drummond, Perths 33-191. Ardkinglas Ho 26-192. Mote Pk 36-209, 31-190. Tal-y-Garth, Glam 28-183. Belsay Cas, Northumb 33-178. *p.136.*

Dawyck Beech R. Dawyck (Orig) 26-**86**. Kew (Colln) 26-51. E Bergholt Pl 24-51. Nymans (Prospect) 24-66, 27-50. Westonbirt (Willes Dr) 24-44. St John's Coll, Cambridge (Bridge St gate) 22-54. Exbury Ho, Hants 24-75. *p.137.*

Weeping Beech 1826 F. Penjerrick **27**-144. Knaphill Nsy (Orig) 22-103+99. Sherlock Rd, Chichester 14-131. Orchardleigh 26-72. Mill Ct, Lr Froyle, Hants 27-111. Drumlanrig Cas, Dumfries 32-101. Green Pk, Bucks 29-105. *p.137.*

Copper Beech c.1700 C. Capel Mnr 34-156. Chart Pk Golf Co, Surrey 38-167. Hylands Pk 19-170. Blenheim Pal (Cascade) 29-150. Curragh Chase 33-132. Ascott 24-140. Syston Pk, Lincs 19-204 at 1m. Beaufort Cas, Inv 28-183. Dalguise Ho, Perths 38-103. *p.137.*

Fernleaf Beech 1826 F. Melbury **27**-101. Knaphill Nsy (Orig) 22-136. Leigh Pk, Havant 26-120. Tredegar Pk 19-101. Margam Abbey 19-118. Auchincruive 20-140. Tal-y-Garth, Glam 26-130. Coul Ho, E Ross 24-129. Scotney Cas, Kent 26-115. *p.137.*

Oriental Beech 1880 R. Edinburgh RBG 24-68. Kew 18-63. Exbury Gdn 16-62. Talbot Mnr 12-29. Birr Cas 27-58. *p.137.*

Chinese Beech 1911 R. Innes Ho 10-31 at 0.5m. Ardanaiseig 10-25. Westonbirt (Willes Dr) 20-51. Holkham 9-31. W Dean 8-22. *p.137.*

Sweet Chestnut Romans C. A272 E/Midhurst 26-282. Castle Leod 28-246. Studley Royal 16-258. Tortworth Ct 22-363. Howletts Pk, Kent 23-303. Bushey Pk (Glazewood Rd) 11-291. Chilham Pk, Kent 18-283. Croft Cas 23-277. *p.138.*

Golden Chestnut 1844 R. Mt Usher 14-44. Grayswood Hill 18-50. Blackhill, Moray 15-46. *p.139.*

Common Oak N C. Bowthrope Fm, Lincs 12-**383**. Fredville Pk ('Majesty') 19-369. Major Oak, Ollerton 16-329. Eardisley 18-294. Tilford 15-259. Birnam 28-228. Lydham Hall, Shrops 19-374. Kings Sch, Sparkford, Som 25-334. Gathmyl, Powys 18-318. Abbotsbury **42**-147. Leeds Cas, Kent 41-117. *p.140.*
 Fastigiata' c.1860 F. Melbury 28-**86**. Hardwick Pk 23-**112**. Reading Univ (Whiteknights Pk) 24-81. Cliveden 22-89. Sawbridgeworth (River's Nsy, road island) 27-105. Marbury Pk 20-70. Abbotsbury 30-60. Holkham Ho 21-40. Wisley 25-61. *p.140.*

Sessile Oak N C. Whitfield Ho **43**-148. Powis Cas (The Giant) 21-**342**. Cowdray Pk 33-242. Nettlecombe Ct 36-233. Woburn Abbey 24-213. Oakley Pk (Above drive) 27-226. The Michendon Oak, Midd 16-186. Brockhampton Pk 29-223. Mickleham (Swanford Lane) 35-198. Kenwood Ho, London 26-166. Easthampton Fm, Shobdon, Heref 25-314. 'Capon Oak', Jedburgh 18-257. Gray Ho, Dundee 31-230. Croft Cas 35-240. Drumlanrig Cas 32-205. *p.140.*

Downy Oak Early R. Melbury 27-101. Colesbourne 27-78. Ickworth, Suffolk **29**-123. Edinburgh RBG 18-68. *p.141.*

Turkey Oak 1735 C. West Dean (Roche's Arb) 40-115. Knightshayes **44**-243. Sandling Pk (lake) 28-200. Powderham Cas 34-192. Phear Pk, Exmouth 26-186. Arnos Pk 30-160. Bulstrode Pk, Bucks 41-211. Ugbrooke, Devon 30-200. Nettlecombe Ct 23-196. *p.141.*

Chestnut-Leafed Oak 1846 R. Kew 32-**211** (Orig). Batsford Arb 34-104. Windsor Gt Pk (Empire Oaks) 23-60. Coll Rd, Dulwich 15-48. Beauport Pk 24-141. Alexandra Pk 23-110. Glasnevin BG 18-78. *p.142.*

Mirbeck's Oak 1845 O. Melbury **31**-116. Ham Mnr Golf Cl, Arundel 27-**141**. Blenheim Pal (Cascade) 29-92. Holker Pk 23-120. Clock Ho, Enfield 26-119. Kew (Isleworth Gate) 27-116. Osterley Pk 26-81. Alexandra Pk 26-101. Tregrehan **31**-97. *p.142.*

Turner's Oak before 1783 O. Eastnor Cas (drive) **27**-117. River's Nsy 19-120. Kew (nr Gingko) 18-157 at 0.3m, (Colln) 21-58. Osterley Pk 18-97 at 1m. Notcutt's Nsy, Woodbridge 15-89. Chiswick Ho 20-67. Capel Mnr 16-93. Bicton (Drive) 28-**122**. *p.143.*

Lucombe Oak 1765 F. W Dean (Roche's Arb) 33-101. Phear Pk, Exmouth 24-229. Bicton Ag Coll 33-198. Wilton Ho 28-175. Sawbridgeworth (road island) 24-170. Dartington Hall 23-153. Killerton (Park) 25-172, (lawn) 30-153. Innes Ho 28-118. Ugbrooke Pk 26-188. Castlehill, Devon 30-208. Scotney Cas 33-140. *p.143.*

Pyrenean Oak 1822 R. Melbury **27**-88. Clonmannon Ho 28-137. Westonbirt (Willes Dr) 22-67. Wakehurst Pl (Pine) 21-48. Kew (Colln) 18-43. Syon Pk 21-69. Edinburgh RBG 19-59. Holland Pk, London 22-46. *p.144.*

Hungarian Oak 1838 O. Osterley Pk (Woods) 31-120 (Prospect) 20-117. Holker 30-134. Kew (Pagoda Vista) 28-112. Glasnevin BG 22-114. Anglesea Abbey 24-100. Howick 22-66. Monteviot 20-95. Syon Pk 32-129. (S Devon) 25-**142**. Stratfield Saye 33-121. Camperdown Pk, Angus 33-106. Carberry Tower, Midloth 31-129. Avenue Ho, Barnet 24-121, Westonbirt School 22-124. *p.144.*

Caucasian Oak 1873 O. Westonbirt (Mitchell Dr) **29**-74, (Broad Dr) 26-83. Melbury 20-**97**. Sheffield Pk (Queen's Walk) 23-75. Kew (Sundial Lawn) 21-90. Edinburgh RBG 23-70. Talbot Mnr 14-44. Jephson Gdns, Leamington 17-48. *p.144.*

Daimyo Oak 1830 R. Eastnor Cas (S of gdn) 19-47. Trewidden 14-49. Osterley Pk 14-51. Caerhays Cas 18-49. Edinburgh RBG 10-29. Westonbirt (Willes Dr) 16-41. Gunnersbury Pk 16-**61**. *p.144.*

Swamp White Oak 1800 R. Syon Ho 25-96. Kew 21-70. Lyndon Pk, Rutland 20-70. *p.146.*

Bur Oak 1811 R. Kew 21-68, 19-57. Tilgate Pk 25-73. Windsor Gt Pk (Empire Oaks) 12-23. Aldenham Ho (Woods) 17-33. Holland Pk **26**-73. *p.146.*

Water Oak 1726 R. Pylewell Pk 16-**87**. Kew (Isleworth Gate) Cut back 20cm diam. Windsor Gt Pk (Empire Oaks) **17**-47. *p.147.*

Blackjack Oak pre-1739 R. Wakehurst Pl (Serps) 18-**58**, 15-32. E Bergholt Pl 16-37. Caerhays Cas 12-27. Canford Sch 11-20. Osterley Pk **20**-40. Castle Milk 15-24. *p.147.*

White Oak 1724 R. Windsor Gt Pk (Empire Oaks) 18-59. Westonbirt (Willes Dr) 17-36. Cambridge BG 19-55. Edinburgh RBG 14-35. Hillier Arb 9-21. *p.147.*

Red Oak 1724 C. W Dean (Roche's Arb) **34**-117. Osterley Pk 30-114. Roath Pk, Cardiff 22-95. Kensington Gdns 24-95. The Gliffaes 20-154. Norbury (Druids' Grove), Surrey 26-155. Southampton Common (Cemetery) 22-135. Gray Ho, Dundee 22-143. Cowdray Pk 33-137. Howletts Pk, Kent 23-134. *p.148.*

Scarlet Oak 1691 F. Wakehurst Pl (Gdn) 24-61. Sheffield Pk (nr gate) 24-87. Ascott Ho 21-83. Sidbury Mnr 22-81. Trent Pk, Midd 20-82. Syon Pk 24-90. Bramshott Hosp, Hants 25-**101**. Burford Ho, Surrey 26-91. Tockington Sch, Glos 20-84. Osterley Pk 30-61, 24-78.
'Splendens'. Knaphill Nsy, Surrey 20-80. Kew 23-81. Stratford Pk, Glos 26-74. *p.148.*

Pin Oak pre-1770 O. Kew (Palm House) 27-98. Marble Hill 24-82. Coll Rd, Dulwich 20-59. Godinton Pk, Kent 20-102. Claremont Ho, Surrey 21-102. Hall Place, Kent 28-102. Hever Cas, Kent 25-85. Syon Pk 27-87. Hyde Pk 27-88 *p.148.*

Black Oak 1800 O. Wray Cas 23-82. Colesbourne 26-86. Killerton 22-80. Albury Pk 22-73. Edinburgh RBG 22-42. Holland Pk 18-47. Peamore 18-82. *p.148.*

Holm Oak pre-1600 C. Sherborne Cas 25-112. Killerton 21-167, (Chapel) 25-139. Howick 23-**207** at 0.5m, 22-140. Pittville Gdns 23-111. Trelissick 24-133. Bishops' Pal, Chichester 16-133. Frogmore, Berks 16-174. Chilham Cas, Kent 24-239 at 0.3m. *p.150.*

California Live Oak 1849 R. Kew (Syon Vista) **16-63**, (Colln) 15-42. Mt Usher **16**-48. Hillier Arb 13-37. *p.150.*

Cork Oak 1699 F. Antony Ho 20-**145**. Mt Edgcumbe 26-163. Powderham Cas 14-136. Margam Abbey 13-52. Belair Pk, Dulwich 15-48. Tregrehan 22-101. Killerton (Gdn) 20-128. *p.151.*

Chinese Cork Oak 1861 R. Hollycombe Steam Fair **19-53** Kew 13-37. Caerhays Cas 11-40. *p.151.*

Armenian Oak 1885 R. Kew (Colln) 9-42 at 1m. Castle Milk 6-30 at 0.5m. Hillier Arb 4m. Hidcote, Glos 10-57 at 0m. *p.151.*

Willow Oak 1723 O. Kew (lawn) 26-128, (Colln) 26-82. Alexandra Park, Hastings 26-69. Glendurgan 16-58. Knaphill Nsy broken-127. *p.152.*

Shingle Oak 1786 R. Kew 20-54. Bedgebury 18-39. Syon Pk **27**-56. Alexandra Pk 20-**76**. Stowe Pk 18-42. *p.152.*

Japanese Evergreen Oak 1878 O. Caerhays Cas 14-66. Killerton 15-50. Jephson Gdns, Leamington 6-23 at 1m. *p.152.*

Bamboo-leaf Oak 1854 R. Leonardslee (Hill Gdn) 18-24. Caerhays Cas 16-23. Westonbirt (Willes Dr) 6m. Wakehurst Pl (Bethlehem Gdn) 17-32. Hillier Arb 9-16 (main stem). South Lodge, Sussex 17-28+26. Frensham Hall, Surrey 15-**46**. *p.152.*

Sawtooth Oak 1862 O. Highnam Ct **24-68**. Kew (Ash Colln) 20-51. Petworth Pk 21-41. Beauport Pk 19-75. Grayswood Hill 20-53. *p.153.*

Lebanon Oak 1855 R. Bedgebury **20**-43, 18-41. Kew 17-45. Colesbourne 17-**47**. *p.153.*

Wych Elm N C. Castle Leod 24-184. Evancoyd, Presteigne 31-141. Hutton-in-the-Forest 37-88. Levens Hall (riverside) 25-164. Castle Howard 41-120. Ballindean, Perths 35-209. Brahan, E Ross 38-**216**. *p.154.*

English Elm pre-Roman C. Preston Pk, Brighton 27-165. Firle Pl, Sussex 32-152. Belsay Cas, Northumb 32-159. *p.155.*

Cornish Elm pre-Roman C. A 94 E/Elgin 26-130. Firle Pl 30-146. Tynninghame 26-99. *p.156.*

Wheatley Elm 1836 C. Preston Pk 31-116 in avenue of 26 trees. Edinburgh RBG 29-65 (1985). Suamarez Pk, Guernsey 21-114 (1986). *p.156.*

Chinese Elm 1794 R. Dyffryn Gdn **17**-33. Wakehurst Pl (Oaks) 14-28. *p.157.*

Siberian Elm 1860 R. Colesbourne 18-71. Edinburgh RBG 15-58. Mote Pk, Kent 19-55. Benenden, Kent 18-**76**. *p.157.*

Caucasian Elm 1760 O. Hyde Park Corner 22-113. Victoria Park, Bath 27-102. Worlingham (Park Drive) 27-216 at 1m. Chudleigh Knighton (roadside, old A38) 26-169, (Pitt Fm) 34-198. Bicton Ag Coll 31-200, 35-172. Capel Mnr 32-140. Syon Ho 35-165. Langley Pk 29-65. Regents Pk 29-89. Valley Rd, Ipswich 28-208. Halliford Pk, Midd 31-144. *p.158.*

Cutleaf Zelkova 1892 R. Jephson Gdns, Leamington 12-39. Crathes Cas 11-38. Wakehurst Pl (Coate's Wd) **18**-41. Glasnevin BG 10-37. *p.158.*

Keaki 1861 O. Tilgate Pk 19-73. Horsted Keynes (roadside Lr Sherriff Fm) 19-90. Lr Coombe Royal 17-89. Kilmacurragh 16-**96**. Hergest Croft 22-76. *p.159.*

Chinese Zelkova 1920 R. Wisley 12-37. Kew (Brentford Gate) 15-**61**. Talbot Mnr 7-23. Witham Hall 10-30. Holkham Hall 11-34. Alexandra Pk 15-48 at 1m. *p.159.*

Hackberry 1656 O. Bicton **15**-48. Cannizaro Pk, Wimbledon 13-48. Oxford Univ pks 12-24. *p.159.*

Southern Nettle-tree c.1796 O. Borde Hill (S Park) **16**-48. Grove Rd, Shirley, Southampton 12-**83** at 1m. Lacock Abbey (orchard) 15-76. *p.159.*

Common/Black Mulberry c.1500 C. Withersdane Hall 16-98 at 1m. Scotney Cas 9-65. E Bergholt Pl 11-68 at 1m. Denman Coll 8-71 at 1m. Forty Hall 8-**73** at 1m. Gt Dixter 9-52. Preston Pk, Brighton 11-51. Hatfield Ho 4-95 at 30cm. Cedars Pk, Chestnut 5-61 at 1m. *p.160.*

White Mulberry ?1596 O. Kew **15**-57. Oxford BG 14-**67** (bole horiz). Owston Pk 7-40. Victoria Pk, London 11-25. Finborough Hall 10-53 at 1m. *p.160.*

Osage Orange 1818 R. Cambridge BG 13-36. Bowood 13-21. Change Ho 11-29. *p.160.*

Southern Magnolia 1734 C. (Free-growing trees) Cockington Ct 11-41. Powderham Cas 9-69 at 0.5m. Nonsuch Pk, Epsom 10-**70**. *p.162.*

Chinese Evergreen Magnolia 1900 R. Caerhays Cas **18**-52. Borde Hill (Kitchen Gdn) 13-53. Abbotsbury 13-27. Hyde Pk (Nursery Border) 6m. Trewidden 12-31+24. *p.162.*

Japanese Bigleaf Magnolia 1865 O. Trewidden **16-76**. Savill Gdn, Windsor 16-41. Wisley (Woodl Gdn) 12-31. Wakehurst Pl (Valley) 15-41. Chobham Pl 14-40. Westonbirt (Circular Dr N) 16-26. Lanhydrock, Cornwall 15-57. Arduanie, Argyll 17-57 at 0.3m. *p.163.*

Bigleaf Magnolia 1800 R. Savill Gdn, Windsor 12-22. Bodnant 11-28. Nymans (Wall Gdn) 11-21. Sheffield Pk 11-17. Holker Pk 9-21. Leonardslee (Top Gdn) 9-19. Killerton 18-30. *p.163.*

Cucumber Tree 1736 O. Mote Pk, Maidstone 26-67, 20-85. Brockenhurst Pk 21-**96**. Tilgate Pk 26-65. Wisley 20-54. Wakehurst Pl (Serps) 23-58. Kew (nr Main Gate) 22-80. Margam Pk 27-69. Lingholm, Cumb 17-70. *p.163.*

Northern Japanese Magnolia 1892 O. Kew (Beeches) 15-**63**, (Magnolias) 15-60. Trewithen 14-60. Winkworth Arb 13-33. *p.164.*

Willow-leafed Magnolia 1892 O. Nymans (Magnolia Gdn) **18**-35. Savill Gdn, Windsor 15-**38**. Bodnant **18**-30. Winkworth Arb 14-30. Kew (Victoria Gate) 14-31. Talbot Mnr 11-23. *p.165.*

Veitch's Hybrid Magnolia 1907 O. Caerhays Cas 29-67, 22-90. Bodnant 20-82. Borde Hill (below Kitchen Gdn) 24-55. Trewithen 21-74. Lanhydrock 19-70. *p.165.*

Campbell's Magnolia 1868 O. Borde Hill (below Kitchen Gdn) 21-48. Abbotsbury (Valley) 19-58. Exbury 15-73. Westonbirt 15-58. Kilmacurragh (Wall Gdn) 13-73. *p.165.*

Tulip Tree c.1650 F. Leith Pl 33-197. Stourhead (W of lake) 36-189. Leigh Pk 32-205. Mote Pk, Maidstone 29-183. Margam Abbey 30-151. Golden Gr, Carmarthen 24-**254**. Kitlands, Surrey 33-190. Deans Ct, Dorset 28-187. Deepdene, Surrey 28-183. *p.166.*

Chinese Tulip-tree 1901 O. Ashford Chase 24-75. Abbeyleix 25-53. Kew (Bell Lawn) 24-40. Borde Hill (N Gdn) 26-79. Mt Usher 22-68. Fota, Co Cork 26-78. *p.166.*

Spur-leaf 1901 R. Caerhays Cas 12-41+40. Cambridge BG 13-30. Edinburgh RBG 11-40. *p.166.*

Katsura Tree 1881 F. Westonbirt (Victory Gl) 27-44+39. Petworth Ho 20-40 at 1m. Sandringham Pk 18-36+28. Howick 16-32+27. Ashford Old Mnr 19-39+32. Cannizaro Pk, Wimbledon 19-38. Ashbourne Ho, Cork 21-60+57. Leny Ho, Perths 19-57. Tynninghame 18-52+49. *p.167.*

Winter's Bark 1827 F. Kilmacurragh 18-43+32. Bosahan 17-32. Lr Coombe Royal 16-**70**. Howick 10-18. Ashbourne Ho **20**-29. Castlewellan 17-48. Clyne Cas, Glam 15-44. *p.168.*

Bay 1562 C. Margam Abbey **21**-29, 19-34. Abbotsbury 12-22. Kensington Gdns 11-28+27. Regent's Pk 10-26. East Pk, Southampton 10-31. Knowle Pk, Devon 11-27+21. *p.168.*

California Laurel 1829 O. (IOW) **22-115**. Borde Hill (Gdn) 16-85. Langley Pk 16-46. Holland Pk 17-61. Greenwich Pk 15-41. Lydhurst 21-60. Townhill 17-39. Gunnersbury Pk 18-70. *p.169.*

Sassafras 1630 R. Cannizaro Pk, Wimbledon 21-68, 20-57. Kew (nr Pagoda Vista) 13-57. Hillier Arb 10-29. Caerhays Cas 12-23. *p.169.*

Chinese Sweetgum 1884 R. Killerton **21-40**. Caerhays Cas 16-38+24. Osborne Ho 11-28. Hillier Arb 11-18. The Grange, Kent 16-31. *p.170.*

Sweetgum 1651 C. Syon Pk **30**-88. Kew 28-70. Osterley Pk 26-65, 21-52. St Fagan's, Cardiff 21-49. Roath Pk, Cardiff 16-48. Abbotsbury (Lr Pool) 23-55. Stratfield, Saye 28-**100**. *p.170.*

Persian Ironwood 1840 F. Dyffryn Gdn 11-37. Petworth Ho 8-39. Cannizaro Pk, Wimbledon 10-30+28. Lingholm 5-42 at 1m. Tilgate Pk 12-43. Abbotsbury **14**-40. Wakehurst Pl 10-48. *p.171.*

Gutta-Percha Tree 1896 O. Kew (nr flagstaff) 14-54. Wisley 11-32. Talbot Mnr 11-31. Dyffryn Gdn 9-26. Oxford Univ pks 10-30. Hillier Nsy 12-44. *p.171.*

Oriental Plane c.1550 F. Rycote 21-**274**. Weston Pk 24-233. Corsham Ct 28-225. Jesus Coll, Cambridge 28-164. Exton Pk 24-139. Melbury 23-195. Woodstock Pk, Kent 28-260. Duntish Ct, Devon 28-245 at 0.3m. *p.172.*

London Plane c.1680 C. Bryanston Sch 47-183, **48**-179. Mottisfont Abbey 33-365 (dble tree?), 33-224 (gd bole). Ely (Bishop's Pal) 35-281. Ranelagh Pk 40-252. Winchester Coll 36-205. Riverside Gdns, Richmond 40-177, 34-195. Osterley Pk 31-177. Festival Walk, Carshalton 42-217. Witley 38-208. Pusey 32-240. Cirencester Abbey 36-194. Kew (Rhodo Dell) 35-181. Lydney Pk, Glos 33-270. Chilton Foliat (A419) 16-250. Wotton Ho, Surrey 31-213. *p.173.*

Hawthorn N C. Cockington Ct 10-58. Weston Pk 11-48. Hyland Pk, Writtle 9-61. Ware Pk 8-56+56. Hall Place, Kent 16-**78**. *p.174.*

Cockspur Thorn 1691 R. Hillier Arb 8m. Kew 5-21. Cannizaro Pk 8-28. *p.175.*

Broadleaf Cockspur Thorn pre-1797 C. Langley Pk 9-33. Alexandra Pk, Hastings 9-30. Oxford Univ pks 9-30. Kew 6-35. Emmetts, Kent 9-52. *p.175.*

Hybrid Cockspur Thorn pre-1880 F. Bath BG 9-50. Edinburgh RBG 9-36. Howick 7-33. Milford Lo, Wells 11-51. Victoria Pk, Bath 12-55. Marble Hill 15-45. *p.175.*

Himalayan Tree-Cotoneaster 1824 O. Nymans **17**-35. Regent's Pk 8-**51**. Arnos Pk, Midd 8-25. Cockington Ct 7-24. Pitgaveny, Moray 16-32. Gray Ho, Angus 15-51. *p.176.*

Rowan N C. Sandling Pk **18**-22. Chilworth Mnr (Univ of Southampton BG) 14-63. Welland Pk 16-45. Sandford Pk 15-52. *p.177.*

True Service Tree Very early O. Oxford BG 16-75, 16-67. Arley Cas 20-**106**. Colesbourne 19-57. Owston 17-51. Winkworth Arb 18-36. Witham Hall, Lincs 18-60. Wootton Ho, Surrey 17-80. *p.177.*

Japanese Rowan 1906 O. Edinburgh RBG 15-41. Wisley 16-30. *p.178.*

Chinese Scarlet Rowan c.1908 C. Sheffield Pk (Bluebell Dell) **17-50** at 1m. (nr Conifer Walk) 14-36. Savill Gdn 13-30. Winkworth Arb 11-27. Thorp Perrow 13-41. Hatton Cas, Aberdeens 15-33. *p.178.*

Sargent Rowan 1908 O. Westonbirt (Broad Dr) 11-46 (above graft). Windsor Gt Pk (Valley Gdns) 10-26. Rowallane 9-46 at 0.5m. Trewithen 9-51. Keir Ho, Perths 10-31. *p.178.*

Joseph Rock' 1933 F. Wisley (Orig) 16-38. Hillier Arb 8-21. Savill Gdn, Windsor 8-10. Calderstone Pk 10-23. Ness BG 10-21. *p.179.*

Hupeh Rowan 1910 F. Borde Hill (N Garden) 14-50. Bodnant 14-30. Thorp Perrow 13-40. E Bergholt Pl 13-37. Hidcote 15-38. Singleton Abbey, Glam 12-40. Edinburgh RBG 13-41. *p.179.*

Vilmorin's Rowan 1889 F. Crarae 9-26, 8-30. Nymans (Wild Gdn) 8-29. Inverewe, W Ross 9-22. *p.180.*

Wild Service Tree N O. Gatton Manor Golf Co 27-72. Petworth Pk 19-66. Crittenden Ho 16-68. Parsonage Fm, Udimore, Sussex 20-**133**. Hall Place, Kent 26-120. Markshall, Essex 20-80. *p.180.*

Bastard Service Tree Unknown O. Savill Gdn, Windsor 17-44. Westonbirt (Clay l) 18-28. Hollycombe 20-71. Sedlescombe Ch, Sussex 17-78 at 0.3m. Hyde Pk 11-51. Green Pk (London) 9-55. *p.181.*

Swedish Whitebeam Very early C. Borde Hill (below Kit Gdn walls) **18**-54. Fountains Abbey 15-**85**. Powis Cas Gdns 16-66. Glasnevin BG 12-60. Old Forge, Westonbirt 14-84. Calderstones Pk, Mersey 17-76. *p.181.*

Whitebeam N C. Wakehurst Pl (Woodland Valley) **23**-48. Ashford Chase 19-47. Battersea Pk 20-61. Colesbourne 16-58. Trawsoed 18-59. Sandford Pk 14-49. Wotton Ho 12-69 at 1m. Castle Ashby 22-87 at 1m, 11-78. *p.182.*

'Majestica' 1858 F. Westonbirt (Willes Dr) **21-68** at 1m. Kew 14-49. Primrose Hill, London 16-57. *p.182.*

'Wilfred Fox' c.1920. Innes Ho **12-33**. Hillier Arb 9-21. Bristol Zoo 6-12. Tortworth Ct 14-31. *p.182.*

Service Tree of Fontainebleau N O. Holker Pk **22**-47, 16-55. Glasnevin BG 16-80. Edinburgh RBG 16-65. Borde Hill (S Pk) 12-77. Oxford BG 20-86. Kilkerran, Ayrs 7-84. Battersea Pk 17-58. *p.182.*

Himalayan Whitebeam 1820 R. Westonbirt (Morley Ride) **21**-51, (Circular Dr) 17-47. Borde Hill (below Kit Gdn walls) **21**-86. (includes *S. thibetica* 'J Mitchell'). Stourhead 17-60. Burford Ho 23-68. Alexandra Pk (Bohemia) 17-48. *p.183.*

Folgner's Whitebeam 1901 R. Westonbirt (Holford R) 14-26, (Circular Dr) 12-17. Sheffield Pk 16-29. Caerhays Cas 20-32, 18-38. Crarae 9-24. Borde Hill (Kit Gdn wall path) 11-32. *p.183.*

Japanese Crab 1862 C. Waddesdon Ho 10-39. Hylands Pk 8-41. Chobham Ch 10-50. Leicester UBG 8-51. Horsham Pk 12-56. *p.184.*

Purple Crab pre-1900 C. Kew 11-45. Glasnevin BG 10-48. *p.184.*

Chinese Crab pre-1780 O. Cambridge BG **13-71**. *p.185.*

Siberian Crab 1784 O. Aldenham Pk 15-69. Wakehurst Pl 10-39. *p.186.*

Hupeh Crab 1900 O. Westonbirt (Broad Dr) 17-26. Savill Gdn, Windsor 12-54. Wakehurst Pl 16-53. Longstock Pk 10-34. Singleton Abbey, Glam 11-58. The Grange, Kent 19-53. Holker 12-51. *p.186.*

Pillar Apple 1897 F. Westonbirt (Clay I) **18**-30. Knaphill Nsy 15-**46**. Thorp Perrow 17-29. Regent's Park (Rose Gdn) 12-18. Cathays Pk 14-22. Cambridge BG 12-30. *p.187.*

'Jown Downie' Crab 1875 C. Westonbirt (Mitchell Dr) 11-30, (Downs) 9-40. Wisley 8-32. *p.187.*

Willow-leafed Pear 1780 C. Kelvingrove Pk **14**-45. Victoria Pk, London 12-45. E Bergholt Pl 13-40. Hall Place, Kent 11-**67**. Prince's Pk, Liverpool 6-41. *p.188.*

Common Pear Very early C. Leatherhead (pk) 18-58. Thorp Perrow 17-36. Forthampton Ch, Glos height unmeasured **1m** diam. Holland Pk, London 18-65. Tickners Gr **21**-73. *p.188.*

Wild Cherry N C. Prior's Mesne **31**-71. Studley Royal 18-**170**. Hatfield Forest 18-73. Antony Ho 23-53. Trelissick 16-81. Riverhill, Kent 25-86. Mote Pk 16-86. Belvoir Cas 28-50. *p.189.*

Sargent Cherry 1890 C. Sheffield Pk (nr ent) **15**-61. Leonardslee 10-80, 18-70. Bodnant 11-61. Rowallane 11-70. *p.189.*
'Accolade' 1925 C. Longstock Gdn 8-31. Savill Gdn, Windsor 6-26. Waterer's Nsy, Bagshot 6-**46**. Wisley 9-35. Valley Gdns, Windsor 10-34. *p.189.*

Myrobalan Plum Early C. Kew 9-32. Thorp Perrow 6-35. *p.190.*

Pissard's Plum c.1880 F. Victoria Pk, Bath **12**-35. Langley Pk, Slough 11-54. Leicester BG, 8-58. Bromham Hosp, Bedford 8-**64**. *p.190.*

Winter Cherry pre-1909 C. Savill Gdn, Windsor **11**-29. Bath BG -58cm. Brockenhurst Pk 9-42. Cambridge BG 5-33. Singleton Abbey 11-**78**. *p.190.*

Yoshino Cherry 1902 F. Westonbirt (Morley R) **11**-34. Kew (Palm Ho) 7-**57**, (Victoria Gate) 9-54, (Museum) 5-46. Bristol Zoo 5-51. Knightshayes 10-56. *p.191.*

Tibetan Cherry 1908 O. Petworth Ho 12-28. Westonbirt (Clay I) 10-**44**. Bodnant 11-42, 9-57 at 1m. Killerton 8-33. Wisley 9-37. Crathes Cas 10-61 at 1m. *p.191.*

'Kanzan' Cherry 1914 C. Savill Gdn, Windsor 9-55. Birr Cas (Formal Gdn) 4-63. Bath BG 5-40. Leonardslee 10-81. Highdown 9-60. *p.192.*

Manchurian Cherry 1910 O. E Bergholt Pl 14-74. Wisley 9-41. Hillier Arb 9-20. Cluny Gdn, Perths 19-46+28. *p.194.*

Black Cherry 1629 R. Kew 20-**65**. Savill Gdn, Windsor 16-45. Wakehurst (Willes Dr) 20-56. Hever Cas, Kent **24**-60. *p.195.*

Bird Cherry N F.
'Watereri' N F. Sandling Pk 16-40. Westonbirt (S/ Willes Dr) 15-**40**. Glasnevin BG 9-36. Thorp Perrow 11-31. Hergest Croft **27**-61. *p.195.*

Judas Tree pre-1600 F. Muntham Crem, Findon 51cm (half of split bole). Bath BG 12-56. Gordon Ho, Twickenham 9-100 at 1m. Nonsuch Pk, Surrey 10-60. *p.196.*

Yellowwood 1812 R. Wakehurst Pl (below Bethlehem Gdn) **17**-40. Bath BG 13-**41**. Cambridge BG 11-37. Jephson Gdns, Leamington 10-28. Hyde Pk (SE) 9-38. *p.196.*

Robinia c.1636 C. Kew (E Wall) **29**-104, (lawn 1762 tree) 15-**150**. Brookwood Necropolis, Surrey 19-125. Bayfordbury 28-101. Hampton Pk, Surrey 26-215, forking. *p.198.*
'Frisia' c.1945 C. Kew (lake W) 14-26. Bath BG 15-30.Marble Hill 16-38. *p.198.*

Honey Locust 1700 O. Victoria Pk, Bath **25-129** at 0.5m. Avington Pk 19-61. St James's Pk 22-56. Glasnevin BG 19-71. *p.199.*
'Inermis' ?1700 O. Emmanuel Coll, Cambridge **23-74**. Cambridge BG 20-66. West St, Chichester 15-60. Lexden Rd, Colchester 17-51. Kew 20-58. Avenue Ho, Barnet 22-69. *p.199.*

Pagoda Tree 1753 O. Oxford Univ pks 17-92. Jephson Gdns, Leamington 13-86. Anglesea Abbey 18-70. Dulwich Pk 17-74 at 1m. Caversham Pub Lib 16-80 at 0.5m. Kew (Bell Lawn) 19-71. Roath Pk, Cardiff 19-63. Syon Pk (Wilderness) 27-158. *p.199.*

Kentucky Coffee Tree 1748 R. Nymans (Magnolia Gdn) **18**-50. Mote Pk, Maidstone 11-51. Victoria Pk, London 13-29. Victoria Pk, Bath 16-48. Dulwich Pk 12-30. Dulwich Lib 12-44. Jephson Gdns, Leamington 13-41. Oxford BG 14-46. Leigh Pk, Hants 14-35. Battersea 15-47. *p.201.*

Japanese Cork Tree 1863 R. Edinburgh RBG 17-56. Glasnevin 13-38. Kew 11-51. Auchincruive 13-82 at 0.5m. Talbot Mnr 12-31. *p.202.*

Amur Cork Tree 1856 R. Kew (bamboos) 19-60. Cedar Pk, Chenies 8-50 at 0.5m. Tilgate Pk 10-39. *p.202.*

Euodia 1908 O. Glendoick **24-100**. Greenwich Pk 20-90. Glasnevin BG20-61. Edinburgh RBG 15-71 at 1m. Anstey Lane, Alton 9-39. Bodnant 15-71 at 1m. Victoria Pk, London (playground) 9-41. *p.203.*

Tree of Heaven 1751 F. Bury St Edmunds Abbey (gate) **26**-105. Oakley Ch, Bedford 25-**106**. Lexden, Colchester 23-101. Belton Pk 25-82. Univ of Exeter (Streatham Hall) 23-95. Dulwich Pk 18-81. Bishop's Pal, Wells 20-104. *p.204.*

Downy Tree of Heaven 1897 R. W Dean (gdn) 26-75. Kew (Broad Walk) 20-72. Edinburgh RBG 13-40. Cambridge BG 19-48. Glasnevin BG 14-43. *p.204.*

Picrasma 1890 R. Kew 9-50 at 15cm. Westonbirt (E Mitchell Dr) 9-13+12. Muntham Crem, Findon, Sussex 8-18. Wisley 4-5. *p.204.*

Chinese Cedar 1862 R. Pencarrow 22-46. Kew 17-70. Hergest Croft **27**-67. Cambridge BG 18-64. Glasnevin BG 16-70. Edinburgh RBG 14-34. *p.206.*

Varnish Tree 1874. O. Cambridge BG **19**-60. Stanage Pk 16-**64**+61. Wakehurst Pl (Jap Gdn) 18-62. Hergest Croft 18-48+40. Glasnevin BG 16-44. Westonbirt Ho 21-70. Witham Hall, Lincs 13-81 at 1m. *p.206.*

Chinese Varnish Tree 1907 R. Westonbirt (Clay I) **17-56** at 0.5m, (Holford Ride) 15-27+26. Bath BG 13-50. Hyde Pk (Nursery Border) 9-30. Mount Ho, Glos **24-80**. *p.206.*

Box N C. Birr Cas (hedge) 12-19. Chiswick Ho 9-18. Westonbirt (The Waste) 8-13+12. Audley End, Essex 11-20. Norbury Pk (Druids' Gr) 12-21. *p.207.*

Balearic Box 1780 R. W Dean Ho **11**-23+22. Abbotsbury 8-13+12. Cambridge BG 5m. Bath BG 6-21. Paignton Zoo 6-10. *p.207.*

Holly N C. Staverton Thicks, Suffolk 23-75. Horsham Pk 20-39. Johnstown Cas 21-21 (main stem). Rotherfield Pk 19-52. Sandling Pk 18-56 (main stem). Hatfield Ho 17-51. Claremont 16-81 at 1m. Ashburton Pl 25-37 *p.208.*

Highclere Holly 'Hodginsii' 1838 C. Ballamoar 22-50. Westonbirt (Wigmore) 14-49. Tatton Pk 16-41. Killerton (N fence) 18-48. Colaton Ralegh, Devon 22-32. *p.209.*

Himalayan Holly 1840 R. Wakehurst Pl (Woodl Vall) 15-40. Abbotsbury 13-34. Linton Pk, Kent 17-**55**. *p.209.*

Norway Maple pre-1683 C. W Dean (Roche's Arb) **30**-87. Cobham Hall 23-91. Westonbirt (Holford Ride) 29-85. Cawdor Cas 22-84. Dunrobin Cas 25-80. Clapton Ct 22-81. Castle Fraser, Aberdeens 26-118. *p.210.*

'Schwedleri' 1870 C. Westonbirt (Main Dr) **25-80**. Waddesdon Ho (NW Dr) 23-79. Ascott Ho 22-70. Abbotsbury (Euc W) 24-60. Alnwick Cas (River W) 19-55. Osterley Pk (Prospect) 20-73. *p.210.*

Sugar Maple 1735 O. Hackwood Pk 25-83. Mt Usher 21-77. Blenheim Pal (Rose Gdn) 19-60. Bedgebury 15-57. Holkham 16-30. Eastnor Cas 16-73. Westonbirt (Circular Dr N) 22-47. Glasnevin BG 17-40. Moncrieffe Ho, Perths 22-75. *p.211.*

Miyabe's Maple 1895 R. Bedgebury **18-52**+41. Batsford Pk 15-45. Glasnevin BG 12-31. *p.211.*

Lobel's Maple 1838 O. Edinburgh RBG 20-80. Abbeyleix 26-50. Westonbirt 24-63. Regent's Park 13-41. Talbot Mnr 23-46. Eastnor Cas **30-116**. Ashridge Pk, Herts 26-82. Battersea Pk 22-82. *p.211.*

Cappadocian Maple 1838 F. Westonbirt (Morley Ride S) **26**-61. Leigh Pk, Havant 19-**87**. Trentham Pk 14-104 at 1m. Victoria Pk, Bath 18-66. Howick (Drive) 13-80. Castle Leod 15-72. Glasnevin BG 18-72. Dulwich Pk 20-52. *p.211.*

Sycamore Early C. Drumlanrig Cas 35-225. Birnam 32-230. Cobham Hall 36-193. Belton Pk (Field) 31-146. Trelissick 16-157. Dunrobin Cas 28-105. Royal Windermere Yacht Cl 28-137. Bargany, Ayrs 26-188. Tolpuddle 18-183. *p.212.*

'Brilliantissimum' Kew (Boathouse W) 13-37. Tredegar Pk 7-31. St Fagan's, Cardiff 8-24. *p.212.*

Van Volxem's Maple 1873 R. Westonbirt (Willes Dr) **27**-81, (Broad Dr) 25-73. Edinburgh RBG 17-91. *p.212.*

Italian Maple 1752 O. Balloan **23**-102. Smeaton Ho 22-95. Kew 18-96 at 1m. Victoria Pk, Bethnal Green 16-53. *p.213.*

Horned Maple 1880 R. Westonbirt (Main Dr) **15-35**. Hillier Arb 12-32. *p.213.*

Balkan Maple 1865 R. Westonbirt (Broad Dr) 19-64, (Willes Dr) 15-47. Oxford Univ pks 15-39. *p.213.*

Oregon Maple 1827 O. (Co Tipperary) 20-125. Trinity Coll, Dublin 16-108. Westonbirt (Circ Dr) 24-97. Thorp Perrow 20-46. Victoria Pk, London 17-77. Colesbourne 16-46. Edinburgh RBG 25-64. *p.214.*

Trautvetter's Maple 1866 R. Edinburgh RBG 21-61. Glasnevin BG 14-60. Winkworth Arb 16-32 at 1m. *p.214.*

Heldreich's Maple 1879 R. Hergest Croft (Ave) **23-86**. Edinburgh RBG 21-54. Hillier Arb 10-25. *p.214.*

Silver Maple 1725 C. Westonbirt (Willes Dr) **34**-94. Kew (Jap Gate) 27-**130**. Wisley (Pine) 30-108. Osterley Pk 30-110. Haste Hill, Haslemere (roadside) 28-108. Ascott Ho 27-95. Cotehele 30-116. Finsbury Pk 22-110. *p.215.*

Deep-veined Maple 1881 R. Hollycombe Steam Fair **14**-**34**. Muncaster Cas 6-13. Savill Gdn, Windsor 9m. *p.215.*

Smooth Japanese Maple 1820 C. Leonardslee **18**-42. Westonbirt (Main Dr) 16-**45**, (Loop Walk) 17-48 at 0.5m. Blagdon 12-43 at 0.5m. *p.216.*

Zoeschen Maple 1870 R. Kew 19-71. Winkworth Arb 14-52. Westonbirt (Willes Dr) 13-40. Glasnevin BG 16-67. Abbeyleix **24**-60. *p.216.*

Field Maple N C. Mote Pk, Maidstone 22-**135**. Kensington Gdns 17-81. Cannizaro Pk, Wimbledon 19-45. Hughenden Mnr (field nr ch) 17-95. Kinnettles 27-81. Wimpole Ho, Cambs 18-90. Abbeyleix 27-107. *p.216.*

Père David's Maple 1879 O. Savill Gdn, Windsor 17-38+32. Holkham Hall 17-37. Dyffryn Gdn 14-40. Bury St Edmunds Abbey 14-46. Wakehurst Pl 14-43. *p.218.*

Hers's Maple 1924 F. Wisley 16-40 (Battleston H). Winkworth Arb 16-40 at 1m. Wayford Wood, Somerset 17-36. Talbot Mnr 12-39. Trewithen 14-30. Howick 12-38. *p.218.*

Red Snakebark Maple 1894 O. Westonbirt (Waste) **13**-26. Winkworth Arb 11-**36**. Exbury Ho 12-35. *p.218.*

Moosewood 1755 O. Bath BG 11-28. Crarae 11-22. *p.218.*

Grey-Budded Snakebark Maple 1879 O. Bodnant 11-**33**. Nymans (wild gdn) **13**-28. Kew (Middle Walk) 11-23. *p.218.*

Birch-Leaf Maple 1901 R. E Bergholt Pl 11-34. Wisley (Bat Ho) 20-32. *p.220.*

Lime-leaf Maple 1881 R. Grayswood Hill 11-25. Westonbirt (off Broad Dr) 11-20. *p.220.*

Red Maple 1656 F. Westonbirt (Willes Dr E) **24**-50. St Fagan's, Cardiff 24-83. Cowdray Pk 20-77. Regents Pk (Boating Lake) 14-28. Ken Wood, London 18-50. *p.221.*

Trident Maple 1896 O. Norham End, Oxford **15-56**. Kew 14-41. Borde Hill (N Park) 14-44 at 1m. Bedgebury (Hill's Ave) 10-31. Trentham Pk 12-51. Cannizaro Pk, Wimbledon 11-19. *p.222.*

Tartar Maple 1759 R. Hillier Arb 8-12. Cannizaro Pk, Wimbledon 4-10. Edinburgh RBG 6-16. Drummond Cas, Perths 7-20. *p.222.*

Montpelier Maple 1739 O. Kensington Gdns (Head of Lake) 14-58. Above St Briavel's Common, Glos 13-70. Osterley Pk 11-51 at 1m. Cannizaro Pk, Wimbledon 10-32. Kew (nr Lion Gate) 12-48. Singleton Abbey 15-62. *p.223.*

Cretan Maple 1752 R. Tregothnan 8-52. Kew 10-31. Cambridge BG 9-28. *p.223.*

Hornbeam Maple 1879 O. Wakehurst Pl (below Bethlehem Gdn) **11**-13+11. Westonbirt (Main Dr) **11**-30. Crarae 4m. Auchincruive 6-19. *p.223.*

Nikko Maple 1881 O. Exbury **16**-32. E Bergholt Pl 14-**43**. Sheffield Pk (W of gate) 15-42. Trewithen 14-38. Killerton 12-39. Howick (Rhodo Gdn) 8-20. Westonbirt (Mitchell Dr E) 15-36, (Main Dr) 14-37, 14-36. *p.224.*

Rough-Barked Maple 1923 R. Trewithen **11**-28. Westonbirt (N of Down Gate) 10-25. Winkworth Arb 7-10. Thorp Perrow 8-10. Fota 9-14. Hillier Arb 12-18. *p.224.*

Vineleaf Maple 1875 R. Wakehurst Pl (Woodland Valley) 13-27. Westonbirt (Morley Ride) 12-60 at 0.3m, (Mitchell Dr) 8-40. Dyffryn Gdn 8-21. Howick 8-20. Trewithen 11-41. *p.224.*

Paperbark Maple 1901 F. E Bergholt Pl **14**-25. Dyffryn Gdn 10-**60**. Edinburgh RBG 10-37. Howick 11-27 at).5m. Leonardslee (drive) 13-50. *p.225.*

Ashleaf Maple 1688 C. Wardour Cas **17**-43. Kew 16-**80**. Enfield Chyd 11-35. Melksham Sports Cl 13-42. Victoria Park, London 12-41. Linton Pk 18-80. Ramsbury Ch. Wilts 12-70. Peckover Ho. Cambs **19**-44. *p.225*

Horse Chestnut c.1615 C. Ashford Chase **39**-111. Hurstbourne Priors Ch 36-**213**. W Dean Ho 26-197. Fredville Pk 20-197. Cawdor Cas 19-163. Dunrobin Cas 30-105. The Promenade, Cheltenham 24-138. Ickworth Ho 26-166. Kilkerran 33-164. Wrest Pk 30-157. The Rectory, Much Hadham 37-181. Moncrieffe Ho 28-212 at 1m. Kingston Lacey 35-175. *p.226.*

Red Horse Chestnut pre-1818 C. Endsleigh **28**-90. Sandling Pk **20**-**108**. Westonbirt (Picnic site) 23-81. Battersea Pk (S of Terraces) 22-89. Melksham Sports Cl 13-99. Haddo Ho 18-83. Victoria Pk, Bath 16-89. Kew 19-105. *p.227.*

Japanese Horse Chestnut pre-1880 O. Westonbirt (Clay I) **25**-63, (Entr) 23-59, (Circular Dr) 20-**82**. Thorp Perrow 19-52. Birr Cas 14-41. Sidbury Mnr 16-65. Castle Milk 12-26. *p.227.*

Sunrise Horse Chestnut 1924 O. Westonbirt (Offices) **10**-24, (Mitchell Dr) 8-14. Cambridge BG 8-24 at 0.5m. Kew 7-12. Hillier Arb 9m. *p.227.*

Yellow Buckeye 1764 F. Bath BG **23**-85 at 0.5m. Pencarrow 18-77. Bury St Edmunds Abbey 20-69. Trentham Pk (N of lake) 14-65. Denman 18-70. St Margarets, Twickenham 23-**96**. *p.227.*

Hybrid Buckeye pre-1815. O. Battersea Pk **21**-**71**, 21-62. Pittville Gdns, Cheltenham 15-53. Cambridge BG 18-52. Kilmory Cas 19-61. *p.228.*

Indian Horse Chestnut 1851 F. Westonbirt (Loop Walk) 21-65. Kew (Main Gate) 15-80, ('Sidney Pearce') 13-61. Killerton 17-39+29. Ickworth Village Green 13-52. Cannizaro Pk, Wimbledon 15-52 at 1m. Hidcote, Glos 18-**85**. Townhill Pk, Hants 21-**85**. *p.229.*

Red Buckeye 1711 R. Goodwood Pk (Drive) 12-**40**. Kew (Colln) 9-20, 12-30. Nymans **14**-26, 13-28. *p.220.*

Broad-leafed Lime N C. Victoria Pk, Bath **34**-101. W Dean Ho 32-183. Deene Pk 26-121. Belton Pk (car park) 27-117. Clumber Pk (nr middle ave of Common Lime) 33-120. Haddo Ho 20-166 at 0.5m. Cathays Pk 25-83. Pre Hotel, St Albans 27-112. Exbury 24-103. Thorp Perrow (Spring Wood) 30-92. Pitchford Ho, 'Tree House', Shrops 14-**236**. Longnor Ho, Shrops 30-192. *p.230.*

Common Lime Unknown C. Duncombe Pk **46**-121. E Carlton Pk 29-**213**, 22-196. Gatton Pk 44-159. Scone Pal 30-181. Levens Pk (river) 40-152, (Ho) 29-172. Hutton-in-the-Forest 40-145. Borrow Ho 37-164. Ware Pk 32-171. Croft Cas 41-180. Scotney Cas 32-**186**. *p.230.*

Small-leafed Lime N F. Dodington Pk (above Dr) 38-**121**. The Rye, H Wycombe 37-110. Brampton Bryan 22-**186**. W Wycombe (car park) 35-128. Oakley Pk 32-181. Wrest Pk (lawn) 35-134. E Carlton Pk 24-150. Regent's Pk (boating lake) 22-78. Theobalds PK, Midd 34-**19**. Whitfield Ho 30-107. Tottenham Ho, Wilts **40**-117, 34-117. Petworth Ho 38-104. *p.230.*

Crimean Lime pre-1866 F. Kew (E Border) 20-52, (Colln) 16-**80**. Westonbirt (Willes Dr) 20-52. Queen's Rd, Cambridge 19-48. Osterley Pk 19-72. Antony Ho 16-54. Victoria Pk, London 12-48. Nymans (Terrace) **22**-44. *p.230.*

Silver Lime 1767 F. Westonbirt (The Downs) 30-101. Tortworth Ch **35**-**145**. Kensington Gdns 28-83. Green Pk 26-86. The Rye, H Wycombe 29-63. *p.232.*

Silver Pendent Lime 1840 F. Bath BG 34-123. Beauport Pk 32-**148**. Orchardleigh 33-134. Wray Cas 21-108. Trentham Pk 19-92. Jephson Gdns, Leamington 27-100. Green Pk, Bucks **37**-113. Hall Pl **37**-125. Magdalen Br, Oxford 28-118. Egrove Ho, Kennington 35-123. *p.232.*

Von Moltke's Lime 1872 R. Kew **23**-67. Killarney Ho 19-**101**. Glasnevin BG 22-58. *p.232.*

American Lime 1752 R. Westonbirt (Willes Dr) 24-52, 21-40. Winkworth Arb 19-37. Windsor Gt Pk (Totem Pole Ride) 12-24. Kew (Flagstaff) 17-67. Grayswood Hill, Sy 23-**80**. *p.232.*

Oliver's Lime 1900 R. Westonbirt (Spec Ave) **26**-**55**, (Acer GI) 21-44. Kew 11-48. Killerton 18-34. *p.232.*

Amur Lime 1925 R. Westonbirt (Morley R) 21-42. *p.233.*

Mongolian Lime 1880 R. Kew 19-50. Thorp Perrow 20-47. Edinburgh RBG 16-39. Wakehurst Pl (Coates' Wood) 21-48+39. *p.233.*

Nymans Hybrid Eucryphia 1915 F. Leonardslee (front) 22-36. Killerton 16-24. Logan BG 17-32. Nymans 17-31. Birkhill, Fife **23**-33. Priestwood, Bucks 18-20. *p.234.*

Deciduous Camellia pre-1878 O. Killerton 15-**45**. Winkworth Arb 11-23. Savill Gdn, Windsor 9-17. Dawyck 8-16. *p.235.*

Chinese Stuartia 1901 R. Tilgate Pk 14-35. Borde Hill (below Kitch Gdn) 18-24, (Kitch Gdn wall) 13-34. Dyffryn Gdn 12-25. Wakehurst Pl (pond) **18**-40. Innes Ho 4-11. *p.235.*

Castor Aralia 1864 O. Dyffryn Gdn 15-61. Exbury 14-60 at 1m. Greenwich Pk 16-52. Wakehurst Pl 16-52. Kew 14-51+45. *p.235.*

var. maximowiczii 1890 O. Durris Est, Kincards (roadside) 17-**72**. Dawyck 38-54. The High Beeches, Sussex 20-41. Bodnant 13-22. Killerton 12-21. Leckmelm, W Ross 12-64. Stobo, Peebles 18-50. Ramster 17-50. *p.235.*

Pride of India 1763 F. Chelsea Physic Gdn 10-**76**. Battle Abbey (path) **16**-53. Sandford Pk, Cheltenham 14-37. Joyce Green Hosp, Dartford 13-41. Oxford BG 14-38. Battersea Pk 12-42. *p.236.*

Pittosporum Unknown F. Lochinch 16-38. Abbotsbury 12-43. Powerscourt 14-37. Howick 9-32 at 1m. Culzean Cas 14-58 at 1m. *p.237.*

Idesia 1865 R. Stourhead (nr Zigzag) **20**-35. Wakehurst Pl (Slips) 15-28. *p.237.*

Orange-Bark Myrtle 1844 O. Abbotsbury 16-27+27. Rowallane 12-34. Trelissick 12-21+21. Culzean Cas 11m. Penlee Pk 13-43. Chyverton 10-38 at 1m. Tresco Abbey 20-27+27, 16-61 at 1m. *p.237.*

Blue Gum c.1800 F (Irl). Eccles Hotel, Glengarriff approx **46**-200. Powerscourt 41-96. Bangor Cas 37-110. Laxy Glen 36-125. Garron Pt, Co Antrim 31-**241**. *p.238.*

Cider Gum c.1845 F. Sidbury Mnr 22-**148**. Lochinch 30-121. Wakehurst Pl 27-109. Somerleyton Hall 20-95. Howick 22-40. Alexandria Pk, Sussex 22-60. *p.239.*

Snow Gum F. Kilmun For Gdn **23**-36. Logan BG 16-34. Hillier Arb (Valley) 12-28. Crarae 24-33. *p.239.*

Urn Gum pre-1860 R. Mt Usher **36**-101. Castlewellan (Wall) 23-110, (Woods) 34-85. Crarae 22-48. Kilmun For Gdn 25-36. Arduanie, Argyll 31-83. Stonefield, Argyll 26-123. *p.239.*

Broad-Leafed Kindling Bark c.1945 O. Mt Usher 25-62. Kilmun For Gdn 23-36. Suamarez Pk, Guernsey 21-50. Ashbourne Ho 25-94. *p.239.*

Tupelo 1750 O. Sheffield Pk (E of Con Walk) 25-57, (gate) 21-53. Chatsworth Ho (hillside) 20-65. Bicton 17-64. Kew (Pagoda Vist) 19-60. Killerton 14-33. Borde Hill (Bentleys) 22-40. *p.240.*

Dove Tree 1904 O. Westonbirt (Loop Walk) 18-62. Minterne 17-43. Pencarrow 18-49. Fosbury Mnr, Wilts **22**-47. Tregrehan 15-81 at 0.3m. *p.240.*

var. vilmoriniana 1897 F. Borde Hill (warren) 21-43. Hergest Croft 23-48+46. Tilgate Pk **25**-42+41. Rowallane 19-48+41. Nymans (Magn Gdn) 17-34+34. Wayford Wood 21-40. Trehane, Cornwall 17-**87**. Burncoose, Cornwall 17-50. *p.240.*

Pacific Dogwood 1835 O. Embley Pk Sch **14**-20. Edinburgh RBG 12-27. Hillier Arb 10-33+31. *p.241.*

Bentham's Cornel 1825 O. Mt Usher 14-51. Glendurgan 12-30. Antony Ho 12-32. Coleton Fishacre 16-41. *p.241.*

Table Dogwood 1890 O. Westonbirt (Main Drive) 17-52. Clapton Ct 10-21. Abbotsbury 17-46. Greenwich Pk 13-56. *p.241.*

Strawberry Tree N F. Sandringham Pk 11-28. Cannizaro Pk, Wimbledon 11-28+20. W Lavington Ch, Sx 10-23+20. Leonardslee **16**-33. Hurn Ct 9-75 at 0.5m. *p.242.*

Hybrid Strawberry Tree c.1810 O. Glasnevin BG 13-40+36. Highdown, Sx 11-56. Sandling Pk 9-46. Bodnant 13-61+41. E Bergholt Pl 10-50 at 0.3m. Knaphill Nsy 16-50+42. Trent Pk, Midd 9-38. *p.242.*

Cyprus Strawberry Tree 1724 R. E Bergholt Pl 10-23. Highdown, Sussex 7-14. W Dean Ho 10-27. Jenkyn Pl, Bentley 9-37 at 0.3m. Notcutt's Nsy, Suffolk. 7-18. *p.242.*

Pacific Madrone 1827 O. Killerton 20-60. Roydon Pk 14-**119** at 1.3m. Bath BG 11-49. Bodnant 13-41. E Bergholt Pl (gate) 14-47. Innes Ho 15-42. Hergest Croft 25-69+49. "Savannah", Bagshot 25-70. Coverwood, Surrey 25-86. *p.242.*

Sorrel Tree 1752 O. Sheffield Pk **19**-34. Fota 18-53. Leonardslee (Valley Gdn) 18-37. Borde Hill (Warren) 16-22. Cannizaro Pk, Wimbledon 9-22. Holker 15-33. *p.244.*

Snowdrop Tree c.1897 F. Savill Gdn, Windsor (Rosea) 15-27. Tilgate Pk 11-35+31. Winkworth Arb 13-50 (dble). Wisley 10-34. *p.244.*

Snowball Tree 1862 F. Caerhays Cas 14-36+25. Chyverton 12-24. The High Beeches, Sussex 11-22. Tregothnan **15-43.** *p.245.*

Bigleaf Storax 1879 O. Ladhams, Goudhurst 16-**32.** Holker 12-15. Chobham Pl 11-20. *p.245.*

Hemsley's Storax 1900 O. Hollycombe Steam Fair **14**-22. E Bergholt Pl 9-20. The High Beeches, Sussex 10-21. Caerhays Cas 13-22. *p.245.*

Common Ash N C. Cockington Ct 37-116. Clapton Ct 12-**223.** Rotherfield Pk 35-135. Chollerton Vill 24-167. Bwlch-y-Cibau. Llanfyllin 25-192. Ascott Ho 29-139. Peasmarsh, Sussex 36-167. Petworth Ho 39-90. Glenlyon, Perths 30-211. *p.247.*

Single-leaf Ash O. Wardour Cas 27-73. Cawdor Cas 25-59. Kensington Gdns 24-97, 26-86. Victoria Pk, Bath 24-84. Culcreuch Cas, Stirling **32-128.** Avenue Ho, Barnet 21-105. *p.247.*

Manna Ash 1710 F. Hyde Pk 22-81, 19-77. Roath Pk, Cardiff 17-54. Victoria Pk, Bath 24-84. Kensington Gdns **26**-73. Haremere Hall 23-**105.** *p.247.*

Narrowleaf Ash c.1800 O. Melbury **31**-68. Chiswick Ho 29-**100.** Battersea Pk 25-70. Victoria Pk, London 22-81. Stowe Pk 26-83. *p.248.*
'Veltheimii' Kensington Gdns **23-**78, 22-76. Kew 23-68. Battersea Pk (Play Area) 14-54. Westonbirt (Broad Dr) 18-41. *p.248.*

Caucasian Ash 1815 O. Glasnevin BG 18-56. Knaphill Nsy 21-64. Kew 19-63. *p.248.*
'Raywood' Kew 19-33. Hillier Arb 17-32. Winkworth Arb 14-30. *p.248.*

Oregon Ash 1870 R. Kew 20-79. Regent's Pk (Boating Lake) 18-70. Edinburgh RBG 25-58. *p.248.*

White Ash 1724 O. Kew (Bell Lawn) **32-86.** Batsford Pk 30-61. Victoria Pk, London 19-50. Glasnevin BG 22-53. Colesbourne 23-56. Deene Pk 19-32. *p.249.*

Red/Green Ash 1783 R. Kew (Bell Lawn) **28**-72. Oxford BG 26-**86.** *p.249.*

Chinese Privet 1794 O. Kensington Gdns (Marlb Gate) 12-45 (dble) Battersea Pk 15-64+41. Gloucester Ave, Enfield (st trees) 9-29. Victoria Pk, London 12-38. Waddesdon, Bucks 16-67. *p.250.*

Phillyrea 1597 O. Cambridge BG 9-23+21. Studley Cas 8-41. Sandringham Pk 8-40. The Vyne, Hants 8-36. *p.250.*

Date-Plum pre-1633 R. Westonbirt (Mitchell Ave) **18**-40. Glasnevin BG 13-31. Pylewell, Hants 12-40. Kew 14-30, 11-40. *p.251.*

Persimmon pre-1629 R. Oxford BG **17-60.** Glasnevin BG 10-40+31. Kew 15-34. *p.251.*

Northern Catalpa 1880 O. Wakehurst Pl (Pergola Walk) 20-52. Radnor Gdns, Twickenham 20-**109.** Broadlands 20-91. Tilehurst Rd, Reading 9-43. Manor Pk, Aldershot 10-53. Ascott Ho 12-58. West Pk, Southampton 11-48. Bicton 16-52. *p.252.*

Indian Bean Tree 1726 F. Melbury **19**-51. Chiswick Ho 14-108. Westminster Pal 12-**110.** Kew (Bell Lawn) 12-90, (Palm Ho) 11-85. Copdock Hotel, nr Ipswich 12-85. Central Cross Dr, Cheltenham 13-76. Hever Cas 16-103. Bath BG 12-91. *p.252.*

Hybrid Catalpa 1891 F. Bishop's Pal Gdn, Chichester 13-70+42. Hergest Croft 18-92. *p.252.*

Yellow Catalpa 1849 O. Killerton 14-51. Leatherhead (town centre) 13-66. Ashstead Pk Sch 13-53. Syon Pk **22-80.** *p.252.*

Farges's Catalpa 1900 R. Westonbirt (Loop Walk) **20**-33. Kew 18-**58**, 13-31. Longstock Pk 7-27. *p.252.*

Paulownia 1838 F. Westonbirt (Spec Ave) **26**-71. Rowallane 16-66. Goodwood Pk 16-58. Battersea Pk 15-68. Chilham Cas 19-78, 20-71. Linton Pk 20-76. Mottisfont Abbey 16-62. *p.253.*

Cabbage Tree 1820 C. Logan BG **16**-41, 12-**75.** Morrab Gdns, Penzance 10-66. Bishop's Ct IOM 10-49. Kilmacurragh 13-53. Claremont Gdns 6-11. Mt Stewart 6-61. Tresco Abbey 15-68. *p.254.*

Chusan Palm 1836 F. Abbotsbury (Vict Gdn) 13-**23.** Muntham Crem, Sx 11-21. Penrhyn Cas 10-21. Cliveden Ho 10-20. Trebah **16**-20. *p.254.*

Locations of notable trees

(NT) indicates a National Trust, and (ST) a Scottish National Trust, property.

Abbeyleix, Co. Leix
Abbotsbury, Dorset
Abbotswood, plots, Forest of Dean (For Comm)
Abercairny, Crieff, Perthshire
Achamore, Gigha I, Argyll
Achnacarry, Inverness
Adhurst St Mary, Petersfield, Hants
Aigas House, Beauly, Inverness
Aira force, Ullswater, Cumbria (NT)
Aldenham Park (Woods) Elstree, Herts
Aldourie Castle, Inverness
Alexandria Park, Hastings, Sussex
Alnwick Castle, Northumberland
Althorp, Northants
Alton Towers, Cheadle, Staffs
Anglesea Abbey, Cambridgeshire
Antony House, Tor Point, Cornwall
Ardanaiseig House, nr Taynult, Argyll
Ardross Castle, nr Alness, Easter Ross
Arduaine, nr Oban, Argyll
Ardverikie, Lagganside, Inverness
Arley Castle, Bewdley, Worcs
Armadale Castle, Isle of Skye
Arnos Park, Midd
Ascott House, nr Leighton Buzzard, Beds (NT)
Ashbourne House Hotel, Cork
Ashford Chase, nr Petersfield, Hants
Ashford Old Manor, nr Petersfield, Hants
Ashridge Park, Berkhampstead, Herts
Ashtead Park (School) Ashtead, Surrey
Auchincruive Agricultural College, Ayr
Avington Park, nr Winchester, Hants
Avondale Ho, Rathdrum, Co Wicklow

Balfour Manor, Sidmouth, Devon
Ballamoar, Isle of Man
Ballindalloch, Banff
Ballogie Estate, Aboyne, Aberdeen
Ballywalter, Co Down
Balmacaan, Drumnadrochit, Inverness
Balmoral Castle, Ballater, Aberdeenshire
Bangor Castle, Bangor, Co Down
Bargany, Ayrshire
Bath Botanic Garden, Avon
Batsford Park, Moreton-in-Marsh, Glos
Battersea Park, London
Battle Abbey, Battle, Sussex
Bayfordbury House, Bayford, Herts
Beaufort Castle, Inverness
Beaufront Castle, Hexham, Northumb
Beauport Park, Battle, Sussex
Bedgebury National Pinetum, Goudhurst, Kent
Belair Park, Dulwich, London
Belsay Castle, Hexham, Northumb
Belton Park, Grantham, Lincs
Belvoir Castle, Leics
Belvoir Castle, Co Down
Benenden School, Kent
Benenden Village, Kent
Benmore Arboretum, nr Dunoon, Argyll
Bicton Garden, East Budleigh, Devon
Bicton House Agricultural College, East Budleigh, Devon
Biddulph Grange, Staffs, nr Congleton, Chesh
Birnam, Dunkeld, Perths
Birr Castle, Birr, Co Offaly
Bisham Abbey, Marlow, Bucks
Bishop's Court, Isle of Man
Black Rock Gorge, Novar, Evanton, E Ross
Blackmoor House, nr Liss, Hants
Blair Castle, Blair Atholl, Perths
Blair Drummond, Doune, Perths
Blaise Castle, Henbury, Bristol
Blagdon House, nr Newcastle-on-Tyne
Blenheim Palace, Woodstock, Oxon
Bodnant, Tal-y-Cafn, Conway, Gwynedd (NT)
Bohunt Manor, Liphook, Hants

Bolderwood Arboretum, Lyndhurst, Hants (For Comm)
Bonskeid House, Loch Tummel, Perths
Borde Hill, Hayward's Heath, Sussex
Borrow House, Derwent Water, Cumbria
Bosahan, Manaccan, Cornwall
Boultham Park, Lincoln
Bowood Park, Calne, Wilts
Bowthorpe Farm, Bourn, Lincs
Brahan House, Muir of Ord, E Ross
Brampton Bryan, nr Knighton, Heref
Branklyn Garden, Perth (ST)
Brickenden Grange (Golf Club), Hertford, Herts
Broadlands, Romsey, Hants
Broadwood, Dunster, Somerset
Brockhampton Park, Bromyard, Heref (NT)
Brockenhurst Church, Hants
Brockenhurst Parkm Hants
Brocklesby Park, Immingham, Lincs
Brook House, Londonderry, Co Derry
Brookwood Necropolis, Woking, Surrey
Broxwood Court, Sarnesfield, Heref
Bryanston School, Blandford, Dorset
Bulkeley Mill, nr Llanrwst, Gwynedd
Bulstrode House, Gerrards Cross, Bucks
Burford House, Tenbury Wells, Worcs
Burwood Estate, Walton-on-Thames, Surrey
Bwlch-y-Cibau, Llanfyllin, Powys

Caerhays Castle, Tregony, Cornwall
Cairnsmore (roadside Pinetum) Newton Stewart, Kirkcud
Caledon Castle, Caledon, Co Tyrone
Cambridge University Botanic Garden
Canford School, Wimborne, Dorset
Cannizaro Park, Wimbledon, Surrey
Canon's Park, Edgware, London
Capel House, Enfield, Midd
Capenoch, Thornhill, Dumfriesshire
Carclew, Penryn, Cornwall
Carshalton Park, Surrey
Castle Ashby, Northampton
Castle Fraser, Aberdeens
Castle Horneck, Penzance, Cornwall
Castle Kennedy, Stranraer, Wigtowns
Castle Leod, Strathpeffer, E Ross
Castle Milk, Lockerbie, Dumfries
Castlehill, Barnstaple, Devon
Castlewellan, Newcastle, Co Down
Cathays Park, Cardiff, Glam
Cawdor Castle, Cawdor, Nairn
Cedars Park, Chesnut, Herts
Central Cross Drive, Cheltenham, Glos
Central Park, Bournemouth
Change House, Hadleigh, Sussex
Chatsworth House, Edensor, Bakewell, Derbys
Chelsworth, Lavenham, Suffolk
Chiltlee Estate, Liphook, Hants
Chilworth Manor, University Botanic Garden, Southampton
Chiswick House, London
Chobham Place, Chobham, Surrey
Chollerton Village, Wall, Northumberland
Chudleigh Knighton, Newton Abbot, Devon
Chyverton, Truro, Cornwall
Clapton Court, Crewkwerne, Somerset
Claremont Gardens, Surbiton, Surrey
Claremont Park, Esher, Surrey (NT)
Cliveden House, Wooburn, Bucks (NT)
Clock House, Enfield, Midd
Close Walks Wood, Midhurst, Sussex
Clonmannon House, Wicklow, Co Wicklow
Clumber Park, Worksop, Notts (NT)
Clunie Castle Garden, Aberfeldy, Perths
Cobham Hall (School), Rochester, Kent
Cockington Court, Torbay, Devon
Coed Coch, Abergele, Clwyd

Colesbourne, S of Cheltenham, Glos
Colebrooke Manor, Brokenborough, Co Fermanagh
Conon House, E Ross
Coolhurst (School), Horsham, Sussex
Copdock Hotel, Ipswich, Suffolk
Corsham Court, Corsham, Wilts
Coull House, Aberdeens
Coverwood, Ewhurst, Surrey
Cowdray Park, Midhurst, Sussex
Cragside, Rothbury, Northumb (NT)
Craigievar Castle, Aberdeens (NTS)
Crarae Garden and Forest Garden, Furnace, Argyll
Crathes Castle, Deeside, Kincards (ST)
Cricket House (Wildlife Park), Crewkerne, Somerset
Crowthorne Avenue, B3348, Crowthorne, Surrey
Crittenden House, Matfield, Tonbridge, Kent
Culcreuch Castle, Fintry, Stirling
Culdees, Forfar, Angus
Culzean Castle, Maybole, Ayrshire (ST)
Curragh Chase, Askeaton, Co Limerick

Dalguise House, Dunkeld, Perths
Darnaway Castle, Forres, Moray
Dartington Hall, Totnes, Devon
Dawyck Castle, Stobo, Peeblesshire
Dean's Court, Wimborne, Dorset
Deene Park, Corby, Northants
Denman College, (WI), Marcham, Abingdon, Berks
Dochfour, Inverness
Dodington Park, Chipping Sodbury, Glos
Downton House, New Radnor, Powys
Drum Castle, Aberdeen (ST)
Drum Manor, Cookstown, Co Tyrone
Drumlanrig Castle, Thornhill, Dumfriesshire
Drummond Castle, Crieff, Perths
Drumtochty Glen, Auchinblae, Kincards
Dunans, Glendaruel, Argyll
Duncombe Park, Helmsley, N Yorks
Dunkeld House (Hotel), Dunkeld, Perths
Dunorlan Park, Tunbridge Wells, Kent
Dunrobin Castle, Golspie, Sutherland
Duntish Court, Honiton, Devon
Dupplin, Belle Wood, Perths
Durris Estate, Banchory, Kincards
Dyffryn Garden, St Nicholas, Cardiff, Glam

Eardisley Village, S of Kingston, Herefords
East Bergholt Place, East Bergholt, Suffolk
East Carlton Park, Corby, Northants
East Malling Church, Kent
East Park, Southampton City, Hants
Eastnor Castle, Ledbury, Herefords
Ebernoe House, Petworth, Sussex
Eccles Hotel, Glengarriff, Co Cork
Edinburgh Royal Botanic Garden
Eilean Shona (Island), Ardloe, Argyll
Elvaston Park, Derby
Embley Park (School) nr Romsey, Hants
Emmanuel College, Cambridge
Endsleigh House, Milton Abbot, Tavistock, Devon
Eridge Castle, Frant, Kent
Errol House, Perths
Esher, River Drive, Surrey
Evancoyd, Evenjobb, New Radnor, Powys
Ewhurst Church, E Sussex
Exbury House, Beaulieu, Hants
Exeter University, Devon
Exton Park, Oakham, Rutland

Fairburn House, Muir of Ord, E Ross
Fallbarrow Park, Bowness, Cumbria
Fasque House, Fettercairn, Kincards
Festival Walk, Carshalton, Surrey
Finborough Hall, Great Finborough, Suffolk
Fingask, Perths
Forty Hall, Enfield, Midd
Fota Island, Cobh, Co Cork
Foulis Castle, E Ross

Fountains Abbey, Ripon, N Yorks
Fredville Park, Hythe, Kent
Frensham Hall, Shottermill, Surrey
Furzey House, Beaulieu, Hants

Garnons, Byford, Herefords
Garron Pt, Co Arntrim
Garston House, Watford, Herts
Gathmyl, Newtown, Powys
Gatton Manor (Country Club) Ockley, Surrey
Gatton Park (School) Reigate, Surrey
Gayhurst, Newport Pagnell, Bucks
Glamis Castle, Angus
Glasnevin Botanic Garden, Glasnevin, Co Dublin
Glen House, Peeblesshire
Glenapp, Ballantrae, Ayrshire
Glendoick, Errol, Perths
Glendurgan, Mawnan Smith, Cornwall (NT)
Glenferness, S of Forres, Moray
Glengarry Hotel, Invergarry, Inverness
Glenlee Park, New Galloway, Kirkcud
Glentanar, Aboyne, Aberdeenshire
Gliffaes, The, Crickhowell
Gnaton House, Newton Ferrers, Devon
Godalming Town Meadow, Surrey
Goodwood Park, Chichester, Sussex
Gordon Castle, Fochabers, Moray
Gosford Castle, Markethill, Co Armagh
Gothic Lodge by Wimbledon Common, Surrey
Grantley Hall, Ripon, N Yorks
Grayswood Hill, Haslemere, Surrey
Great Dixter, Northiam, Sussex
Great Missenden Abbey, Amersham, Bucks
Green Park, Aston Clinton, Bucks
Green Park, London
Greenwich Park, Greenwich, London
Grimston Hall, Tadcaster, Yorks
Gunnersbury Park, London

Hackwood Park, nr Basingstoke, Hants.
Haddo House, Old Meldrum, Aberdeenshire (ST)
Haffield House, Donnington, Herefords.
Hafodunas, Abergele, Clwyd
Haggerston Castle, Berwick-on-Tweed,
    Northumb
Hall Place, Kent
Halliford Park, Sunbury, Midd
Hallyburton House, Coupar Angus, Perths
Ham House, Petersham, Surrey.
Ham Manor Golf Club, Arundel, Sussex.
Hampton Court, Middlesex.
Hampton Park, Seale, Surrey
Hanford House, Blandford, Dorset.
Hardwicke Park, Bury St Edmunds, Suffolk
Haremere Hall, Etchingham, Sussex
Hatfield Forest, Takeley, Essex
Hatfield House, Hatfield, Herts
Hatton Castle, Aberdeens
Headfort, Kells, Co. Meath
Heanton, N Devon
Heckfield Place, Hants
Heligan, St Ewe,Cornwall
Hergest Croft, Kington, Herefords
Hester Park, Cheltenham, Glos
Hermitage, Inver, Dunkeld, Perths (ST)
Hever Castle, Kent
Hewell Grange, Bromsgrove, Worcs
High Beeches, Handcross, Sussex
Highclere, Kingsclere, Hants
Highdown, Goring, Sussex
Hillier Arboretum, Ampfield, Romsey, Hants
Holker, Cartmel, Cumbria
Holkham Hall, Wells, Norfolk
Hollycombe Steam Fair, nr Liphook, Hants
Holme Lacey, Hereford
Honeyhanger, Shottermill, Haslemere, Surrey
Horsley Towers, East Horsley, Surrey
Howick, Alnwick, Northumb

LOCATIONS OF NOTABLE TREES

Howletts Park Zoo, Canterbury, Kent
Hughenden Manor, High Wycombe, Bucks (NT)
Hurstbourne Priors Church, Whitchurch, Hants
Hutton-in-the-Forest, Penrith, Cumbria
Hyde Park, London
Hyland Park, Writtle, Essex

Ickworth House, Suffolk
Inchmarlo, Banchory, Kincards
Innes House, Lhanbryde, Moray
Inveraray Castle, Argyll
Inverewe Garden, Poolewe, Wester Ross (NTS)

Jenkyn Place, Bentley, Hants
Jephson Gardens, Leamington Spa, Warwicks
Jesus College, Cambridge
Johnstown Castle, Wexford, Co. Wexford
Joyce Green Hospital, Dartford, Kent

Kailzie Castle, Peebles
Keir House, Dunblane, Perths
Kelvingrove Park, Glasgow
Kennedy Arboretum, New Ross, Co. Wexford
Kensington Gardens, London
Kenwood House, Highgate, London
Kew Royal Botanic Gardens, Kew, Richmond,
    Surrey
Kiftsgate, Chipping Campden, Glos
Killarney House, Killarney, Co. Kerry
Kilkerran, Maybole, Ayrshire
Killerton, Silverton, Exeter, Devon (NT)
Kilmacurragh, Rathdrum, Co. Wicklow
Kilmory Castle, Lochgilphead, Argyll
Kilmun Forest Garden, Dunoon, Argyll
Kilravock Castle, Croy, Nairn
Kilruddery, Bray, Co. Wicklow
Kilve Priory, Williton, Somerset
Kincardine Castle, Auchterarder, Perths
Kinfauns Castle, Perths
Knaphill Nurseries, Knaphill, Woking, Surrey
Knole Park, Sevenoaks, Kent (NT)
Knowle Park, Sidmouth, Devon
Kyloe Wood, Beal, Northumb

Lacock Abbey, Lacock, Wilts (NT)
Ladham House, Goudhurst, Kent
Lamellan, St Tudy, Cornwall
Langley Park, Slough, Berks
Langleys, Chelmsford, Essex
Lanhydrock, Bodmin, Cornwall (NT)
Laxy Glen, Isle of Man
Leeds Castle, Kent
Leigh Court, Bristol, Avon
Leigh Park, Havant, Hants
Leigh Village, Kent
Leighton Park, Welshpool, Powys
Leith Place, Leith Hill, Surrey (NT)
Leny House Hotel, Callender, Perths
Leonardslee, Lower Beeding, Sussex
Levens Hall, S of Kendal, Cumbria (NT)
Lexden, Colchester, Essex
Lingholm, Derwent Water, Cumbria
Lochanhead (Hotel), SW of Dumfries, Kirkcud
Loch Inch, Castle Kennedy, Stranraer, Wigtowns
Lochnaw (Hotel), W of Stranraer, Wigtowns
Logan Botanic Garden, S of Stranraer, Wigtowns
Longfords Castle, S of Salibury, Wilts
Longleat House, Warminster, Wilts
Longnor Hall, Shrops
Longstock Gardens, N of Stockbridge, Hants
Lower Coombe Royal, Kingsbridge, Devon
Lower Sherriff Farm, Horsted Keynes, Sussex
Lowther Castle, Penrith, Cumbs
Lude House, Blair Atholl, Perths
Lydham Park, Shrops (Hall)
Lydhurst, Warninglid, Sussex
Lyndford Arboretum, Mundford, Norfolk
Lynhales, Kington, Herefords

Manor Park, Aldershot, Hants
Marble Hill Park, Twickenham, London
Marbury Park, Nantwich, Cheshire
Margam Abbey, Margam, Glam
Meikleour House, Meikleour, Perths
Melbourne Hall, Melbourne, Derbyshire
Melbury Park, Evershot, Dorset
Merlewood Grange, Grange-over-Sands, Cumbria
Moncrieffe House, Bridge of Earn, Perths
Moniac Glen, Beauly, Inverness (now labelled
    Reelig Glen)
Monk Coniston, Coniston, Cumbria
Montacute House, Yeovil, Somerset (NT)
Monteviot Pinery, Jedburgh, Roxburghs
Monzie Castle, Crieff, Perths
Morrab Gardens, Penzance, Cornwall
Morton House, Bideford, Devon
Moss's Wood, Leith Hill, Surrey (NT)
Mote Park, Maidstone, Kent
Mottisfont Abbey, Romsey, Hants (NT)
Mount Congreve, Co. Waterford
Mount Edgcumbe, Tor Point, Cornwall
Mount House, Alderley, Glos
Mount Stewart, Newtownards, Co.Down (NT)
Mount Usher, Ashford, Co. Wicklow
Much Hadham Rectory, Herts
Muckross Abbey, Killarnev, Co. Kerry
Muncaster Castle, Ravenglass, Cumbria
Munches, New Abbey, Dumfries
Muntham Crematorium, Findon, Sussex
Murthly Castle, Dunkeld, Perths
Myarth, nr Crickhowell, Powys
Mylor Church, Penryn, Falmouth, Cornwall

Ness Botanic Garden, Neston, Cheshire
Nettlecombe Court, Williton, Somerset
New Court, Topsham, Devon
Nonsuch House, Bromham, Wilts
Norham End, Norham Road, Oxford
Notcutt's Nursery, Woodbridge, Suffolk
Nuneham Arboretum, Nuneham Courtenay, Oxon
Nymans, Hand Cross, Sussex (NT)

Oakley Park, Ludlow, Shrops
Ochtertyre, Crieff, Perths
Orchardleigh, Frome, Somerset
Osborne House, Isle of Wight
Osterley Park, Hounslow, London
Owston, Doncaster, Yorks

Paignton Zoo, Torbay, Devon
Pain's Hill, Cobham, Surrey
Parkhatch, Hascombe, Surrey
Patshull House, Burnhill Green, Wolverhampton,
    Staffs
Patterdale Hall, Ullswater, Cumbria
Peamore, Exeter
Pencarrow, Bodmin, Cornwall
Penjerrick, Falmouth, Cornwall
Penlee Park, Cornwall
Penrhyn Castle, Bangor, Gwynedd
Peper Harow School, Godalming, Surrey
Pershore College of Agriculture, Worcester
Petworth House, Petworth, Sussex (NT)
Phear Park, Exmouth, Devon
Pitcarmick, Strathardle, Perths
Pitchford House, Shrewsbury, Shrops
Pittville Park, Cheltenham, Glos
Portmeirion, Portmadoc, Gwynedd
Possingworth Park, Waldron, Sussex
Powderham Castle, Kenton, Devon
Powerscourt, Enniskerry, Co. Wicklow
Powis Castle, Welshpool, Powys (NT)
Pre Hotel, St Albans, Herts
Prested Hall, Kelvedon, Essex
Preston Park, Brighton, Sussex
Princeland House, Coupar Angus, Perths
Priors Mesne, St Briavels, Glos

Puck Pits, New Forest, Hants
Pusey House, Faringdon, Berks
Pylewell House, Lymington, Hants

Queenswood, Hope-under-Dinmore, Herefords

Radley College, Abingdon, Berks
Radnor Gardens, Twickenham, London
Raehills, Annan, Dumfries
Ramster, Chiddingfold, Surrey
Randolph's Leap, Nairn
Ranelagh Park, Barnes, London
Reading University (Whiteknights Park) Berks
Red Rice College, nr Stockbridge, Hants
Reelig Glen (Moniac) Beauly, Inverness (For Comm)
Regents Park, London
Rhinefield Terrace, Lyndhurst, New Forest, Hants
Rhododendron Wood, Leith Hill, Surrey
Ribston Hall, Knaresborough, Yorks
Riverside Gardens, Richmond, Surrey
Rivers's Nursery, Sawbridgeworth, Herts
Roath Park, Cardiff, Glam
Roche's Arboretum, West Dean, Sussex
Roezel Manor, Jersey
Rosehaugh, Black Isle, Inverness
Rosehill Park, Falmouth, Cornwall
Rossie Priory, Dundee, Perths
Rowallane, Saintfield, Co. Down
Royal Well, Cheltenham, Glos
Roydon Park, Neston, Cheshire
Rycote, Thame, Oxon
Rye, The, High Wycombe, Bucks

Saltram House, Plympton, Devon (NT)
Sandford Park, Cheltenham
Sandling Park, Hythe, Kent
Sandon Park, Stone, Staffs
Sandringham Park, Norfolk
Savill Garden, Windsor Great Park, Berks
Scorrier House, Redruth, Cornwall
Scotney Castle, Lamberhurst, Kent (NT)
Selborne Church, Hants
Sheffield Park, Uckfield, Sussex (NT)
Sherborne Castle, Sherborne, Dorset
Shinners Bridge, Totnes, Devon
Sidbury Manor, Sidford, Devon
Singleton Abbey, W Glamorgan
Skelgill Wood, Ambleside, Cumbria (NT)
Smeaton House, East Linton, E Lothian
Somerleyton Hall, Lowestoft, Suffolk
South Place, Lr Beeding, Sussex
Speech House, Coleford, Glos (For Comm)
Speymouth Forest (Wisharts Burn) Fochabers, Moray
Sports Club, Melksham, Wilts
Stanage Park, Knighton, Heref (Powys)
Stanway, Winchcombe, Glos
Stonefield, Tarbert, Argyll
Stourhead, Mere, Wilts (NT)
Stowe Park (School), Bucks
Stratford Park (Sport Centre), Stroud, Glos
Streatham Hall, Exeter University
Strete Ralegh, Ottery St Mary, Devon
Strone House, Cairndow, Argyll
Stuckgowan, Luss, Dunbartons
Studley Castle, Redditch, Worcs (Warwicks)
Studley Royal, Ripon, N Yorks
Suamarez Park, Guernsey
Sunningdale Nurseries, Windlesham, Surrey
Sutherland's Grove, A 828, Barcaldine, Oban, Argyll
Syon House, Brentford, Midd
Syston Park, Starnford, Lincs
St Fagans, Cardiff, Glam
St James's Church, Patterdale, Cumbria
St James's Park, London
St John's Isle of Man
St Ronan's School (Tongs Wood) Hawkhurst, Kent

Tal-y-Garn, Pontyprydd, W Glam
Talbot Manor, Fincham, Norfolk
Tannadyce, Angus
Tatton Park, Knutsford, Cheshire (NT)
Taymouth Castle (Gardens) Kenmore, Perths
Terling Place, Witham, Essex
Terrace Gardens, Richmond, Surrey
The Fen, Cambridge City
Theobalds Park, Enfield, Midd
Thorp Perrow, Bedale, N Yorks
Tickford Gra, Guildford, Surrey
Tigh-na-Bruich, Invergarry, Inverness
Tilgate Park, Crawley, Sussex
Tongs Wood (St Ronan's School), Hawkhurst, Kent
Tottenham House School, Savernake Forest, Wilts
Trawsoed, Aberystwyth, Dyfnant
Trebah, Mawnan Smith, Cornwall
Tredegar Park, Newport, Gwent
Tregothnan, Tresillian, Truro, Cornwall
Tregrehan, Par, Cornwall
Trelissick, King Harry Ferry, Truro, Cornwall (NT)
Trengwainton. Penzance, Cornwall (NT)
Trentham Park, Trentham, Staffs
Trent Park, Enfield, Midd
Trewidden, Penzance, Cornwall
Trewithen, Probus, Truro, Cornwall
Tring Park, Tring, Herts
Tullymore Park, Newcastle, Co Down
Tyninghame, East Linton, E Lothian

Ugbrooke Park, Chudleigh, Devon
Ulcombe Church, Kent
University Parks, Oxford

Vernon Holme School, Canterbury, Kent
Victoria Park, Bath, Avon
Victoria Park, Bethnal Green, London
Victoria Park, Leicester
Vivod House and Forest Garden, Llangollen, Clwyd
Vyne, The, Basingstoke, Hants (NT)

Waddesden House, Aylesbury, Bucks (NT)
Wakehurst Place, Ardingly, Sussex
Walcot Park, Lydbury, Shropshire
Wardour Old Castle, New Castle, Tisbury, Wilts
Ware Park, Ware, Herts
Warnham Court, Horsham, Sussex
Wayford Manor, Crewkerne, Somerset
Wayford Woods, Crewkerne, Somerset
Welford Park, Newbury, Berks
Welland Park, Market Harborough, Leics
Wells Hall, Reading University, Berks
West Dean House, Chichester, Sussex
West Kingsclere Farm, Kingsclere, Berks
West Lavington Rectory, Midhurst, Sussex
Westonbirt Arboretum, Tetbury, Glos (For Comm)
Weston Park, Shifnal, Shrops
West Park, Southampton
Whiteknights Park, Reading University, Berks
Whitfield, Thruxton, Herefords
Whittingehame House, Haddington, East Lothian
Wilton House, Wilton, Wilts
Wimpole House, Cambridge (NT)
Winkworth Arboretum, Godalming, Surrey (NT)
Wisley, RHSG, Ripley, Surrey
Witley, Surrey
Witham Hall, Witham-on-the-Hill, Lincs
Withersdene Hall, Wye, Kent
Woburn Abbey and Evergreens, Woburn, Beds
Woodhill, Kirkmichael, Perths
Woodhouse, Uplyme, Devon
Woodstock Park, Sittingbourne, Kent
Woolbeding, Midhurst, Sussex (NT)
Wotton House, Dorking, Surrey
Wray Castle, Ambleside, Cumbria (NT)
Wrest Park, Silsoe, Beds
Wythenshaw Park, Manchester

Index of English names

The first page reference is to the tree's main treatment; the second to its appearance in the list of notable British trees.

INDEX OF ENGLISH NAMES

Index of Scientific names